ST MARTIN'S

TRUE CRIME
CLASSICS

Paul relived that macabre moment in the bedroom again and again. Nervousness as he opened the door; Monica's brown eyes fixated on his frightened, confused blue ones. The shotgun—her body, flying into the air, soaring, then crashing violently, blood gushing. Words were superfluous: the shotgun told instantly of all the unhappiness and pain, leaving no room for talk.

Farmington and state police officers intermixed, measuring blood spots, collecting evidence. Officers buzzed almost, but not quite out of Paul's earshot. Finally, what they were saying slowly penetrated his fog.

"You can't kill yourself with a shotgun!" "She's too tiny to reach the trigger."

"Monica would never kill herself!"

GRAVE ACCUSATIONS

A TRUE STORY OF
LIES, FAMILY SECRETS, AND DEATH

ANDREA EGGER
IN COLLABORATION
WITH PAUL DUNN

St. Martin's Paperbacks

Published by arrangement with New Horizon Press.

GRAVE ACCUSATIONS

Copyright © 2001 by Andrea Egger and Paul Dunn.

Cover photograph of graveyard by Carl Purcell c/o Mira.com.

ISBN: 0-312-98524-X
EAN: 978-0-312-98524-0

Library of Congress Catalog number: 2001089169

Printed in the United States of America

New Horizon Press edition published 2001
St. Martin's Paperbacks edition / February 2004

St. Martin's Paperbacks are published by St. Martin's Press, 175 Fifth Avenue, New York, NY 10010.

10 9 8 7 6 5 4 3

AUTHOR'S NOTE

This book is based on the experiences of Paul Dunn and reflects his perceptions of the past, present and future. The personalities, events, actions and conversations portrayed within the story have been taken from his memories, extensive court documents, interviews, testimony, research, letters, personal papers, press accounts and the memories of some participants.

In an effort to safeguard the privacy of certain people, some individuals' names and identifying characteristics have been altered. Events involving the characters happened as described. Only minor details have been changed.

TABLE OF CONTENTS

PROLOGUE

"I'm filing battery charges against you today."

Monica Dunn looked out the window, her perfect face hidden from her husband. Such a simple word, battery. But it could end a police officer's career. Even one with a fifteen-year record of dedication and honesty.

"What in the world are you talking about?" Paul Dunn asked, trying to hear over the resounding crunch of cereal and laughter from their four-year-old and five-year-old daughters in the nearby kitchen. Monica continued to stare out at the street as the sun glinted off her shiny, dark curls. Her carefully made-up brown eyes and delicate cheekbones radiated an energy of their own. She didn't answer her husband. She didn't even flash those sparkling, bedroom eyes at him.

Her back to Paul, Monica's silence seemed to grow deafening. She finally whirled around and spoke. "Look at me. I'm bruised all over."

She stood there only moments, then strode past him toward what had been the bedroom they'd shared for so long before their separation two weeks ago. Now he didn't belong. Stunned, Paul watched her hips swivel in the fitted, deep purple dress that clung to her breasts and tiny waist, snugly fitting around those luscious hips. The button-down dress accentuated every curve. Her legs swirled endlessly in high-heeled, spiked pumps. Paul remembered those pantyhose-clad legs wrapped around him during moments of abandon.

"Are you kidding? You know I never hit you," responded Paul, his blue eyes darkening as he marched down the hall after the vision in purple.

"What are you saying, Monica?" Paul called out, desperation in every syllable. Anxiety and panic spun around in the thirty-five-year-old police officer's head and turned his thoughts to confusion. He was answered only by a sharp click. *She's locking the bedroom door*, Paul thought.

"Monica! Please let me in. We have to talk," Paul pleaded. When there was no reply, he pounded on the door, muscles bulging underneath his sport shirt. "Please, Monica. What are you trying to do to me?" The sound of his pounding heart drowned out all other thoughts.

"You miserable bastard!"

Anger seared the air. Her words—then silence. Even in his numb state, he knew he had to do something fast. "Monica! Let me in, damn it!"

He heard a click a few seconds later. Her husky voice called out.

"Come here."

Paul opened the door. A glance showed him the water-bed with its maroon quilt and oak headboard—and Monica. Then he saw the shotgun. He knew it was loaded, because guns were always loaded in his house. He had told Monica to keep them that way. Invoking the code of the Old West, some of those he arrested became violent and threatened to pay him or his family back.

A second became a lifetime as a nightmare followed in slow motion. The shotgun, the blast, buttons exploding, blood spurting on the quilt, onto the purple dress. Monica's body flew backwards, skimming the air like a swan, then crash-landing, blood spilling onto the floor. *This can't be happening*, he thought. But it was. Monica's blood flowed from her body.

A scream echoed. It took a moment for Paul to realize it came from his own throat. He ran to the unconscious Monica and tried to lift her, but she was covered in blood and slipped from his hands. She gasped weakly, the only sign of life he saw or heard. But her body's feeble attempts at living couldn't bring Monica back to the instant before the shotgun blast violated the body men once would have sold their souls to possess.

PART ONE

INTENSE PASSIONS, IMPULSIVE ACTIONS

How dreadful knowledge of truth can
be
When there's no help in the truth!

—Sophocles

CHAPTER 1

SPRINGTIME

By the time April rolls around Farmington, New Mexico, winter says a hasty good-bye in its dashing way of fur-trimmed coats one day and sleeveless attire the next. Roaring dust devils cause northwestern New Mexicans to chew more earth than chewing tobacco, as the monsoon season has not yet begun. Once overflowing rains turn the swirling dust devils to memory, New Mexico appears to be more of a rain forest than a desert. Flash floods surprise drivers on the interstates and cracked dirt roads. Then, they too are gone and made into another memory as the bone-dry desert sucks in the water and only thirst survives.

Farmington is known for its oil, stunning landscape, and the San Juan River. Rocky hills surround the small town, which is right at the tip-top of the state in a region known as the Four Corners. If you go to the right place, you can stand in four states at once—New Mexico, Utah, Colorado and Arizona. While Farmington has its share of the rich, it also has its share of the farmers and ranchers who make their living off the land. Signs along Highway 64 remind you of that in bold, unprofessional-looking writing. "Hay 4 Sale" handwritten in red brightens one white sign. Another sign for peaches didn't have enough room for the whole word so the sign glares "Peach's" in black letters.

Still another sign down the road a piece corrects the spelling error and helps people figure out where the peaches are located by including arrows. Flea markets line the sides of the road.

Many easterners consider New Mexico to be the epitome of the Wild West, filled with cowboys and Indians. But many Native Americans wear cowboy boots and hats, while a lot of Anglos wouldn't be caught dead dressing "cowboy style." A large amount of the population in the state is split between Native Americans, Anglos and Hispanics, with a small percentage of African-Americans. Some New Mexicans try to act as if they're not inherently racist while also striving to erase that racism inherent in all humans and replace it with a culture of tolerance.

Despite modern areas, some of the Wild West image still clings to New Mexico with its vast unpopulated stretches of land. Billboards posted around offer a $20,000 reward for information on one or another killer. Traditional Indian dances with colorful dress and painted faces ensure that Native American heritage will not be forgotten. One of the biggest such displays of Indian heritage is the Inter-tribal Ceremonial, held annually in August in Gallup, two hours south of Farmington, where millions of people worldwide come to view the dances. In fact, Gallup features free Indian dances, with all their bright colors and beautiful velvet fabrics, feathers and face-painting, every evening during the summer. While seemingly ages away from Farmington, Gallup would become an ominous part of Paul's future.

Along some highways, such as Interstate 40, which runs through Gallup, drivers tune their radios to 530 AM to listen to "Hear New Mexico," featuring actor Ricardo Montalban describing the sites. Some listen to the broadcast just to hear Montalban's husky voice or reminisce about his sexy, white suit and manly chivalry on the old television show, *Fantasy Island*. Others prefer to remember him as the virile villain in the "Star Trek" film, *The Wrath of Khan*.

Interstate 40 serves as a thoroughfare from the East to the West Coast and replaced the famed Old Historic 66, which still exists in Gallup and some other places.

To Paul Dunn, who was born June 19, 1958 in Albuquerque, New Mexico, those roads led home. He lived in Santa Fe during his early childhood. Then his parents, Jane and Harvey "Buzz" Dunn, and his older sister, Robin, moved to a small farm in Nambe, New Mexico when Paul turned thirteen. There, his brother Mark was born.

Paul's boyhood was happy and typical. He went to Pojoaque Junior and Senior High Schools, where he played basketball. After school, he learned to ride horses and take care of the other animals on the farm.

On Paul's sixteenth birthday, while working part-time as an attendant at a gas station, he met some New Mexico State Police officers who stopped in for soft drinks. One of the officers invited the eager teen to go riding along with him to see what fighting crime was all about. Paul accepted the offer and rode with him several times. Those experiences shaped Paul's ambitions and then his career for the next two decades.

After graduating from high school, Paul took law enforcement courses at New Mexico State University in Las Cruces for a year. In late August 1977, the City of Santa Fe hired him as a jailer. He was working there when, at twenty, he met and married Juliet Martinez. In September 1979, to his great pride, he became a Santa Fe police officer.

Beautiful, dark-haired Juliet gave birth to a daughter, April, on June 7, 1981. Though their marriage was troubled, Juliet attested to the fact that Paul never hit her or abused her in any way during their marriage. In 1982, Paul moved to Farmington, New Mexico after being hired by the police department at higher wages than in Santa Fe as well as the opportunity for advancement.

In these years, Paul focused on being the best cop he

could be and the best turned-out, with polished, high boots and a perfectly pressed uniform with shiny buttons, glossy, well-cut hair and a "can do" attitude. He felt he owed this to the public he served and those who hired him. Though he had some friends, many of his co-workers just tolerated him and in private some labeled him arrogant. Some were jealous of Paul's unusual, virile quality, which often attracted women's admiring glances. Few understood that Paul actually felt lesser, but compensated for that by his confident air. Because he sometimes seemed cocky, some people misinterpreted his actions at times. For instance, while other police officers waved at Paul as they drove past him, the motorcop brushed his hand through the air in what some said disdainfully was a regal manner.

Paul felt it wasn't arrogance—on a motorcycle one must keep both hands on the handlebars, so to ensure one's own safety and the safety of others a wave had to be quick. But Paul worked hard to improve his appearance. He spent hours at the gym, practically bursting his muscles in an effort to put more bulk on an already hulkish form as if the better he looked, the better he would feel about himself and the better others would feel about him. He didn't know why he felt such emptiness. It wasn't until much later in his life that he would come to terms with the black hole of loneliness in his heart and the ways he had tried, and failed, to fill it.

One officer's wife who disliked him didn't mince words: She called him an asshole. Moreover, his hatred for those who broke the law caused him to get into fights with suspects. When he matured, he called it the "beast" in all of us, the "fighter spirit," the "evil." Deeply committed to his job, he worked both patrol and traffic and became an expert in accident reconstruction. To become more proficient, he took courses in firearms training. That was the same year Paul met Monica Sanchez Cortez.

Monica Sanchez had grown from a lovely child into a

beautiful young woman. When she became pregnant at fifteen, Monica married the baby's father, Patrick Cortez, her high school sweetheart. Monica divorced Cortez in the early 1980s. Later, Cortez died in a motorcycle accident when a drunk driver crashed into him and his bike. Monica never got over his sudden death. A depressing shadow seemed to spread across her life. Perhaps that is why she clung too tightly to people with whom she was close.

A dutiful daughter, Monica visited her parents' house every day and kept in touch with her siblings. Though some called her standoffish, others said she had a ready smile and a full stash of candy for everyone who passed her desk in the municipal court.

On a Saturday in the early springtime of 1982, Paul Dunn zoomed into the Farmington Police Station on his motorcycle. His dark blue, perfectly pressed uniform and high, polished boots complemented his blue eyes and brown hair, red highlights glinting in the New Mexico sun. That morning Paul had written an excess of tickets and had to go back to the station for another citation book. "Occupational hazard," he murmured as he walked downstairs. He noticed the side door to the municipal clerk's office was open. Puzzled, Paul decided to see what was up. One of the court clerks, Monica Cortez, sat at her desk, tears streaming down her cheeks. She didn't know Paul was there until he spoke.

"Are you all right? Is there anything I can do?"

"My cousin's been in a car accident. He's seriously injured. I don't know if he'll make it."

Paul listened sympathetically, all the while taking in her soft, dark curls curving around her beige, flawless skin—even tear-stained. She was crying so hard Paul almost couldn't comprehend her words as he stared at her. He knew she had worked at the courthouse for a long time, but he worked the graveyard shift so he rarely saw her except when he had to appear there. Though Paul and his wife were not getting along, they were still married. So, after Paul murmured soft words of comfort to the distressed woman, he went about his duties.

That afternoon Paul saw fellow motorcop Lawrence "Dusty" Downs, his expressive blue eyes and sparkling dark-blonde hair, as always, perfectly groomed.

"That's some beauty in Municipal Court," Paul commented.

"Oh, you mean Monica. She's dating Hawk, so be careful."

"Hawk" was their sergeant, Mark Hawkinson.

"She was crying her eyes out. Said it was about some cousin who'd been injured," Paul said as he went about removing his uniform and putting on workout clothes.

Later, Magistrate Terry Pearson formally introduced Paul and Monica.

Time passed. One day Paul found himself once again in Municipal Court, this time for a hearing. Once more he saw that vision of beauty sauntering toward him, eyes smiling in recognition.

Monica certainly wasn't oblivious to the attention her looks created, said a police officer's wife who found Monica too obvious. She didn't try to hide her body under rags, that was for sure. She never wore an outfit more than once—or so it seemed. Monica bought new, expensive clothes more often than the rest of Farmington combined, joked another officer's wife. Wherever she went, Monica had to be the best-dressed woman and she never dressed in "grubbies," even around the house. She didn't cook or clean very often. To those who knew her well, what she did best was look beautiful and sexy. She turned heads—and took many men's thoughts away, at least temporarily, from their wives.

The only photo of herself Monica allowed people to see was a professional, glamorous portrait she'd had taken. She didn't like being photographed. Even though she was quite capable with hair, makeup and clothes, Monica wouldn't settle for anything less than the expensive photo session in which the photographer used special lighting and touched up any facial flaws.

To men who saw Monica, it appeared she was born to defy the assumption that "Gentlemen prefer blondes." Her voluptuous body was neither fat nor model-thin, at least for the 1990s. To some Monica appeared to be a current-day, Hispanic version of Marilyn Monroe.

As Monica approached him and smiled, Paul wondered, *Is she flirting with me?* He couldn't believe it. Not one to mince words, Paul responded bluntly to her coyness.

"You're Hawk's."

"Hawk and I broke up."

Despite telling himself that he should walk away, Paul found himself asking to see her again. This was Paul's first break with his "moral code"—seeing Monica while still married to his first wife. He did not yet know that act would affect the entire course of his life.

Monica's perfection was not lost on Paul. Raised around Hispanic women, he liked their dark, often sultry looks. Monica's thick, luscious brown curly hair shone and her sparkling brown eyes twinkled when she smiled. This precipitated Paul's nickname for her: "Smiling Eyes." He thought her perfectly formed breasts and tiny waist completed the picture. She was twenty-two, he was twenty-five. Their flirting progressed rapidly from subtle, never obvious touching in front of people and maintaining knowing eye contact. Sexual tension burned between them.

On the first evening they were together, Paul drove to a rustic canyon. Each could see fire in the other's eyes. It didn't take long before clothes fell and bodies intertwined in that private haven.

After that, when Paul wasn't on duty, he and Monica were inseparable. Monica even helped Paul through his divorce in 1984. About the only thing Paul felt wasn't perfect about Monica was the way she recoiled from his daughter April, who lived with her mother. She was just a four-year-old when Paul and Monica first met. Monica wouldn't say things directly to April's face, but she'd loudly whisper to Paul in April's hearing, "When is she going home?"

That Monica hated April and treated the little girl horribly was something April kept from her father. Years later, April confessed about all the verbal abuse she'd received at Monica's hands. Monica always made it clear to April her presence wasn't wanted. April told Paul she kept quiet because she was protecting *him* from information that might cause a fight between him and Monica.

Paul couldn't understand Monica's jealousy of a child. He tried not to think about it as he and Monica planned for their marriage and the babies he proudly knew they would make together. Paul and Monica were so wrapped up in each other—and in themselves—the world ceased to exist for them. They saw no danger in this; they couldn't predict the precarious future which satisfying their every desire would make a reality. While ecstatic and in love, Paul was beginning to become isolated from his friends, but he didn't really care. Outside of Monica, he didn't want to be with anyone else. Their isolation was the first sign of trouble. Neither knew it.

CHAPTER 2

"GRINGO"

It was Valentine's Day 1986 when Paul and Monica married. He didn't care that some of her family members didn't like him and referred to him as a "gringo," a racist slur some Hispanics use to describe Anglo people. If Monica noticed, she did nothing to stop this. And Paul was so high on his new life that he didn't care.

Every Sunday Monica visited her parents at their home. After they were married, Paul was expected to go with her or show up there after work. Each time, he noticed the nasty looks her brother and sisters gave him. They treated him like a second-class citizen. They spoke Spanish, which he didn't understand, around him all the time to let him know he wasn't wanted.

Sometimes Jerry, Diane and Theresa glared at him; at others they ignored him. There was never a welcoming, "Hi, how are you?" but an implicit dismissal: *Go about your business. You might be here, but we don't have to acknowledge you.*

Her siblings never gave Paul a chance. But Monica's parents, Dora and Torry Sanchez, as well as Monica's Uncle Clyde, treated Paul well and Paul loved them.

After Paul and Monica married, she kept her job as a municipal court clerk and Paul remained a police officer.

Soon he took a second job as a security guard for former Governor Tom Bolack. He had to. Monica shopped at exclusive stores. She wouldn't be caught dead at stores like Kmart, according to one police officer's wife. She dressed better than some attorneys' wives did, although Paul didn't make as much money, even with two jobs. Even when she went to a very casual event like a baseball game she was "dressed to the nines" while other women wore shorts or jeans.

Paul wanted to please Monica more than anything. One day, Paul put a $250 muslin jumpsuit on layaway for her at Mary Murphin's, an exclusive boutique.

"That was a lot of money for me to spend for one jumpsuit," Paul admitted. "Oh, but she looked fantastic in it."

To work first at the court and then at the bail bond office for an admiring boss, Monica wore pant suits, jumpsuits—she dressed professionally. She didn't dress provocatively, but no matter what she put on, men found her irresistible. Paul didn't care how much money he spent on his wife's wardrobe and ego. Whatever Monica wanted, he gave her. He saw her as a sweet, loving, passionate woman. They laughed together, spent many good times together and loved each other. He found her passion for life irresistible.

Two years into their marriage, Paul and Monica planned for a home, a child and all the dreams of young love. They weren't really trying to have a baby, but the news that Monica was pregnant was a cause for them to celebrate—they were on a roll.

Monica glowed through her pregnancy despite six weeks of wretched morning sickness and the inevitable weight gain. Paul wouldn't have believed it possible, but to him pregnancy made Monica even more beautiful. *It can't get any better than this!* Paul kept thinking. Paul didn't know that Monica secretly was set on never having another baby. She wasn't going to ruin her body with stretch marks.

The labor was long and protracted, but Monica's face

glowed when she held little Diane Dunn on September 3, 1988, a few months after Paul and Monica's second wedding anniversary. Such plans they had for that little picture of perfection. She was their princess.

Paul soon learned that, to Monica, the baby was more a doll to be played with than a living child with needs of its own. Paul was the one to wake up with Diane in the middle of the night, soothe Diane's upsets and change her "crappy" diapers. Monica's delicate nature couldn't handle the sleeplessness, smell and mess. Paul couldn't have known then that he would eventually do all the vacuuming, dish washing and laundry, and work two jobs. He just knew he was happier than he had ever been. His ladies, those two beautiful faces. *What did I do to be rewarded with such a blessing?* Paul asked himself over and over. He knew he would work as hard as he needed to without ever complaining if only he could keep them. He would do anything.

In late 1988, after Diane's birth, Paul joined a school program known as Adopt-a-Cop, formed by the Country Club Elementary School's Parent–Teacher Organization president, Sharon Lee. She and her husband, Larry, became and stayed good friends with Paul. Paul worked as an "adopted cop" for kindergarten, first, third and fifth grade classes over the next several years. He photographed eager students sitting on his motorcycle and even played basketball and volleyball with students during his off-duty time. He also wrote traffic tickets in the thousands during that time. Scrupulous to obeying the rules, he felt when someone broke the law on his watch the person had to be punished. When the department issued trading cards with police officers' pictures, Paul's card was popular and collectible. Many times he was the guest speaker at Farmington schools and the Fox School of Driving. His expertise in accident investigation was called upon by the state police, the San Juan County Sheriff's Department and the Bureau of Indian Affairs.

The night his second daughter, Racquel, was conceived is forever etched into Paul's memory. It was the night their home burned to the ground, igniting their possessions and their dreams as the couple watched helplessly. They stayed at Monica's parents' home. That night, despite their losses, they made ecstatic, joyful love for the first time since their first daughter Diane's birth.

But three months later, when Monica learned she was pregnant again, she was filled with an unquenchable fury at Paul, at her condition, at their life. She balked at another pregnancy so soon after Diane's birth. No, she wouldn't stand for her body growing huge and clumsy again. Monica wanted an abortion. Paul wouldn't even discuss it; the idea of the life they'd created being murdered, as he saw abortion, was abhorrent. Monica saw it as a sane way out. Usually the one who gave in, this time Paul refused. A grumbling, ever-complaining Monica prepared for the morning sickness and weight gain of childbirth for the second time in less than a year.

In one sense, Paul may have won the battle, but he lost the war. To get Monica to agree to go through with the pregnancy, he agreed to have a vasectomy so they would never have another child.

Seven months into her pregnancy, as if to punish Monica for her distaste of being pregnant again, Monica's appendix swelled and almost burst. Doctors said she needed an emergency appendectomy, which would mean a simultaneous cesarean section. If Monica's appendix burst before the cesarean, Monica and the baby would die of toxemia. And if something went wrong with either surgery, they still might die. The odds weren't great, but there didn't seem any better choice. Luckily, the plan worked; the cesarean was performed first, the appendectomy immediately after. A healthy baby, Racquel Dunn, was born August 3, 1989.

Paul Dunn was a loving, giving father. He worshipped April and, later, Diane and Racquel. But many police officers and other people who knew Paul didn't see his parental affection. They didn't see the softer side.

A handful of Farmington residents appreciated Paul's courtesy and gentleness when he came to their homes at their time of need—when a family member had a heart attack or other emergency. Some people who received traffic tickets from the good-looking cop practically thanked him for the ticket because his demeanor was so kind and professional. Many people wrote letters on his behalf to the chief over the years. Paul knew he was far from perfect, but he was slow to judge people, even those who criticized him unjustly.

But he couldn't seem to satisfy his wife. Monica was horrified by the scars from the appendectomy and the cesarean. She had always believed you couldn't be too rich, too womanly, too glamorous, too sought-after, too sexy. She never let outsiders see her without her makeup. Paul, of course, saw her natural face and he thought her even more beautiful that way, although Monica never believed him.

After Racquel's birth, Monica's passion for life also carried with it the capacity for deep anger, which caused her to freeze out her husband for long periods of time, punishing him with bitter silence or angry words. This led to a push-pull relationship: Paul always trying to get her to talk quietly about problems and Monica fleeing such encounters—even when they were in bed.

Not only Paul's attitude, but her own physical appearance now irritated Monica. Her sagging breasts became a constant complaint of Monica's after Racquel's birth. Monica knew after nursing a baby a woman's breasts rarely return to the same firm, high-pointing shape. "I don't care," Paul told her. "Your breasts still excite me." But Monica began to talk about getting breast implants.

"I was perfectly content with what she had before. Her

breasts felt real. But this was something she needed to do for *her*, for her psyche."

Monica got her wish. Paul had heard the typical locker room banter that implants felt hard, not real. He found out the gossip was true. After the operation, Monica's larger breasts never felt as soft and responsive.

However, Paul saw Monica's self-esteem leap. She loved to throw back her shoulders and show off her new shape in tight-fitting sweaters.

Paul concealed his disappointment.

More disappointments followed and Paul was silent about these as well. Monica told him her boss at the bail bonds company for which she worked at the time had bought the $3,000 implants. When Paul, in exasperation, asked why, she said it was a bonus. Paul didn't think to ask what she did to deserve a bonus. He did not hear then about the rumors of backrubs at her desk . . . and more.

CHAPTER 3

THE GREEN-EYED MONSTER

"Are you fucking her?"

Monica's words struck Paul like four stabs in the back. She snarled the words as she sat ramrod-straight inside her van parked next to his police motorcycle that day.

Paul played dumb to avoid a scene. "What's wrong? Gosh, babe! That's Kelley. You know Kelley."

"No, I don't." Monica's words spat bile. "We haven't met."

Paul had just left the police station to have lunch with Monica when Kelley Hatch, a local television reporter, stopped to ask for some facts about a car accident. Paul got out his clipboard and gave her the information. Monica stormed off to the van, slamming the door loudly.

He had a lot of explaining to do when he got in the van, believing that words that hurt you are imprinted in your memory. That a woman he considered so perfectly feminine and womanly could utter such language astounded Paul. As beautiful as everyone knew her to be, however, something seemed to bring out the green-eyed monster in Monica. She never seemed sure she really had Paul.

Their relationship began unraveling as their girls grew into their toddler years and beyond. Paul found that if he was going to keep peace in the house, he had to keep his mouth shut. If he wanted to resolve a problem, he learned the only way to do so was to swallow his grievances and forget about them. Although in the early stages of the relationship he had been content to spend all his time alone with Monica, now that they were a family, he felt things should be different. But Monica only allowed Paul and the girls to see those of whom she approved—*her* friends and family. Slowly, she had distanced Paul from his friends and family. Sure, one could say he let her. He had isolated himself from everybody, leaving no room in his life for anyone but her—her and those who met with her approval.

"I had to account for all my time," Paul admits in retrospect about Monica's authoritativeness.

In early 1990, Monica pushed Paul into being best man for her best friend's fiancé. "I think he's a jerk. I'd sooner kick his butt," Paul griped. Monica said, "Do it for me." End of discussion. He did it.

By the time the wedding took place, Monica had returned to her job at the courthouse, but Paul and Monica's relationship had further deteriorated.

And if he ever so much as glanced at another woman, he never heard the end of it. Slowly, chip by delicate chip, Monica broke Paul's self-esteem. "There were lots of good times, but always jealousy." He thought, *She'll get over this*, but she didn't. Slowly, his spirit dissolved. Words, like acid, burned. Why did he let her do it? Paul cannot, to this day, answer that question.

"I felt like her property. I had to go here. I had to do this," Paul said miserably.

Life at home was getting so strained, he just couldn't handle it anymore. "Outwardly, it all looked normal. Inwardly, it was more than I could bear."

Since Paul was a body builder with as many female eyes on him as male ones focused on his wife, Monica was ever vigilant. She wanted his entire attention focused on her alone. When Paul and Monica went out, for instance to the comedy club, she watched her husband like a hawk. If he even glanced at another woman, she exploded.

"Do you want her? Do you think she's *that* great? Go get her!"

To avoid her condemnation, Paul found himself constantly looking down whenever he was with her so as not to inflame Monica's jealousy by accidentally making eye contact with a member of the opposite sex.

Jealousy is a strange predator that boosts the ego at first, but slowly, ever so slowly, strangles its prey. "Initially, it's flattering that your mate thinks you're so attractive that she's protective. After a while, it's like, 'God, I can't breathe!' "

But Monica's jealousy of Paul's glances at other women also shot an insecure Paul's self-esteem through the sky. He felt Monica wanted him completely. No one else did, or so he thought. He needed her.

He also learned that she needed him when she told him she had been molested by a relative as a child. Not knowing much about sexual abuse survivors, he later decided this might explain why she had such trouble with issues involving love, sex, security and relationships. Monica had been convinced by her abuser that she must give in to his demands, because she was too beautiful for him to resist, that she was created to tempt men and she must submit. Monica told Paul he was the only one with whom she shared her experiences as a child sexual abuse survivor. It made him want to protect her all the more, but it didn't stop them from fighting.

One day, Paul was lying on the couch in their home when Monica returned from baseball practice. Monica was an extremely good pitcher for a local team. She poured a soft drink into a heavy glass goblet and sipped from it, standing in the doorway between the kitchen and living room. They spoke about picking up his daughter April to stay with them for an extended period. Monica made a snide comment about April; Paul made a snide comment back.

In the next instant, using all the strength in her pitching arm, Monica tossed the glass goblet at Paul's head. Paul threw his arms in front of his face as the goblet struck him. He ran to Monica and grabbed her.

"Don't you ever do that again!" he roared.

Mid-sentence, Paul felt his thighs being kicked. He looked up and realized he had lifted Monica off her feet and up in the air. She kicked his thighs again as hard as she could. *What the hell is happening to us?* he thought. He reacted in panic and dropped her. Monica slammed to the ground and sprained her ankle. Paul feared his anger and what it had made him do. He felt guilty about Monica's spraining her ankle. He never knew whether Monica felt guilty about throwing the weighty glass at him. They never talked about the incident again.

Paul was determined, however, never to become angrily physical again. He tried to remain passive during the rest of their relationship and Monica mainly used the silent treatment when Paul angered her.

But perhaps the fight started bad habits. It was definitely battery and, yes, Monica had started it. However, battery, according to New Mexico law, simply means a "rude or insolent" touching of another person. It doesn't have to be a punch or a slap. A shove can be considered battery. Grabbing someone's arm? That's battery. Barring someone from leaving a room is battery. Whether or not Paul would admit it, he and Monica had committed battery against each other. On some level, because he knew the law so well, he also knew they had done so. Monica knew it, too.

By now they had stopped even trying to communicate, except for Monica's heated declaration one night: "If you ever leave me, I'm going to destroy you and then I'm going to kill myself."

Of course, he felt it was only her temper flaring. He didn't believe her. But he grew more silent, more lonely.

CHAPTER 4

ALL HALLOWS EVE

Anita Harris and her friend were riding their horses along the property line separating Anita's and the former governor Tom Bolack's land when they saw Paul Dunn, his blue and white pickup truck parked nearby. Anita noted the Farmington Police badge on the dashboard inside the truck. Paul was chainsawing his way through a pile of wood.

"Are you a cop?" Anita asked, staring at the good-looking, muscular guy in front of her.

Paul nodded. "I'm a police officer, but I'm working part-time as a security officer for Mr. Bolack."

Anita eyed the chainsaw with a small, superstitious shiver, since it was All Hallows Eve. *There's something a little eerie here*, Anita thought. *But he's awfully cute*.

The women rode on, not introducing themselves. Paul did not offer his name, either.

Just before Anita got divorced, she met Paul again. She was riding near the river and had crossed over onto the former governor's property. Paul motioned for her to stop.

"Mr. Bolack is having problems with vandalism and no one is allowed in this area," he told her.

Unintimidated, Anita replied, "He's given me permission to ride here."

Paul looked at her as if he didn't believe a word she

said. *What an impudent little snot!* she thought. But she couldn't help noticing once again what an attractive man he was. Boldly, she asked his name so she could complain to Bolack about him—at least, she would know the cutie's identity.

Later, Anita asked her sister, Margaret, to ask her fireman husband, Andy, to find out about Paul Dunn.

A few days later, Andy told Margaret, "He said he'd clear a place for Anita to ride anytime, but the guy's married with three children."

Anita was disappointed. She didn't know until much later the problems Paul and his wife were having or the unfulfilled needs Paul had.

At Christmas, Andy and Margaret threw their annual holiday party for city co-workers and friends. That night Anita saw Monica and Paul together. Anita noticed Monica's possessiveness immediately.

"She was holding his arm. She watched him and she watched the other women at the party with a wary expression, like she was looking for something. It was clear: He was her property. There was no happiness in her face. You didn't get the feeling you could go up to her and spend some time chitchatting, as people do at parties. She was closed off."

Later at the Christmas party, Paul's eyes met Anita's from across the room and he remembered seeing the spunky woman when she'd ridden her horse on Tom Bolack's vast San Juan County ranch land. Before they knew it, they were standing in front of the sparkling tree talking.

"Have you been riding lately?" Paul asked.

Anita nodded. "I still ride on Bolack's land all the time."

Paul desperately needed a friend to talk to at that point in his life. Though he was continuing to work the Bolack security job to supplement the income he made as a cop and Monica's income as a court clerk, Monica spent his money and her own faster than they could make it. Besides the jobs, he was doing all the housework. Monica was queen over all she surveyed—except Paul's soul, though he didn't have the strength of spirit to realize that yet. It seemed nothing he did pleased Monica anymore. He felt completely inadequate, although he was doing more than everything he could to keep their marriage going.

Paul wasn't thinking of beginning an affair with Anita Harris that night. He just felt grateful for a sympathetic ear.

Anita knew immediately she and Paul would click. It was a first impression combined with her belief and knowledge of auras. She had learned from a psychologist that when a person meets someone or something new, the brain asks three questions. *What is it? Have I seen it before? Is it going to hurt or help me?* Looking at it that way, Anita believed first impressions were vital to survival.

Soon after the party and away from Monica's vigilant eyes, Paul and Anita met again on Bolack's land and poured out the stories of their lives to each other. For Paul, there was finally someone to whom he could tell all the feelings he had kept concealed for so long. With her strawberry hair and ivory complexion, the compassionate Anita quickly became an ally. Paul had never really talked openly to a woman before. Although his body had experienced physical love many times, a spiritual connection had never completed the picture until Anita, with her earthy attractiveness, entered his life.

Anita felt money was a large part of Paul's problems with Monica. They had separate checking accounts. He had no idea where Monica's money went, but she had no qualms about spending his. The bills were all his responsibility. "He never said anything openly about resenting it, but I got the impression he felt it would be nice to have some support. Cops don't make a lot of money," Anita notes.

Paul and Anita never touched during those first weeks

as their friendship grew. Finally, they discussed a relationship. Paul made it clear that if he got divorced, he would lose his girls. "I can't lose my babies," he said, always referring to the girls as "his babies." Anita understood.

Sometime after that, Paul fell in love. It wasn't the kind of fiery, out-of-control love he had once felt for Monica. That love had died because of a lack of communication. "I know now we just had sex," he sadly admitted to Anita. With Anita, Paul felt he could walk through life with her forever in his soul.

Anita learned of Paul's generosity, his ability to listen and how safe she felt around him. Having survived an abusive marriage, it took Anita a long time to trust again. She wasn't about to choose another violent man and she knew the signs to watch for. Never in her relationship with Paul did he menace her, and she loved the positive male influence he had on Josh, her fourteen-year-old son.

Anita also learned about Paul's caring nature. Paul also served as a male nurse for the former governor, who had suffered several strokes and was in a wheelchair. Paul did things for Bolack that many people hired to provide security would simply never do.

Seeing this gentle, caring side of Paul made Monica's treatment of him infuriate Anita. A woman's true beauty, Anita knew, was more than skin deep. It radiated from her inner self. Independent but caring, Anita didn't hold grudges and tried to think of others while respecting their privacy. So she couldn't believe Monica's self-centeredness. Monica treated Paul more like a servant than a husband.

While Anita couldn't believe Paul could love a woman like Monica, some people who knew Paul just couldn't see him with Anita. Most people remember her spending every free moment of time riding a horse and wearing old jeans and boots. In fact, she sometimes related better to animals than people. A free spirit, she usually wore a natural look, with no makeup and her red, glossy hair curled below her shoulders, casually blowing in the wind.

Sometimes when Anita looks at me, I can feel her beauty, Paul thought.

Anita's beauty was reflected in her soul and her personality. Her easy self-confidence—in exact opposition to Monica's neediness—her poise, her dignity—these elements made up Anita. She wasn't cocky, but she believed in herself—which was attractive to Paul in itself. Anita possessed a natural loveliness that shone through the simple T-shirts and jeans she threw on in five minutes.

It took Monica two hours to get ready to go anywhere. Her clothes, makeup and hair had to be perfect. If they weren't, she would not go.

"Anita's not what people call 'drop-dead' gorgeous. It's everything, the whole package. Monica's beauty was only exterior," Paul divulged.

Had Monica known Anita, she would have joined the rest of the people in town in not understanding why Paul was attracted to the woman. Anita saw men as shallow and immature, always needing to show off the trophy they had won, which is exactly how many perceived Monica—a trophy. For Monica, natural and internal beauty were not concepts she knew of or cared about. Monica's sweet, innocent face and ladylike hospitality made everyone describe her as an angel, as someone who never entertained an evil thought. Most people didn't know her well. They had never seen her blistering anger or jealousy.

Paul's intense guilt didn't stop his having an affair with Anita. Not that Paul didn't try. He wrote several drafts of "Dear John" letters to Anita trying to cut the relationship off, but he never could bring himself to send them.

Paul and Monica now had only the children in common. Since he had to work two jobs to make ends meet, the couple rarely saw each other.

Emotionally, Paul and Anita grew closer. Anita never

forgot the first night they made love. It was perfect. They drove her sedan one March night to the river; cottonwood trees formed a canopy overhead. She reclined the car's leather seats and their pent-up love and passion combined with the beautiful scenery as bodies and minds intertwined.

Anita hoped that some knowledge she had gained through therapy after her abusive marriage might help Paul. She gave Paul the book *Co-dependent No More* by Melody Beattie. Anita's therapy had helped her recognize unhealthy relationships and steer clear of them. She hoped Paul might do the same. Later, he told her he had stayed up all night reading the book.

"I can see everything so much clearer after reading the book," he said. "I've never been in therapy, but I can see myself on almost every page," he revealed to Anita.

Pleased that the book helped him, Anita still panicked at what happened next.

CHAPTER 5

A BOMBSHELL

Before Anita gave him the book about codependency, Paul knew the balance between his work and Monica's work on the marriage was "a bit off." He knew he deserved better, but he didn't know to what extent or how to get it. The book answered those questions for him. And he realized how unhappy he was with Monica the way things stood.

Paul terrified Anita by jumping into action too quickly after reading the book. He decided he didn't need therapy or other help. He would act.

"He went immediately from Point A to Point C," Anita noted. "He began talking about leaving Monica right away and getting his own apartment. I was like, 'Whoa! Slow down.'"

In February of 1994, Anita stepped out of the whirlwind and broke up with Paul. After a bad marriage, she didn't need a relationship growing more serious by the minute with a man in an unhealthy and destructive marriage. In one sense, she feared commitment. If he divorced Monica, that would change everything. Anita felt she wasn't in love with him then and she relished her hard-won freedom. She needed to date others to be sure of her feelings. She needed to fulfill her own needs now that she was master of her own life.

. . .

Soon afterwards, Paul began writing Anita a love letter, saying he always wanted to be with her but wouldn't push her into anything if that's not what she wanted. Paul expected to wait until six months or so after he polished the last version of the letter on March 7, 1994, before giving it to Anita. He estimated that the date he would send it to her would be around September 25. Why he picked that date, he couldn't explain. But he wanted to give his relationship with Anita time. Anita was afraid, he knew, of getting involved with someone so obviously caught in a codependent, unhealthy relationship with his wife. Although Anita had already broken up with Paul, they were still seeing each other as friends during this time. Paul believed Anita would change her mind and their relationship would again begin to blossom—especially after he and Monica divorced. He wrote in the letter that if she was reading it six months after he wrote it, then he and Monica were probably divorced.

As he penned those words, he had no idea what was about to happen during the months to follow.

Paul expressed his deep love for Anita in the letter and lamented the fact that Anita didn't feel the same way.

"Why is it so hard to say or express that you love me?" he wrote. "Because you don't? If you're reading this, it must be the truth. I've thought very hard about what I am going to do next and it is not without great sadness that I must write this."

That night in March when Paul actually wrote the letter, Anita went on a date with another man.

"I can't compete with the other men you date," the letter went on, "who are better looking than me. I'll never be able to offer you anything more than my love, my care, my strong back and mind."

He assured Anita that he wouldn't want to own her, because of what she had taught him about codependency.

"I've come too far for that, but I do—and always will—desire you."

He wrote that his love for her must not be enough if he had decided to give her the letter after all. "If you're reading this, it means I give up."

He told Anita they would've been great together, but he wouldn't live a lie with her. He wouldn't live with a soul mate who saw him as nothing but "safe," as she had once told him. He said they'd always be friends and he thanked her for helping him recover from being dependent on Monica.

Then he told her how saddened he was to realize she wasn't joking when she told him the Saturday before he wrote the letter that she didn't love him. When she went out with another man the next night, he realized she really meant she didn't want the serious relationship that he wanted.

"I know how Monica felt at the end of our love, grasping for something that was dead, trying to hold onto love lost . . . I'll miss your counsel, your feisty spirit and your body more than you know. But I guess it's time to let you go."

Paul told Anita to call him if he was wrong about her needing to be free. He wrote he'd never forgive her ex-husband for abusing her physically and emotionally to the point that she might not ever be able to handle a committed, serious relationship.

"I love you and always have since the day we first met and, as in the ruby you wear, you will always have a piece of my heart. This is not a 'Dear Anita' letter, it is a letter of freedom on your part, because I finally realize I can't hold your hand and walk life's path side by side with you. I'll miss you and Josh deeply. Give him my love, for I do love and respect him immensely. Forever yours, Paul."

The irony was that Paul mainly wrote the letter to get his feelings out. He wasn't sure he would ever send it. He put the letter in the glove compartment of his truck, mistakenly assuming it would be safe from the scrutiny of others.

Meanwhile, Paul dropped what must have seemed to Monica to be like a nuclear bomb. The macho-on-the-outside, passive-on-the-inside man became assertive and began openly questioning the state of their marriage. "I'm doing all the giving in our relationship," he said, "while you receive everything." His defiant comments and questioning caused Monica's suspicions to jerk and she started looking for reasons for the change in her husband.

She took to searching his things. She went through the pockets of his trousers and jackets hanging in the closet; she checked under the pile of shorts and T-shirts in his drawers; she rifled through the desk where he kept mail and bills. On March 7, not finding anything in the house, she checked his truck. After first running her hand underneath the seats, she popped open the glove compartment and swept the contents out onto the floor of the cab. Immediately, she found the letter to Anita. It was all she could do to restrain herself from ripping it open. Then, finding that the envelope wasn't sealed, she carefully extracted the letter, sickened at the sight of Paul's handwriting filling the pages. Words of love to another woman! The letter held her transfixed. Whether or not Monica missed the gist of the letter, which was that Paul intended to end the affair, she focused entirely on the word "love." Paul loved Anita. That meant he didn't love Monica. How could any man resist Monica? How could Paul love someone else when he had Monica? More than furious, she felt deserted and very much alone as she read about Paul's secret life.

Little did Paul and Anita know, Monica had a secret life of her own.

Later on, after she discovered the letter, Monica showed up at the Farmington bank where Anita worked as a loan officer. Anita immediately recognized her as Paul's wife. She had some friends in tow and was looking intently around the bank lobby. When Monica spied Anita's nameplate, the group headed her way.

She has a sense of purpose on her face like she's on a mission, Anita thought. *I hope this confrontation doesn't get too ugly right here in front of my co-workers.*

Monica looked beautiful that day. She had finally lost the weight she'd gained from her pregnancies and looked terrific in a softly tailored tan jumpsuit, her makeup flawless.

"I'm Paul Dunn's wife. I just wanted to meet the woman who's breaking up my marriage," she said, loudly enough for all those around to hear.

Monica blazed on while Anita tried to gather her thoughts. While she spoke, Monica fingered an enormous ruby heart she wore on a gold chain.

"Is yours as big as the one I'm wearing?" Monica had also found a bill from a jewelry store for a smaller ruby heart like the one she wore.

"I'm not sure I understand what you're talking about," Anita answered calmly.

She did, of course. Paul had given Anita a gift of a small ruby heart on a gold chain.

"How can you live with yourself being with another woman's husband?" Monica screeched, not mincing words.

"I'm not with him. I'm not seeing him anymore," Anita replied softly.

It was true, but Anita could tell that Monica didn't believe her. Suddenly Monica stopped and looked around at the craned necks and fascinated faces. She seemed to have no more questions. She had already achieved her aim of creating a scene.

"I think you should talk to your husband," Anita said quietly.

Just then a heavyset woman came out of another office. She had no idea what was going on at Anita's desk, but her face brightened when she recognized Monica. She came over and said hello.

Monica gushed, "Oh, hello. It's so good to see you, Nancy." She glanced at her watch. "I'm sorry, I have to go now. Bye!"

With that, Monica and her friends strode out of the bank.

Relief spread throughout Anita's tensed body as she slowly lowered herself to her chair. As she thought about it through the day and the entire scene sunk in, anger overtook her. She snatched up the telephone and called Municipal Court, asking to speak to Monica Dunn. *She walked into my world; I can call her in her world*, Anita fumed silently.

Monica was upset at the call and asked how Anita got the number, as if it were unlisted.

Anita spoke her piece. "I don't have any designs on Paul. I'm not the reason he's leaving you."

The phone call was short and to the point. Monica was outraged.

Afterward, though, Anita felt humbled, because she knew Monica was right. She had absolutely no business being with another woman's husband.

Later, after Anita found out that Monica had had an affair while married to Paul, gotten pregnant and had an abortion, she fumed. "The monumental gall of that woman to come down on *me*."

When Paul returned home that night, Monica confronted him and told him to leave. As always, he did as she said.

If Monica felt emotional turmoil, she masked it when

she visited attorney Victor Titus, Paul's friend. Soon after, she and Paul separated. She announced she was going to be seeking a divorce and contacting another lawyer who was not so close. She never made any claims of spousal abuse to Titus nor did she say anything about his affair or her own.

A few days later, Monica went to visit handsome Farmington Police officer Lawrence "Dusty" Downs. "She came into my office in the detective division and asked if she could talk to me about something," Downs said, explaining it had to do with Paul. "Monica had a bruise on the right side of her face," Downs said. "When I noticed the bruise on her face, that was the first time I had physically seen her. It had been common knowledge throughout the department, throughout the building I should say, that she and Paul were having marital difficulties. When she walked in the room, it was an assumption on my part the bruise may have been partially related to that."

Her sister's boyfriend accompanied Monica. On the occasion, Downs said, Monica spoke for the first time of having suffered abuse at her husband's hands and confided she thought he was taking steroids. Downs took photographs of her and gave her a domestic violence packet.

Downs said that after Monica's disclosures he was concerned for her safety and her well-being. Monica hadn't bothered to mention to Downs that a few days before, she had found in Paul's truck a letter proclaiming his love for Anita.

But Monica was not always so upbeat. Her best friend, Vicki Maestas, who knew Paul because Vicki's husband and Paul were casual acquaintances, said that Monica often came to work with tears in her eyes or eyes reddened from crying. Vicki worked with Monica for eight years and had been close to her during the time they were court clerks and even during Monica's brief stint working for a bail bondsman. Monica told Vicki Paul constantly came over to the house to talk to her after she told him to move out and that he "harassed" her at home and work by calling or stopping by unannounced. "He was driving by, trying to find out where she was all the time and just constantly bothering her."

Paul's actions angered Monica. Maestas didn't describe fear in Monica's demeanor. Monica told Maestas she had snooped in Paul's truck and found a letter Paul wrote to Anita. That they had had an affair was obvious. Maestas described Monica's fury at finding out about the affair. Monica told her she'd made copies of the letter, keeping one and giving the other copy to her father.

One day at work, Monica seemed especially sad to Maestas. She and another co-worker decided to visit Monica at home after work. Paul showed up at the front door while the two clerks were inside. Paul and Monica spoke at the front door. Soon, Monica's co-workers heard the two former lovers arguing over a document Paul needed. Maestas intervened, offering to get the document for Monica. In a moment, Maestas returned to the front door with the document. Maestas stepped outside and after handing the document to Paul, told him he needed to tell Monica once and for all if he wanted out of the relationship or not. Paul said he loved Monica, but he didn't think he was in love with her anymore. Before Paul could say anything else, Monica came out of the house and told Paul to leave. He left.

As that stormy March spun by, a troubled Paul devoted himself to his children. He went to his and Monica's house every Monday and Tuesday to see the girls. Just as he had done when he lived there, he did the laundry and cooking, and bought groceries, which seemed to please Monica, who also went off one weekend to Las Vegas. And she seemed to have a good time when she went with Paul to a movie on March 29, and met him at a neighborhood pub on March 30.

Paul went to see Maestas and asked her who Monica

had gone to Las Vegas with a few weeks earlier. Maestas said she didn't know. Paul persisted.

"Am I going to have to look at this person every day? Do I work with him?" Paul asked.

Maestas repeated she didn't know who Monica had gone to Las Vegas with. In that conversation, Paul also made reference to divorce and said he wasn't going to "get screwed over" as he did in his first marriage. He didn't get custody of April when he divorced his first wife. This time he would fight to get custody of Diane and Racquel.

On April 1, after filing divorce papers, Monica went out to lunch with Dusty Downs. That Friday, Paul stopped at Monica's office and told her he'd pick up the girls Monday morning. He also planned to cut the grass, clean out the hot tub and go grocery shopping for Monica.

Monica's mood darkened and became explosive on the night when she and her daughter, Amanda, followed Paul to Anita's house. Perhaps she had been expecting that an obviously suffering husband would want to return home to her and his children.

Late in the day on April 3, Monica's family had a barbecue at which Monica saw her friend Paula Jacquez, a nurse in Farmington whom she and her sister had known from their school days.

Paula and Monica had much in common as Paula explained. "I was kind of distraught over my husband. He and I had been separated for six months and my oldest son had gone out with a friend and had been away for a couple of hours. When Monica showed up at her uncle's barbecue, she could tell I was worried. I explained to her how it was hard to gain control of a teenage boy whose dad isn't around, and Monica and I got to talking and got to crying. We went off into the bedroom, and we spent probably two or three hours just, you know, discussing what breaking up is like after being married for so long. There was a lot of heartache and a lot of understanding between us."

Paula went on: "There was a lot of time we were crying, and there were a few times we could smile, but Monica could talk and start something and I could finish her sentence and she could do the same for me." Paula noticed Monica had lost a lot of weight. Monica complained that it was real hard for her to take care of herself physically as well as mentally. Paula explains, "I talked her into coming into my office and seeing my doctor and possibly getting something to help her sleep. Monica was concerned that Elaine, another nurse who worked for the same doctor and who was a friend of Paul's, would get hold of her records and give them to Paul, which would make a difference in the fight over custody of her children. I reassured her that I was sure my doctor wouldn't let that happen."

An upset Monica also told Jacquez, "I went to Anita Harris's place and saw Paul's truck there."

"It was there," Paula says, "she showed me a place on her elbow and on her side where she said she had been thrown into a mirror and broke it. She described the situation as him being a Jekyll-and-Hyde type of person. One minute he was the loving man that she married, the next minute it took next to nothing to make him fly off the handle." At one point, the two women laughed bitterly over the fact that it is okay for a man to go off and have a relationship with another woman, but when the woman tries to get on with her life, it's not okay; she's wrong to do it. "We shared the same belief that in society it is okay for your spouse to screw around, but if you go out to dinner with somebody, then it makes you evil."

Later, when Paul stopped by Monica's house to drop off some Easter treats for the girls, he gave Diane and Racquel a dollar and Amanda five dollars. Monica said she also needed some money, so without counting it, he handed her the rest of the cash from his wallet.

All seemed peaceful for the moment between the two former lovers, but it was the calm before the storm. Paul had heard that she was depressed. Of course, what he didn't know was the trigger had been Monica seeing him at Anita's. Paul asked Monica if he could come into the house for some water. At first she was reluctant, asserting he could get a drink anywhere and wanting to know why he felt the need to come into her house for that. But then she gave in. As they walked through the house, Paul asked how work was going on the remodeling of the master bedroom. He quickly entered the room with Monica nervously trailing behind. When he noticed the master bathroom door was closed he approached and tried to open it, but Monica jumped in front of it. Her quick movement knocked down a mirror hung on the door and it broke. Later, Paul admitted he tried to get to the bathroom to see if a man was hiding inside, but Monica blocked his way. Paul left after the mirror broke and didn't see Monica until Monday. He didn't know Monica had seen him at Anita's.

"You don't care. He hurt me and you don't care." She repeated the words but would never explain who hurt her. Paul got the impression that she was raped on the trip she had made to Las Vegas unbeknownst to him. In his rage and frustration about her being raped and refusing to name her attacker, he punched a hole in the wall. He had no idea at the time and would have thought anyone crazy who said Monica *had* to get herself bruised somehow if she was going to make the battery theory fly and set him up for murder.

That Easter Saturday, Monica called her friend Vicki Maestas around 8:30 P.M. Monica blurted out that "it" happened again. Maestas asked Monica why she didn't call the police about Paul's abuse. Monica said Paul threatened to kill her if she reported his violence, because he risked losing his job. "She was very afraid of Paul. She was scared. In our conversations, she was scared."

Monica told Vicki she had a domestic violence packet and she planned to file charges against Paul on Monday, despite the threats. She said she was scared about what Paul would do once he was notified about the charges, Vicki said.

Monica never talked to Maestas about suicide, not that night and not before.

On Easter Sunday, Monica paged Dusty Downs while he was at church and he called her back.

Downs commented, "Monica seemed distraught, somewhat upset." They arranged to meet at the police department around noon. Monica arrived with Rick Jacquez, her sister's boyfriend.

"She advised me that there had been an incident on the previous day and she now wished to go ahead and proceed with filing charges and a formal report. I explained to her again, uh, what would happen by the filing of this, this offense report would automatically start an administrative investigation. And I wanted her to be aware of that, that these people would be contacting her, uh, interviewing her in regards to that. I wanted [her] to be aware of that. I also informed her of her own personal safety that she needed to seek the civil remedy which is the domestic violence petition which would restrain Paul from any further contact with her. I even provided her with what we call the Domestic Violence Package to facilitate that."

Downs explained she would have to file the papers in court. Monica promised to do so. She asked Downs to call her early Monday to ensure she didn't back down.

But that never happened. Instead, the last explosive episode between Monica and Paul intervened.

On that Monday, at 5:30 A.M., Paul left Anita's house and went to his apartment to change and get some cereal and milk for his daughters' breakfast. He arrived at his former home about 6:40 A.M., just as Monica was backing out of the driveway with the girls in the van. Monica saw Paul and pulled back into the driveway.

"What did you expect me to do with three dollars?"

Monica demanded as she left the car. The girls remained inside the van, Diane wearing her Catholic school uniform.

"I didn't know I only had three dollars left when I handed you the cash." Monica told him she was taking the girls to their grandmother's house before she went to work. This puzzled Paul after the plans they'd made for him to watch the girls.

He got the girls out of the van, and they all followed Monica into the house. The girls started eating the cereal Paul poured for them. Monica asked Paul to dispose of some spoiled meat in the refrigerator and he did as he was told.

When Paul had finished the task, Monica made her angry announcement that she was filing charges against him.

CHAPTER 6

BLOODSTAINED HANDS

Guilt-ridden and grief-stricken, Paul surveyed the blood-stains from Monica on the walls and furniture. He tried several times to pick Monica up, but the gushing blood made her body slippery—blood yet another barrier between the one-time lovers. After one of those desperate moments, he looked up to see his fifteen-year-old stepdaughter, Amanda, wet hair dripping from her shower. Hatred loomed at him, her arms tightly crossed around her towel-wrapped body.

"What did you do to my mom?" she demanded.

"Nothing!" Paul cried hoarsely. "She just shot herself. Call 911! *Don't let the babies back here!*"

Amanda slammed the door. Diane was already calling 911, something her kindergarten teacher had just taught the class. Amanda took over the call. She told the dispatcher exactly what Paul had told her.

Finally, Paul half-dragged, half-carried his wife as he tried to race through the house. But he moved as though every step forced him to pull his shoes out of sucking quick-sand. He tried to ignore the wide-eyed horror in the little girls' eyes as they watched their death-soaked mother and determined father. In the garage, Paul tried to put his wife in the van, but she slipped out of his arms a final time. He felt her body shudder and knew he had no time to head for the hospital. He had to begin cardiopulmonary resuscitation.

Amanda kept the girls away from the garage, where she stationed herself. Her suspicious eyes took in Paul's every move.

After what seemed like hours, sirens roared in the air and an ambulance turned into the driveway. Emergency medical technicians took over CPR and tried to stop the bleeding as much as possible for the quick ride to the hospital. At that point, Paul didn't notice the blood all over his hands. "She died in my arms," he murmured over and over. What he did notice was the faces of the Farmington Police officers who arrived at his house. They were grim. He knew from personal experience that officers are trained to hide their emotions. But these guys could have at least acted a little sympathetically toward him after such an ordeal. Their stony expressions puzzled Paul.

Soon after ambulance personnel wheeled Monica off to the hospital, Paul looked down and saw for the first time his blood-covered hands. "I tried to give her CPR," he said. The other officers ordered him not to wash. Paul, feeling himself in shock, didn't have the energy to take care of himself anyway. And it didn't dawn on him the extent of what was going on in the minds of the officers.

Memories flashed through Paul's mind like dreams. Meeting Monica, dancing so close their heartbeats intermingled, their children's births. Their passionate, almost violent lovemaking, her body glowing afterward in the low light. Her warmth. The most beautiful woman in the world! Those pictures quickly metamorphosed into a bloody, gasping, yet still amazing-looking creature. Even death couldn't erase her beauty.

For two hours, New Mexico State Police officers who had been Paul's comrades questioned him, while Monica's blood dried on his hands. Although his fellow officers wouldn't let him go to the hospital to be with his wife in her last moments of life, he felt as if he had been there when the last of her body's physical energy joined its spectral.

Paul relived that macabre moment in the bedroom again and again. Nervousness as he opened the door; Monica's brown eyes fixated on his frightened, confused blue ones. The shotgun—her body, flying into the air, soaring, then crashing violently, blood gushing. Words were superfluous: the shotgun told instantly of all the unhappiness and pain, leaving no room for talk.

Farmington and state police officers intermixed, measuring blood spots, collecting evidence. Officers buzzed almost, but not quite out of Paul's earshot. Finally, what they were saying slowly penetrated his fog.

"Monica would never kill herself!" "You can't kill yourself with a shotgun!" "She's too tiny to reach the trigger." "Paul always kept loaded guns in his house."

But he didn't understand why Dusty Downs, Chief Richard Melton and Captain Mark McCloskey didn't believe him when he said he didn't hit Monica and that he wasn't taking steroids, another of her accusations to Downs. Paul volunteered to take a polygraph test to prove he never hit her. *I want to do it. Why'd she blame me for that when I didn't hit her? Why'd she tell Dusty I did?*

Paul did everything he was asked to do the morning of the shooting. He gave the New Mexico State Police investigator a urine sample, because they wanted to test for steroid use. He cooperated in their blood test for alcohol or other drug use. Their results wouldn't be finished immediately. They let Paul wash his hands and eventually let him leave. He wasn't under arrest while he was undergoing these tests at the Farmington Police Department and the San Juan Regional Hospital, but it sure felt like it. Moreover, Paul blamed himself for Monica's death because of his affair.

That's nothing unusual in police officers' lives—or many other human beings' for that matter—especially with night shift hours and if they work second jobs to make ends meet. But police officers said later that it was pretty hard to swallow, a beautiful woman with three children and a good job ending it all. Many men and women separate. Some get divorced, some get back together. It's devastating, but most women don't kill themselves because of it. And certainly not with shotguns. Officers say most women, if they plan to "off" themselves, do so by taking a bottle of pills.

While officers weighed the options, Detective Dusty Downs brought some news that Monica had visited him the day before. Downs said she showed him her bruises and told the typical domestic violence story. She feared Paul and was afraid of what he would do if she filed charges against him, so she just took the abuse. Now, she finally had the courage to tell someone about the abuse.

"I didn't shoot her! I didn't shoot her!" Paul kept telling seemingly blind and deaf officers, who now believed Downs' account.

Paul turned to Sergeant Mark Hawkinson. "What is happening here?"

"I don't know, bud." Hawkinson's response wasn't comforting for a "bud." His unemotional speech belied the fact he had once dated Monica. "If I were you, I would get a lawyer working," he concluded.

Paul called his attorney friend, Victor Titus. An arm injury had taken Titus from baseball to law school; a divorce took him from Missouri to New Mexico. By age thirty-eight, Titus had been selected as one of the "Best Lawyers in America" three times, served as president of the New Mexico Trial Lawyers and tried hundreds of cases to decision. But he had never tried a murder case.

Titus wasn't home. A frenetic Steve Murphy, Titus' new

partner who'd just passed the bar, answered instead. Sensing trouble, Murphy didn't want to admit his rising panic.

While Paul's co-workers interrogated him, Titus was watching a Rockies game at Mile High Stadium in Denver, Colorado. When Titus called his office, his secretary told him the news.

A bewildered Murphy shortly hooked up with Titus via Titus' cellular phone, which worked despite a raging snowstorm in Colorado. Titus and Murphy both got the impression the police felt Paul was the murderer. As much law experience and arrogance as linebacker-sized Titus had, he didn't want to admit this was his first murder case, too. And that the client was, of all people, a close friend. As if that wasn't enough pressure, Titus could tell the odds were against Paul. He just might be Paul's only chance.

Titus had another immediate problem. He was snowed in, roads closed. He couldn't make the eight-hour drive back to Farmington until the next day.

At the hospital, Monica's family gathered around the now-dead woman, peaceful in that final, eerie way as if she were Sleeping Beauty. But she had a large hole through her body. And they were convinced her handsome prince was the murderer. They couldn't believe Paul had the nerve to say she shot herself. And with his shotgun, too. The family would never believe their Monica would end her own life. She wouldn't do that to them, to her little girls. In addition, to them as Catholics, suicide was a sin punishable by the fires of hell, or at least the torment of purgatory, a place just above hell. The bodies of suicide victims cannot be buried on holy ground.

After leaving the police department, Paul went to his apartment. He spoke on the phone with his father, Buzz Dunn, and stepmother, Leslie. He spoke with his mother, Jane. He also talked to his sister, Robin. Finally, when the phone wasn't pressed to the accused's ear, it rang.

"What in the hell happened?"

Paul choked up at the sound of her voice. "Anita, she's gone. Monica's shot herself."

Anita already knew. After Monica died, her niece had come to the bank where Anita worked. The niece's words didn't exactly break the bad news gently. "I hope you're happy. That son of a bitch murdered Monica."

Paul felt Anita believed his explanation of what happened. She knew he'd never hit a woman, even though she'd be careful to add, no one should hit anyone—male or female. Still, Monica's death stunned her.

"I just can't believe it. I just can't believe it." Anita repeated the words over and over as if saying it enough would help the awful news sink in.

When Victor Titus finally got home around 5:00 P.M. the next day, the attorney attempted to console his friend, but frankly was appalled. The macho cop was gone; in his place was a fearful, grieving man who seemed to cry every few minutes and could not seem to hold his emotions inside. Titus admitted he'd be a wreck, too, if something happened to his own wife, but Paul's emotional reaction made Titus step out of the friend role and into the lawyer role. "Keep your mouth shut."

What Titus meant was for Paul not to talk to the media or to the police without his lawyer present. Not that Titus wanted to hear too many details of Monica's death. He didn't want his client's story to get him too focused on one theory. Instead, he liked to peruse all the evidence and then try to "trip them up." In effect, he played "devil's advocate" with his clients. Even when that client was a friend. Hell, perhaps *especially* when the client was a friend. Of course, he'd never had a client suspected of murder.

However, Titus didn't know that Paul was having an affair or that Monica just found out about it when she had visited Titus and told him that she and Paul were getting divorced.

It jolted Titus that Paul never told him about the affair. But when Titus put his attorney's hat back on, he realized it was a definite suicide motive. Titus also had a nagging question of his own, a central one. Could Paul have done it?

Paul didn't see Anita until three days after the shooting. By then, Paul was staying at his friend Andy's house. Andy's wife, Margaret, is Anita's sister. Watching him, Anita sat there in dry-eyed shock, her thick, flaming hair framing an ivory face on which makeup seemed foreign. People at work and in the community had already begun to ostracize Anita because of her affair with Paul, which was public knowledge now.

CHAPTER 7

A MEDIA FRENZY

The media was going hog-wild. Stories appeared every day in *The Daily Times,* Farmington's newspaper, in the *Albuquerque Journal, The Albuquerque Tribune, The Santa Fe New Mexican* and newspapers in surrounding states of Colorado, Utah and Arizona. Paul's picture appeared everywhere. Monica's face flirted with readers on the printed page and on television. Articles reported Monica had been shot to death and reported Paul had been put on administrative leave with pay until the investigation was over. The local television station, KOBF, heavily covered the story, as did the bigger stations in Albuquerque.

The media reported the path of Monica's body from the shooting to her final resting place. First, a trip to the Office of the Medical Investigator in Albuquerque for the gruesome, but necessary, dissection of the body known as an autopsy. Although this would only take a couple of hours, it was a crucial part of any police investigation. Murder or suicide often left fingerprints, marring the body while telling a tale.

Monica's body finally returned to Farmington just days after her death. Her funeral was slated for four days later.

To his surprise, Victor Titus was asked to be a pallbearer. He wondered why the family had chosen him. They were close-knit and wouldn't have wanted a stranger. Then it hit him. Monica must have chosen him. *How? When?* he wondered. Victor Titus wondered if anyone knew or cared that he was Paul's friend.

At Monica's funeral, people wore yellow ribbons "so the truth would come out." It was pretty obvious the people wearing the ribbons thought Paul had murdered Monica. Reporters raided Monica's funeral, cameramen and photographers tripping over each other to get shots of little Diane and Racquel, as well as the grieving Dora Sanchez, Monica's mother. No one expected to see Paul at the funeral; stories had already come out saying he wasn't allowed. The police were going to see that he stayed away at the family's request. It seemed that Paul Dunn had no supporters. At least, nobody stood up to defend him. Many of his friends, also friends of the deceased court clerk, appeared at the funeral with somber faces.

The appearance of many friends of both Paul and Monica seemed to exhibit support for the Sanchezes—not Paul. Their disbelief that Monica would commit suicide was a tiny bit greater, or in some cases, quite a bit greater, than their disbelief that Paul would kill anyone. For some people, it had more to do with Monica's religion than morality. Catholics are prohibited from committing suicide. For other people, the suicide question was more about race. They believed Hispanic women don't kill themselves. In the battle of the "lesser of two evils," Paul lost.

Paul was told not to go to his estranged wife's funeral. He spent his energy trying to get Diane and Racquel back from Monica's parents, Torry and Dora Sanchez. They refused to let him see his daughters or even talk to them. He could understand and forgive the Sanchezes' need to protect the children. But what they did to the girls he would never understand nor respect. They separated Diane and Racquel, who were as close as twins, at a time when they needed each other the most. Diane was sent to stay with Torry and

Dora, and Racquel to stay with her Aunt Theresa.

The weekend after the funeral, Monica's nephews Torry and Mike Cortez stood at a Wal-Mart store handing out more yellow ribbons for people to tie to their vehicle antennas in Monica's memory. They had a lot of takers.

Much later, a flag memorial for Monica emblazoned the sky at the city's domestic violence shelter.

At that point, attorney Victor Titus didn't think Paul was guilty of murder, but he couldn't completely erase his question. Monica was the stronger person of the pair, and Titus just didn't believe Paul had it in him to kill someone. The next week, Titus met with Magistrate Terry Pearson and Farmington attorneys Jay Faurot and Bob Graham. Titus sought their help in how to handle the case.

CHAPTER 8

RUSH TO JUDGMENT

District Attorney Alan Whitehead believed he had more than enough motives to ensure Paul Dunn would be charged in his wife's death. In addition, he was being pressured by the Sanchez family. While this is common in families when someone dies, here that pressure was more pronounced. The Sanchez family was a well-known, prominent Farmington family. Phone calls of sympathy and support came from everywhere, even Governor Bruce King's office. Both the governor and lieutenant governor visited the Sanchez home after the shooting. This had to be expected, in a way, because of the political ties of Monica's family. Whitehead, of course, denied political pressure in general and in particular, any coming from the governor.

Instead, when asked by the media, he brought up the domestic violence packet filled out the day before Monica died, which included photos taken by a police officer which revealed bruises on her body. He said it would be almost impossible for someone to kill him- or herself with a shotgun. What kind of awkward suicide weapon was that? He pointed to the specter of a police officer abusing his power, his physical strength. Everyone knew police officers had control problems. Whitehead felt he had everything on his side to file charges against Paul. Meanwhile, Whitehead told callers his office was doing everything in its power to investigate the case. Among them, state police drilled holes in the bedroom wall where the shots wound up. Laboratory tests were being run. All Whitehead had to do was sit back and wait.

However, polygraph tests seemed to be a deciding factor for the San Juan County district attorney's offices as to whether to take the case to the grand jury. In fact, a case-in-point was one which had a strange, serendipitous aspect: the gunshot wound victim also was named Monica. When Monica Eckstein died, her husband, Greg, passed a polygraph test. Strangely, though Whitehead had more evidence against Eckstein than he had against Paul Dunn, the district attorney quickly dismissed the charges against Eckstein. What was different about the two cases was that Monica Eckstein's family was virtually unknown in Farmington, certainly not with any ties to Governor Bruce King. Dora Sanchez was a friend of Democratic chairwoman Helen Singleton of Farmington. Singleton helped bring King and Lieutenant Governor Casey Luna to Farmington to show support for Monica Dunn's family. Their simple presence in Farmington put political pressure on Whitehead to prosecute Paul Dunn.

Superstition doubtfully played a role in anyone's belief about the similarities in the two Monicas' deaths. But the circumstances certainly were an uncanny coincidence.

Both women died tragic deaths by firearms with their husbands and children in the house at the time. Suspicion clouded each case, yet both men passed polygraph tests. There were major differences as well; Whitehead saw to it that Paul Dunn was arrested and charged with murder, but he didn't go this route in the Eckstein case.

When Eckstein passed the polygraph test, Whitehead didn't take the case against Eckstein any further. Whitehead had an unofficial policy in which he usually didn't prosecute a case if the accused passed a polygraph test. This isn't uncommon for district attorneys to do.

Monica Eckstein was a receptionist for the City of Farmington's recreation department with no political ties in Farmington or Santa Fe. Her husband worked for Amoco and also wasn't a political figure.

Evidence found in Greg Eckstein's house seemed more suspicious. At least it was obvious Greg or someone tried to clean up after the shooting. Police found a bloodstained bar of soap and a blood-soaked towel in the bathroom. An Amoco glove with a pinkish stain lay in the trash can.

In her fifth month of pregnancy, Monica Eckstein was found wearing men's underwear. She'd been shot through the right eye with a .22 caliber revolver. She had a bruise to her face and her tongue hemorrhaged before she died. She hadn't written a suicide note. Although investigators say they've seen suicides where the person doesn't leave a note, most people leave notes as their last connection with the living. Greg Eckstein was very open with the press after the initial hoopla died down. He believed his wife shot herself by accident while looking at the gun. Why she'd be looking at the gun around her toddler—or be anywhere near a gun while she was pregnant—is another mystery. Her husband could offer no explanation to that puzzle.

Greg also had no clue why there would be a pink or red stain on one of his Amoco gloves. He wasn't working that day. He couldn't explain the men's underwear, since his wife never wore men's underwear.

He also didn't know why she would have a bruise to her chin or hemorrhaging of her tongue.

After finding his wife dead, he washed the blood off his hands, never figuring he'd be considered a suspect of any crime. He knew his wife was dead when he found her. He said he wanted to get cleaned up before going to the hospital since he couldn't do anything to help her survive.

He was downstairs when he heard the gunshot coming

from their upstairs bedroom. He found his wife bleeding from the eye while their one-year-old son, Jordan, looked on. She had just come upstairs after eating breakfast. She brought the toddler with her. She'd never kill herself on purpose in front of their child. Greg Eckstein was sure of that.

So was Monica Eckstein's family, who still believes Greg had some part in Monica Eckstein's death, even if it was just an accident. The dead woman's sister, Vicki Goodall of Farmington, said she knows her sister didn't kill herself. She doesn't really believe her brother-in-law would kill Monica Eckstein. She thinks maybe they argued over the gun or *he* was cleaning it and accidentally shot her. She wishes Greg would just explain how the accident could've occurred.

A dramatic change in wording of both Monicas' autopsy reports proved to be the clincher for Whitehead, although others saw the alteration of findings a different way. The same medical investigator, Dr. Patricia McFeeley, performed both autopsies. Monica Dunn's report had initially indicated the shotgun was pressed to her abdomen. Later, the medical investigator changed this to indicate the gun was one to three feet away, which was the theory of investigators for the prosecution. The manner of death in the autopsy report for Monica Eckstein was changed from "homicide" to "undetermined" when Whitehead decided not to prosecute.

Family members of both women wondered if two killers were wandering around loose. Family members of the men in question wondered if "justice" was synonymous with "politics." Or was it just like that in Farmington? Of course, money is thrown in there somewhere. To prosecute Paul would eat up a lot of state tax funds. Defense in such a case can cost a great deal. Either way, family members didn't get their answers through the system. Neither did Paul Dunn or Greg Eckstein.

And Whitehead was getting lucky. Unlike the first autopsy report, the final autopsy report beautifully matched the ballistics tests. According to it, the shotgun had to be one to three feet from Monica Dunn's body when it was fired. There was no way anyone could kill themselves with a shotgun that was one to three feet away from their body when fired! A problem was solved for the prosecution. Political pressure could be eased by such an easy case. Whitehead wouldn't have to worry about reelection. Adding to the evidence was testimony of Monica's friends, who were continuously worried about her because of her declining health after she and Paul separated. The last few weeks before her death, bruises appeared on her body and a sullen Monica would only tell her friends that she had fallen. When pressed into explanation, friends said there was no way the bruises could have occurred the way she described. Her friends told the prosecutor they began to suspect Paul had abused her.

To Whitehead it all fit together. A conviction would take a bad cop and killer off the streets. Not to mention what it would do for Whitehead's reputation.

As a Tennessee Williams character once observed, "The unmistakeable smell of mendacity is in the air." Titus may not have had experience in murder cases, but he had an astute nose for such odors. Realizing that his own legal experience was not relevant, he now talked Paul into hiring a more well-known defense attorney, Gary Mitchell.

Gary, born in Santa Fe, is the oldest of five Mitchell boys. His father worked for years in the highway department in Encino, where Gary and his brothers went to "the smallest school in the state."

Mitchell gets his true-blue fighting spirit from his

mother, Manon Mitchell of Ruidoso, New Mexico, and his father, Arney Mitchell. His mother always divided her time between the kids and keeping the books at the Methodist church.

"My mom had this fiery passion about protecting the underdog. My dad was a World War II veteran," Gary states.

His mother's "fiery passion" must have affected Gary, who always spoke up for injustices as a youth and as a general loudmouth. He received a scholarship to Illinois Wesleyan College and went to law school at the University of Seattle, Washington.

"Early in life, my father had a great respect for lawyers. He felt lawyers more than anyone else held freedom in their hands. He felt that if we were strong people and stood up for ourselves, we'd always be free."

Growing up without a television, Gary Mitchell read a lot of books, mostly histories and biographies of people who loved their country and fought to strengthen democracy and rid it of corruption.

"Government is an evil we have to tolerate in order to live together. You have to butcher your cattle in order to eat. You don't want to have to do it, but you do it. The government's the same way."

Mitchell was a prosecutor in Thurston County, Washington, before moving to New Mexico, where he worked his way up from being a "nobody" at low wages to being one of the most well-known New Mexican lawyers of his day.

Mitchell's expertise has kept numerous people from being sentenced to death by lethal injection in New Mexico and kept many others from prison. His supporters believe him to be one of the best lawyers in this country; his detractors call him nasty names, but Dave Pfeffer, the investigator he often employs, says anyone who knows the guy knows he's a cowboy with a heart who would provide a stranger a great meal of his own cattle if he was to visit Mitchell at his Ruidoso home.

Recognizing that proving Paul innocent would be difficult, Mitchell decided he needed the services of private detective Dave Pfeffer. Born in Lodi, California, on a black Angus ranch, Pfeffer was raised by parents Walter and Darlene in Carmichael, California, until his sophomore year in high school. The family then moved to Long Island, New York. At the high school he attended there, he learned at an early age what it's like to be on the outside, looking in. The school was ninety-eight percent Jewish and two percent Catholic. The Protestant Pfeffer was immediately distinguished. Also separating him from his classmates was the fact that he wore "funny" clothes, jeans and wild shirts with belts to match and "frat" shoes, which were basic gym shoes with red, white and blue stripes. The Beach Boys were popular in California and Pfeffer's look emulated them. But the popular people on Long Island wore white shirts, ties, penny loafers and nice slacks underneath their long overcoats.

Nevertheless, it didn't take long for the charismatic Pfeffer to fit in. He started hanging out with the "in" crowd, which were the jocks then. The "in" crowd for teenagers in later years ditched too many classes for parties to be on sports teams.

After graduating high school, Pfeffer moved back to California, this time to Fresno. He started working at Sambos family restaurant chain. His endeavors with the chain led him to move to Roswell, New Mexico, where he managed the restaurant. In his time off, he worked with the Roswell Police Auxiliary. He got status early, because he was placed immediately with detectives. That was initially through no fault of his own—the uniforms just weren't large enough to fit Pfeffer. Later, it became obvious Pfeffer was a natural at the job.

"They liked me working with them because I always

seemed to find things in my searches and was continually able to figure out what the next move of the criminal was."

It was that knowledge without proof that came naturally to him, without Pfeffer having taken his first police academy class. The auxiliary was a volunteer organization and didn't have the funds to send its officers to school.

When the Sambos restaurant chain folded, Pfeffer talked to then–Ruidoso Police Officer Paul Lukens, about becoming a full-time police officer. Lukens couldn't understand—and who could blame him?—why Pfeffer would want to go from making $60,000 a year to $450 a month. Finally, Lukens hired the persistent Pfeffer. The department staff never regretted the hire.

Pfeffer's twenty-year career in Ruidoso was plagued by cases of political pressure. Pfeffer was supervisor over the criminal division and ordered the district attorney and the state police to report what his narcotics officer, who was assigned to a special task force, was doing at all times. Pfeffer was told the narcotics officer's actions were none of his business. Pfeffer responded that if he were not made aware of all the officer's duties—as a supervisor should be—then he would immediately transfer the officer onto another assignment out of the task force.

Almost immediately, the district attorney's office and the state police began an investigation into the Ruidoso Police Department. Pfeffer was accused of stealing a nine-millimeter pistol. It was found in the glove box of Pfeffer's marked police unit. Pfeffer showed it to them, pointed out that it was checked out of evidence and approved by the department's deputy chief, which was later confirmed by the deputy chief, although the evidence card with Pfeffer's signature to show he checked it out was oddly missing. The district attorney's office considered charges against Pfeffer since the evidence card was missing, but the office backed down when Pfeffer hired Mitchell as his attorney.

"They were looking for anything to tag me with, as they

were very upset at my insistence to know what that officer was doing," Pfeffer asserted.

During that time, lots of people were suing police departments and Pfeffer wanted to make sure officers under his supervision performed properly so the department didn't get sued.

In another vendetta in Pfeffer's past, he was accused of being the biggest dope dealer in New Mexico when he ran for sheriff of Lincoln County, Ruidoso's county. "No one in the history of the Ruidoso Police Department had, to that point, ever put more drug dealers into jails and prison than I. Anyone with any sense would know that it would be impossible for me to be dealing drugs and busting drug dealers at the same time."

Then rumors spread that he beat his children and sexually abused his daughters.

"Interestingly enough, they checked the schools and found that all but one of my children, a boy, were getting straight A's and that after questioning them, they had told the officers that their 'daddy was the best daddy in the whole world,' " Pfeffer said, quoting police documents.

Nevertheless, the rumor mill worked. Pfeffer wasn't elected. He believes part of the problem was that his family lived in a beautiful home in the upper canyon area of Ruidoso. Pfeffer's parents had put down a substantial down payment for them, which is how Pfeffer was able to afford it. The home was worth about $125,000 after Pfeffer made some improvements to it. People probably wondered how a police captain in Ruidoso could afford the house. Ruidoso is a beautiful, mountainous area that attracts a lot of visitors because of the horseracing track and the view. It's a vacation spot—and the average home is very expensive there. Nobody bothered to ask Pfeffer how he was able to afford the home.

After Pfeffer retired from the Ruidoso Police Department, he began working as a private investigator. Finally, he opened his own business, calling it "Shamus," an Irish word that means "sleuth" or "investigator." Aside from the meaning, the word sounded to him like a perfect match to his golden retriever named Sherlock Holmes.

Pfeffer's nose as well as his instincts had helped him solve some high-priority cases, like a rape case in Ruidoso because of a bunch of partially smoked Salem 100s strewn about in an obscure area in the stunning, hilly Hondo Valley of New Mexico, not far south of Ruidoso.

Gary Mitchell will never forget that case. "Doggone his hide!" The defense attorney smiled in exasperation speaking of then-Sergeant Pfeffer.

Both Pfeffer and Mitchell believe this old case is one of their most memorable on opposite sides of the law.

Pfeffer worked the case of a woman who was kidnapped late at night from her job as manager of a motel by three unmasked men. Threatening to beat her with nunchuks, a martial arts weapon made of wood and chain, they forced her onto the floor of their car while they drove to a bar and bought beer. Then they drove a few more miles; the woman couldn't really tell because she was on the floor, although she wasn't blindfolded. She could tell they turned off the road and onto a dirt road. Finally they stopped. Each raped her in the back floor of the car. Then they forced her to sit in between them in the car seat. They were smoking. She smoked along with them, she told Pfeffer.

Pfeffer wanted to go to the scene of the crime. Asking the victim to close her eyes, Pfeffer drove her in an unmarked car past her motel onto a road to the only bar he knew of in the vicinity she described, if her left and right turn descriptions were correct. He parked at the bar and went inside to talk to the owner and see if he recognized anyone from her descriptions.

"All of a sudden, I heard this screaming and I mean this ungodly screaming."

Pfeffer raced out of the bar, gun ready for action. A car

was pulling out of a parking space. The woman in his car was pointing at it from the passenger seat.

"That's them!" she screamed hysterically.

Pfeffer, dressed in plain clothes, pointed his gun at the driver. The driver stopped. The ashtray was stuffed with cigarette butts. Pfeffer found a pair of nunchuks under the seat of the car.

Pfeffer arrested the men.

He thought his job was pretty much over at that time, although he didn't have much evidence other than her word against theirs. Or so he thought.

Later he drove the woman past the bar and she told him to "turn soon" when she thought he was near the right place where the men had turned onto a dirt road. Pfeffer found one quickly.

He drove to a fairly secluded spot and parked. Stepping out of the vehicle, he began walking around looking for any evidence. Not far into the walk, he found a patch of ground covered with cigarette butts which appeared to have been tossed out of either side of a parked vehicle. The partially smoked cigarettes still had the Salem 100s markings on them. He knew he had found the right place.

The busy day was not over yet. Pfeffer went back to the police department. An officer told him the prisoners were yelling for cigarettes. Back then, inmates could smoke in their cells; in fact, most places allowed smoking. On a hunch, Pfeffer brought two uniformed officers with him when he went to their cell.

"You want cigarettes?"

"Yeah!"

"What kind do you smoke?"

"Salem 100s."

"Salem 100s?" Dave wanted to make sure he heard right.

"Yeah, that's all I ever smoke."

At the trial, Pfeffer and two uniformed police officers testified about the defendants' smoking preference. Pfeffer and Mitchell believe it was the turning point for jurors, who convicted the rapists.

Mitchell was happy to have Pfeffer share an office with him.

Others of the more famous New Mexico cases the two worked include the murder of nine-year-old Dena Lynn Gore in Artesia by Terry Clark, who awaits death by lethal injection and has begged courts to kill him and get it over with. The investigator for the defense on the case, Pfeffer says even having been a cop for twenty-odd years didn't prepare him for the skin-crawling viciousness of his client.

The "Hollywood Video Murders" is also a famous Albuquerque case Mitchell and Pfeffer worked together in the mid-1990s. Their client was convicted of being an accessory to the murders of three employees in the store. While the murders were occurring, the unsuspecting grandparents of one of the victims were waiting in a vehicle outside the store to pick up their grandson from work. The store was about to close.

The murderers made off with about $136,000.

Then they spotted the grandparents. The killers notched off two more killings on their belts after they forced the grandparents out into the hills and killed the witnesses. Pfeffer's client was convicted.

The day Mitchell and Pfeffer drove from their offices in Ruidoso they strutted into Farmington in cowboy boots, their hats tilted perfectly in that "Evening, ma'am," cowboy-polite fashion. At least a foot taller than everyone else, they were quite a pair. Mitchell wore his golden-brown mustache thick, his knowing, hazel eyes appearing innocent. Pfeffer's baby face contrasted with his large, powerful body. *Lord*, Titus thought, *they're going to get killed for sure*. First for being intimidatingly annoying. Then, they had the nerve to go against the flow and believe in the "impossible"—that Monica killed herself with a shotgun.

It's hard not to like Mitchell if you meet him. His country drawl and reasonable questions make most people who aren't on his side feel at best uncomfortable, at worst, stupid. It's unclear if he *means* to terrify people into spilling their guts with his innocent face or if he doesn't realize how his appearance affects people. However, this time Mitchell asked the wrong questions to the right people and managed to anger police and prosecutors immediately. Titus didn't care what the attorney's personality was. Whatever it was—cowboy charm or horseshit—Mitchell was good. Titus felt like he took his first non-shaken breath since being told of Monica Dunn's death.

Mitchell wasted no time. Next he brought in ballistics expert Nelson Welch of Cochiti Pueblo outside of Santa Fe. These experts look at guns and pictures of wounds, and piece together what happened at crime scenes. They look for signs of who did the shooting and how. Welch and Pfeffer spent most of one day searching the Dunn home, looking for clues the police overlooked. While Mitchell described Welch as honest, police officers and prosecutors have said he's just a hired gun. Welch, very passionate of his convictions and work, would be angered at these criticisms, but would not put much stock in them.

Prosecutors didn't really understand what the defense experts were doing in the Dunn house, because the police had already been there and gathered evidence. Whispers intensified. Surely, they couldn't add to the job the police had done.

Word of mouth was that prosecutors believed they had an open-and-shut case.

Welch believed no such thing. He suggested bringing in forensics expert Dr. Martin Fackler. Fackler worked with another expert together on the wound characteristics trying to ascertain why there would be certain marks on Monica's entrance and exit wounds. The experts were shocked at what they learned.

Titus waited impatiently for them to finish their work. He had plenty of other cases to work on but this one occupied his mind. A dim hope flickered in the experts' minds that if they proved Paul couldn't possibly have killed Monica, the district attorney wouldn't prosecute. Little did they know what was going on on the other side of the fence.

CHAPTER 9

TRUTH, LIES AND LIE DETECTORS

Because they thought it could end the case, Paul's attorneys sent him to Salt Lake City to meet with famed polygrapher David Raskin. That Friday, a choking, sobbing Paul explained the events again—his confusion, Monica's silence, the blood, Monica's body blown backwards by the force of the shotgun, her gasping for air, her final shudder—before Raskin asked him the crucial questions. When it was over, Raskin scored the test while Paul paced and chain-smoked outside. He was a wreck by the time Raskin came out.

"I believe you, and I'm sorry, sorry for what you've been through and the pain you've endured. I'd stake my professional reputation on it: you're telling the truth." Raskin never wavered from that view. But a lot of skeptics in Farmington thought Raskin was a hired gun for the defense and that, of course, he would believe his client innocent and make sure Paul passed the test.

Paul said, "Bless his heart. I've heard that angels come to you and you don't know they're angels. I believe David Raskin is an angel."

Raskin told Paul, "I wish I had videotaped the test, because it is a classic example of someone passing the test." He explained that a negative-six or under is failing, between negative and positive-six is inconclusive and anything above a positive-six is passing. Paul got a positive-eighteen.

Ecstatic wouldn't be a strong enough word to use for Paul's emotions when he heard his score. The prosecution would have to let him go now and give Titus and Mitchell the results. Titus said he would take the polygraph results to Whitehead first thing that Monday morning and hopefully end the case. But Paul wanted to go right then and get it over with.

"Let me be the lawyer," was Titus' unemotional response.

An exhausted Paul went to Officer Bob Fain's house, where his father was staying, to tell him the good news. Later, Anita came over to her sister Margaret's house where Paul was staying. Paul looked to her feeling overwhelmed. "Oh my God, Anita, I have some news."

Anita backed away and crossed her arms. "Did you fail?" Turmoil darkened Anita's face. She backed farther away.

"You need to look at it." He handed her the pages.

Despite passing the polygraph, he asked himself, could Anita think he killed Monica?

Mitchell and Titus took the report to the prosecutor. Unfortunately for Paul, unlike in the Eckstein case, Whitehead this time appeared uninterested in the results of the polygraph test. Whitehead knew he had a case he could win—polygraph or no polygraph. He tossed the results aside.

"I don't care about any of that now! He will be charged!" Whitehead exclaimed.

When Paul learned the district attorney had said the polygraph test didn't matter, he moved around in a morose state. Mainly, he moped about Monica's death, not seeing his babies and the lack of support from the police department.

He couldn't believe his state police officer friend, Noe Galvan, was investigating the case.

When Galvan had problems and almost lost his job, Paul gave Galvan the benefit of the doubt. When he saw Galvan back in uniform after an internal investigation, Paul had made a point to say he was glad to see him back on duty.

"He was my friend." And officers were supposed to stick together. It was kind of an unspoken rule that fellow officers—people who care about and spend time with each other outside of work—share special bonds.

Paul felt intense bewilderment and betrayal at Galvan's heading the investigation. "It was like someone ripped your heart out, stuffed it in your face and said, 'How about them apples?'"

Paul never once tried to get anyone to believe he was perfect, but he felt his record of honesty and loyalty should have counted for something. No one listened when Paul explained Monica shot herself with *his* shotgun.

And he had never been lonelier. The Sanchez family wouldn't let him see Racquel and Diane. They wouldn't even let his father, Harvey "Buzz" Dunn, collect the girls after agreeing to the visit April 14, ten days after Monica's death. They turned Buzz away at the door.

Paul decided to go over there himself. When a Farmington police sergeant called to warn the family Paul was on his way, it caused a panic in the Sanchez household. The only way the sergeant would have known about Paul's visit was if Paul told him. Some friend he turned out to be.

The Sanchezes ended up calling in San Juan County Sheriff's deputies when Farmington police officers told them they didn't have enough officers to watch their house. Why the sergeant who made the call causing all the frantic behavior wouldn't personally "serve and protect" the Sanchezes wasn't clear.

Dora Sanchez called City Councilor Mary Fisher, who promised to straighten out the police department.

Ruth Candelaria, a family friend, wrote in a letter to the Farmington *Daily Times* that the police needed to do a better job protecting its citizens. The gist of her letter made the community's attitude clear. Paul needed no trial. They could have just hung him right there.

She stated: "I can't begin to tell you the fear that ran through the family and the children in this household, not to mention how terrified the female guests in the home felt. Knowing how I felt, I know the Sanchez family was truly terrified."

Deputy Ralph Trotter, now a private investigator in Farmington, later said in his report that the city sergeant just intended to warn that violence might result if Paul appeared. The city sergeant also had warned Paul he'd be arrested if he went to the Sanchez home and he assigned an officer to watch the house where Paul was staying. So why would the department tell the Sanchezes they wouldn't stake out their house? It made no sense.

Titus eventually got involved that night and told Paul to stay away from the Sanchez house. A bereft Paul complied, even though he was supposed to be innocent until proven guilty, hadn't been officially charged with anything and had every right in the world to see his daughters.

Paul stumbled around, not really knowing exactly what he was doing.

"I wasn't over Monica's death. Every fiber in my being was screaming: 'I didn't do it!' Nobody was listening. I was all alone. I felt like a doomed man, condemned to the gallows they were building outside my window and I knew what the morning would bring."

CHAPTER 10

JAILBIRD

Exactly two weeks after Monica's death, Titus called Paul to his office. Titus' partner, Murphy, was with him.

"What's up?" Paul asked, solemn faced.

The attorneys munched on hamburgers from Blake's Lotaburger. Apprehension clouded Murphy's features.

The ever-cool Titus handed Paul a burger. "Here, better eat. You won't have good food for a while." He paused and looked at his friend.

"Whitehead has issued a warrant for your arrest." They were to turn Paul over immediately after eating lunch.

The first night in jail, Paul lay wide-awake on the box springs of a bed with no mattress. He couldn't eat, couldn't sleep.

The jailers left the light on in his lone cell all night. He brooded, paced, cried. Paul quickly learned jailers in Farmington treated the inmates like animals. He had to "raise hell" and scream about his constitutional rights in order to get a shower or see the sun. He understood the jail staffers were busy, but treating people like scum before they were found guilty seemed cruel and inhumane.

. . .

Ten days after a suspect is arrested, by law, there must be a preliminary hearing to determine if the prosecutor has enough probable cause to take the case to a jury trial. The hearing is open to the public. The prosecutor presents evidence and the defense can cross-examine witnesses and present its evidence. The media flocked to the jail for a great shot of the "murdering cop" the day of his scheduled preliminary hearing. Wearing sweatpants and a muscle shirt, Paul Dunn grabbed a towel just before leaving the jail and held it over his head. The Farmington *Daily Times'* photograph hit the wire services soon after the hearing, in which the judge decided not to handle the case.

Meanwhile, a crowd picketed outside Magistrate Court with signs reading "No Bond For Dunn" and "No Plea Bargain for Dunn." Residents thought Paul should have been paraded down the hall wearing an orange jail jumpsuit and handcuffs. They argued he should receive no bond and the children should stay with their grandparents. "Justice for Monica" was what the group demanded.

When the preliminary hearing was canceled, the defense team felt doomed. If they could only present their side of the case to a judge—even the small amount of evidence they'd gathered so far—they believed the judge would dismiss Paul's case. The longer such a hearing was delayed, the more prosecutorial zeal and manipulated public opinion would convict Paul before he was even brought to trial.

Soon, Whitehead informed Paul's attorneys he planned to call a grand jury to investigate the death, because no judge could be found to hold a preliminary hearing. Grand juries serve the same purpose as preliminary hearings except the defense attorney and defendant aren't allowed to be present so the defense can't cross-examine witnesses or present evidence. Grand juries differ from trial juries in that they just indict, or charge, someone with an offense. Grand jurors also can perform investigations and ask questions. These hearings are closed to the public.

When Gary Mitchell learned Whitehead planned to convene a grand jury, he began his series of attempts to "knock some sense" into Whitehead. It fell on deaf ears. Mitchell wrote Whitehead and asked him to reconsider having a preliminary hearing where Mitchell could cross-examine witnesses.

"Our investigation confirms my belief that Paul Dunn is innocent."

Mitchell acknowledged that many people in the community believed Paul killed Monica, but he told Whitehead they weren't aware of all the facts.

"I had hoped to be able to have this matter conducted in a fair and honest fashion, with both parties exchanging discovery early on, so that an innocent man wouldn't continue to be in jail and continue to be prosecuted."

Mitchell reminded Whitehead a district attorney must fight for justice, not just prosecute every suspect who comes along. Often, that meant not filing charges against innocent people, no matter what an angry public demanded.

But Whitehead paid no attention to Mitchell's letter and proceeded to schedule the grand jury hearing. He put Deputy District Attorney Darrel Jiles and Assistant District Attorney Kathleen Carnell on the case. In some respects, Whitehead had no other choice but to proceed. He couldn't very well let a cop get away with murder. Especially not when his wife and her family were so well known not only in Farmington, but by the governor.

CHAPTER 11

PURGATORY

Hot tears. Cold cell. The horrific visions—again and again, Monica's body flying through the air, landing on the bed. Blood, everywhere, blotting out his peace. Dream became reality, reality a dream. Paul didn't know if he was living life in a prison cell or having too real a nightmare.

Days passed slowly. Paul waited for the grand jury to meet. A few phone calls of support came from co-workers. City officials fired him almost immediately after his arrest. Councilwoman Mary Fischer made it known she would demand justice. But justice for who? Wasn't Paul a constituent as well as a police officer? Fischer said she cared about the Sanchezes' supposed "nightmare come true" when Paul wanted to see his daughters before his arrest—which he had every right to do. But she made no mention of Paul's own nightmare.

In his living nightmare, Paul felt alone. Abandonment— he never thought it would happen to him.

Betrayal by his co-workers never occurred to Paul. To him, the realization that those who worked with him for so long would think he'd kill Monica was unfathomable. Why could no one else see this? But many turned their backs on him, even those who once seemed steadfast friends. Even they were afraid to defend him for fear of ridicule or losing their jobs. It wasn't popular to be on Paul's side. If you were, you were thought of as someone who condoned wife-beating. You believed it was okay for police to use their power to the detriment of another. It was a belief in the power of man over woman—the age-old belief that men were supposed to drag their women by the hair into the cave and have their way with them. If the woman protested? Why, beat her. Had these judgmental folks really known Paul Dunn, he knew they would never classify him with wife-beaters. And what ever happened to innocent until proven guilty? Why did they believe Paul had beaten Monica without proof?

When Monica died it was almost as though his enemies, like jealous gods, wanted to destroy him. People seemed almost happy to bring him down because they felt he had such a high opinion of himself.

If an egotist he was, it was a misunderstood one in Paul's mind. Had any of these people, in Paul's greener days on the police force, bothered to find out what the real Paul Dunn was like, they would have seen the insecurities as well as the general sensitive, if self-centered attitude, and later, caring father he was.

But the superficial nature he projected was all anyone saw. Paul had few co-workers over to his house and didn't spend time with very many officers and their wives. He had spent most of his time with his family.

They didn't see the softer side. Farmington Police Officer Cliff Ollum and Farmington Community Service Officer Bob Fain remained steadfast in their belief that Paul would never kill anyone, least of all, Monica. It was hard to see his buddy being labeled a murderer for a crime Ollum knew he didn't commit but one in which Paul might get convicted anyway. Ollum knew and liked Monica, too, but he knew Paul would never kill her. Ollum was worried that in a world where true justice gets sullied by politics, his friend might lose the case.

Titus had lost all doubts about Paul's possible guilt. He didn't think Paul was devious enough to plan Monica's death in such a cold, calculating manner. Knowing Monica as well, Titus also believed dressing up and perfecting her makeup was Monica's last dramatic act before she killed herself. The attorney also believed Paul the "too dramatic" type of guy vulnerable to ordeals such as meeting and marrying a woman like Monica and then getting caught up in her jealousy.

Moreover, Paul's personality seemed to Mitchell that of a giver not a taker. Paul's friends said Paul always put other people in front of himself, to the extent that he would suffer to help another person. Paul would give his last dime to a stranger on the street. He tried never to put anyone down, although he always admitted to being imperfect and having human prejudices. He always tried to see the good in a person and try to figure out why they did what they did. That's why he had such a hard time with one of the state policemen and an incident several years before Monica's death, when the man had almost choked a police dog to death. Paul gave him the benefit of the doubt then. "He was my friend."

Nevertheless, this same friend wrote thirteen pages in his court document requesting Paul's arrest in Monica's death. Why his friend ignored evidence in Paul's favor the jailed officer just could not understand.

That Paul was dedicated to his job—and was good at it—was an understatement. That his talents and professional abilities were known and applauded made it especially hard to understand why *everyone*, from schools to other police agencies, could so easily believe him capable of evil without giving him a chance.

As Paul brooded in his cell, his fevered thoughts spun back to another case. One tragedy which brought some, but not most, Farmington police officers together a few years before Monica's death drove them apart. Gossip about the shocking shooting murder of Community Service Officer Vicki Chavez in 1992 rifled through the department. A punchy, upbeat woman, Chavez was always willing to go the extra mile, but often bit off more than she could chew. This made it even more surprising that while her death made a few officers like Paul and Cliff Ollum nurture and support each other in their grief, other officers withdrew. It was a foreshadowing of how the department would later treat Paul.

Community Service officers like Chavez wear uniforms, but are civilians who handle simple police reports and calls that don't involve foreseeable danger. They aren't certified and don't carry guns. In her career, Officer Chavez often had to explain to her supervisors why she continuously put herself at risk. Often, she acted to help someone in trouble. She usually came out of such situations with flying colors. But not the one which finally ended her life.

The sun shone brightly across the clear, blue Farmington sky the morning Chavez drove up to Kevin Ogden's mother's house in Farmington. The department was handling a special patrol of the house while Mrs. Ogden was out of town. The department handled routine patrols of homes whose residents requested the service while they were out of town. The patrols were a boring job that had to be done.

Kevin Ogden, a mental patient who had had problems with the police in the past, was not allowed in the Ogden house while his mother was gone. The ever-observant Chavez saw Kevin's brown station wagon parked in front of the house and knew trouble was brewing.

"Uh-oh, someone's here w' shouldn't be."

The words she ominously spoke on the police radio didn't reflect the dire trouble in which Chavez soon placed herself.

Chavez parked in front of the house. She didn't know that Kevin Ogden, shotgun in tow, lurked at the window, ready to pounce. Before Chavez got out of her car, Ogden charged at her.

"No . . . don't!" were Chavez's final words in life, captured on her police radio.

Several rounds of bullets fired at close range blew off part of Chavez's left cheek, nose and the left corner of her mouth, which remained frozen in a macabre scream. Eyes that would never again see her loving husband, Ben, children and many friends stared frozen in the photographs taken by a shaking Farmington police officer's hands.

The shotgun pellets traveled around her so-called bulletproof vest on the left side and lodged in her lungs. Some pellets entered the vest and pushed the vest into her body. Any of the wounds were fatal.

Ogden didn't know Chavez; the uniform attracted him. He hated cops. He had a long list of arrests, mainly for disorderly conduct and drugs. Everyone who knew Ogden knew the attractive, tall dark-haired man suffered from some mental illness. To police, he was a nightmare in the making. But no one could predict he would kill.

Paul felt not only grief for the loss of Vicki Chavez, but he felt guilty, as if he could have prevented her death. He was working that day. To Paul's mind, a community service officer shouldn't have handled that patrol at the Ogden house with Kevin's history. He knew Kevin Ogden. He had "danced" (fought) with Kevin many times when Ogden resisted arrest. Perhaps if he and other experienced officers had taken Kevin Ogden more seriously—made sure he spent time in prison—Vicki Chavez would be alive. He knew hindsight was twenty-twenty, but that didn't make Paul feel any better.

Still, the way other officers handled her death amazed Paul. The department scrutinized and criticized Chavez's actions before she was buried. They blamed her for parking at the house when she saw Kevin's station wagon. They criticized her because she didn't leave and call a uniformed officer there. They called her death her own fault. While she did violate department policy, Paul and a few other officers found the department's view of her death sickening. No officers were allowed to take time off to support her family through the trial, which was moved to Gallup, two hours south of Farmington, because of too much pre-trial publicity. Only Officer Kim Shirer, a close friend of Chavez's and her family, took a leave of absence to attend the month-long procedure. She appeared every day at the trial, a stronghold for the family and Farmington Police Department's only example of a heart. Paul and Shirer later discussed the reasons for the callousness. They discussed how many officers probably were jealous of Chavez. She made a lot of officers look lazy. This didn't endear her to her co-workers, although most admitted she was a committed officer.

In the wake of the department's mistreatment of Chavez's death, Paul Dunn shouldn't have been surprised at how so many treated him. Nevertheless, an attitude of caring shone on some officers' faces as they spoke about Paul months after Monica's death. Several officers' eyes teared. They obviously struggled between their loyalty to a fellow colleague and the department's unofficial attitude. However, to the majority, Paul spent too much time in the gym, worrying more about his physique and women, than he did his job. And some officers immediately deemed him a bastard and murderer when allegations of domestic violence hit the news.

Officers frown upon domestic abusers—especially cops who prey on their spouses. Part of the reason is that domestic violence situations are among the most dangerous situations officers face daily. Many officers are shot and killed while responding to domestic calls. Sometimes victims turn on the officers when they learn their loved one, albeit the one who just stabbed them, is going to jail.

Domestic violence among their peers makes the whole

department look bad. It's as if all officers abuse their power
and batter their spouses. Trying to disprove this isn't easy.

No matter what was behind the majority of officers' attitudes, it was clear most officers, the very people who
should have stood behind him, ostracized Paul. This was
never more clear to him than when he found himself in an
isolated cell, with few visitors.

PART TWO

DRAWING SIDES AND POINTING FINGERS

Nor is the people's judgment
Always true!
The most may err as grossly
As the few.

—John Dryden
Absalom and Achitpohel

CHAPTER 12

THE GRAND JURY

Darrel Jiles' dry, aristocrat-stiff manner greeted a group of San Juan County residents on a May morning as they assembled for the much-publicized task of determining Paul Dunn's fate. The fortyish Jiles sat at the prosecution table. Next to him sat the light-brown-haired Kathleen Carnell. Both sported eyeglasses and with their similar mannerisms, Carnell appeared to be Jiles' female twin, although she was at least ten years younger.

No one disputes the evidence the prosecutor presents at grand jury hearings, unless grand jurors want to challenge a witness. Jiles began with an introduction of the court workers the grand jurors saw in front of them and gave them a basic synopsis of the case.

"The proposed charge is an open charge of murder. That means that, in New Mexico, there are four levels of homicide—murder in the first degree, murder in the second degree, voluntary manslaughter and involuntary manslaughter. Those are the four levels of homicide. An open charge of murder means that the charging authority—in this case it would be the grand jury if you find probable cause as to a charge—chooses not to specify any particular level, but indicts the target on the opportunity for the trial jury to choose any of those levels of homicide or, in fact, to find the defendant, or in this, the target, not guilty. And, of course, you have the option of not returning any indictment whatsoever having found no probable cause if that is, in fact, your view of the evidence. So an open charge is you're not specifying what level the target would be charged with if you, indeed, find probable cause but allow the uh, the trial jury, at a later date, when a trial, if one takes place, to make that ultimate decision. If, however, in the course of your deliberations, you feel that—you come to the conclusion that there's probable cause for one particular level and not a higher level, then, of course, you would have that opportunity to return an indictment at that level. Again, this will be explained at the end of the presentation of evidence. But at this point, that's just to advise you."

Many confused, open-mouthed jurors stared at Jiles, not following his intricate explanation.

"Also, I'd like to give you copies, one of which I'll need to mark for an exhibit. You have your manuals there, is that correct? These are the pages upon which you will find the statutes and jury instructions which pertain to the levels of homicide in New Mexico and, this we'll call State's Exhibit Number One in the matter of Paul Dunn. And there's one entered into the record and for the record, I am handing each of the members of the grand jury a copy. This shows where you will find each of the instructions. The instruction that is not in your book, which is firearm enhancement instruction, which is the next to the last item on that exhibit, so as we go through the presentation of evidence today and on Friday, if you wish to refer to the statute or the jury instructions, those are the pages upon which you will find them."

Jiles paused for a breath. "If there are any questions, I will answer them now."

The jurors glanced around expectantly, but no one raised a hand.

Jiles was to call a succession of witnesses, including Gerald Beltran, a fingerprint analyst from the New Mexico State Police Crime Laboratory; Larry Renner, the serology analyst from the New Mexico State Police; Rick Jacquez, the boyfriend of Monica Dunn's sister, who had accompanied her to the police station that last weekend to be photographed; Vicki Maestas, a friend of Monica's; Anita Harris; and Kyle Westall, the range master for the Farmington police, who would testify about whether a police officer would know the damage a shotgun would do—but these were for the most part for staging. The witnesses who would be his star performers were: Dusty Downs, the police officer to whom Monica had told her story of abuse; Daryl Harris, the investigator who had photographed the crime scene; Dr. Patricia McFeeley, the chief medical investigator who'd supervised Monica's autopsy; Police Sergeant Mark "Hawk" Hawkinson, who had been Monica's boyfriend prior to her affair with Paul and also was a friend of Paul's; and Larry Warehime, the police department's tool mark expert. But it was the heart-wrenching testimony of Monica's daughter that was to seal Paul's fate.

Walking slowly to take his place, Jiles began, "For the record, it's 3:57 P.M. and Lawrence Downs has entered the grand jury room."

The jurors looked at him expectantly like eager students. A dropped hairpin would have sounded like a bomb in the courtroom as all eyes watched dark-blonde, blue-eyed Downs take his oath. The broad-shouldered, well-muscled detective sergeant settled into the witness seat.

Downs told grand jurors he'd worked with the Farmington police for sixteen years. He explained that the case initially was investigated by his office, then turned over to the New Mexico State Police the morning of Monica's death. Downs also relayed he knew Monica personally, since she was a municipal court clerk. The clerk's office and police department are in the same building in Farmington. Monica was an acquaintance of Downs. Their conversations became more serious when Monica described the typical domestic violence scenario.

Jiles asked if Downs had a conversation with Monica on March 22, 1994.

"Yes. She came into my office in the detective division and asked if she could talk to me about something," Downs said. "She explained it had something to do with Paul."

"On that occasion, did you notice anything about her physical appearance?" Jiles prompted.

"She had a bruise on the right side of her face," Downs replied, turning toward the jurors.

At Jiles' further prompting, Downs continued. "When I noticed the bruise on her face, that was the first time I had physically seen her. It had been common knowledge throughout the department, throughout the building, I should say, that she and Paul had separated. When she walked in the room, it was an assumption on my part the bruise may have been partially related to that."

"As a result of the conversation that you had about her, did you have any particular concerns?" Jiles asked.

Downs nodded slowly. "Yeah. Obviously, I was concerned for her safety and her well-being," he said quietly.

Downs told grand jurors he called her at home the next day, because he was worried about her from what he had learned in their previous conversation. While he was talking to her on the telephone, Monica told him Paul had just arrived at the house. "And her tone of voice, her demeanor changed instantaneously," Downs said.

"In what way? Can you describe the change in her?"

"I would describe it as pure fear," Downs began. "Her voice was shaking, she was very hysterical and she wouldn't let Paul in the house. He was knocking on the door, knocking on the windows. She told me she was on a cordless phone, she was mobile. She said, 'Should I let him in?' I said, 'By no means, do not let him in.' She even said—she begged me to stay on the phone with her while he was there. I didn't want to get off the phone with her because I was trying to get some help to her. She told me to stay with her on the phone while he was there. She kept telling him to leave. 'Paul, just leave. We have nothing to talk about.' I couldn't understand what he was saying, but I could hear a muffled sound in the background. She was trying to communicate with him that she didn't want to talk to him. She didn't want to have anything to do with him. She asked him numerous times just to leave."

"And you could hear her asking him?" Jiles asked.

"Yes."

"Could you ever tell during the course of that conversation whether it appeared that he did, in fact, leave?"

"She told me that he left."

"Okay."

"She was almost giving me a play-by-play description of what's going on. 'I can see him. He's now at the front door. He's lighting a cigarette by the garage.' Apparently, she had visual with him at some point. 'He's back in his truck, now. I think he's leaving. Yes.' "

"Now, after he apparently left, did you continue speaking with her on the, in the same phone conversation?" Jiles asked.

"Yes, I did. You know, I, I explained to her that, that she . . . I tried to convince her that she needed to leave the residence. She had some children with her. I don't know how many children were with her. But I tried to get her to leave for a motel room or a friend's house or a relative, some place where she wouldn't be readily accessible to Paul."

Throughout Jiles' continuous questioning of Downs, the questions he didn't ask Downs would later be held under the spotlight. He never asked whether Downs talked to Paul or tried to find out why Paul showed up at the house. Or if Downs had asked Paul whether he and Monica had an agreement that he would stay away. Downs never ascertained how often Monica allowed Paul to see the children and if visitation was a problem. He also never discovered how much of Paul's belongings remained in the house, items Paul might have needed to obtain. Downs never heard Paul's words to Monica that day, only her reaction to them.

"And why did you make those suggestions to her?" Jiles queried.

"Well, obviously, for her own safety," Downs said with a small shrug.

"You were concerned about that? Did you offer her any means to communicate with you if in an emergency occurred at that time?"

"Yes, I'd provided her with not only my pager number but the number of my cellular phone, which is something I have with me at all times."

Jiles didn't ask if it was the department's customary policy for officers to take a personal interest in suspected battery cases other than giving the alleged victim a domestic violence packet and suggesting they file for a restraining order.

"Did you take any further steps that evening to ensure her protection?" Jiles asked.

"After I got done talking to her, I contacted Captain Tim Lane, who was working patrol that night, as well as Sergeant Lonnie Anderson. I advised them of the situation, telling them at some point in time throughout the night, they may be contacted or respond to a domestic situation at the Dunn residence, because she elected not to leave the residence. I wanted them to be aware of what was going on, what they may encounter when they get out there and how to respond to it."

After another question from Jiles, Downs related that Monica had come to see him again the next day. Downs didn't say why she stopped, but said he told her she should let the department intervene for her family's safety. He explained the criminal charges she could file. She also could file a civil restraining order, which would land Paul in jail if he violated it. She could ask the police administration to discipline Paul for "behavior unbecoming an officer." Instead, she took no action. Downs said he didn't hear from Monica again until March 31. She told him things had improved after she spoke to Chief Richard Melton.

"She made me aware that Paul had also talked to the chief on a separate occasion. She advised me that she felt things were going better, she didn't think that she would be in harm's way any more, because perhaps now that Paul was aware that the department was aware of the situation, that there wouldn't be any further harm to her. She said she felt better about things. She asked if we could perhaps go to lunch the next day," Downs recalled, adding they did go to lunch on April 1.

Jiles was silent for a moment, seeming deep in thought. Then he looked at Downs with a small smile. "Now, I want to direct your attention to Sunday, April third—this would be the day before Mrs. Dunn's death—and ask if, during the morning of that Sunday you had any contact from Mrs. Dunn."

Downs replied she paged him while he was at church and he called her back.

"Can you describe for the grand jury her apparent emotional state?"

"She seemed distraught, somewhat upset," Downs said, then indicated they had arranged to meet at the police department around noon. Monica arrived with Rick Jacquez, her sister's boyfriend.

"She advised me that there had been an incident on the previous day, which would have been Saturday, in which Paul had injured her and she now wished to go ahead and proceed with filing charges and a formal report. I explained to her again what would happen by the filing of this. The offense report would automatically start an administrative investigation. And I wanted her to be aware of that, that people would be contacting her, interviewing her in regards to that. I also informed her for her own personal safety that she needed to seek the civil remedy, which is the domestic violence petition which would restrain Paul from any further contact with her. I even provided her with what we call the Domestic Violence Package to facilitate that."

Downs explained she would have to file the papers in court. Monica promised to do so. She asked Downs to call her early Monday to ensure she didn't back down. That Monday she was dead.

Downs never explained to the jurors why he took a special interest in Monica's case. He didn't tell them he and Paul were friends. He told them he knew Monica through work, but he didn't explain why he would have broken protocol for her.

Usual protocol, if called by a victim when an officer is off-duty, is to tell the victim to call the department and make a report with an on-duty officer. Paul had his suspicions about the relationship between Monica and Downs. Police officers generally consider other officers' wives off-limits. Another unspoken code. Yet Paul felt Downs exhibited strange behavior with Monica for a police officer and a friend. But grand jurors didn't get to hear Paul's side of the story.

So many questions weren't asked and thus, not answered. If Monica was so worried on Sunday that she called Sergeant Downs out of church, why wouldn't she want him to start the administrative procedures immediately? Was she worried Paul could produce an alibi for the time she received her bruises and therefore vindicate himself at an administrative hearing? Why call Downs on Sunday at all when she couldn't file the papers until Monday? Downs didn't bother to find out. With people lying to the police all the time, it's odd that a veteran officer like Downs was not overly cautious. Downs told jurors Monica was just an acquaintance before confiding in him. In that case, he would have no personal knowledge of her then to make him sure she wasn't lying.

Downs described to grand jurors how he photographed Monica's hips and thighs, supposedly heavily bruised, while alone with her in his office that Sunday. Disregarding usual police policy, no female officer was present. Monica met Downs there with her sister's boyfriend, Jacquez, but he waited outside.

In his testimony Downs said the drapes on the window to his office were open and Jacquez could see no impropriety occurred.

Downs told grand jurors San Juan County had a Domestic Violence Task Force involving prosecutors, law enforcement, medical staff and a crisis hotline. Downs explained the "cycle of domestic violence," that without counseling, arrests or other intervention—sometimes the victim leaving the spouse—the violence escalates, sometimes to death. Monica's situation seemed serious. Jiles asked Downs if Paul Dunn was aware of the department's tough attitude about domestic violence. The sergeant responded that Paul knew family violence led to strict consequences and also knew that the department paid for anger management counseling for its officers.

Jiles turned questioning over to the grand jurors, asking them to introduce themselves first.

Carol O'Day asked, "Were the children at her, at her home when she was abused?"

"Sometimes," Downs replied.

O'Day continued. "So, did they tell the police officers that he—?"

"Police officers were never called," Downs interrupted.

"They weren't called," O'Day repeated. "After she was murdered, did they tell—I mean after she was killed—did they tell anything about any abuse?"

Downs didn't respond to the juror's slip. He said he didn't know what the children told the police.

"Mr. Downs, Leonard Gallegos. Do you believe that Paul Dunn was aware though, towards the end there, of the possibility of Monica taking legal action against him in terms of the domestic violence situation?" Gallegos would later become the jury foreman, known for his hard-hitting questions.

"I don't know if he was ever made aware that she contacted me and expressed that she wanted to follow through, file it in court and take advantage of some of the remedies. I have my own personal belief about that, but whether or not he actually physically knew it, I can't answer that definitively."

Craig Norris asked, "How did she indicate to you that Officer Dunn, her husband, had beat her up or bruised her?"

Downs repeated what he had said earlier, that he took photos of her bruises. Then he told the jurors what Monica had told him.

"Dunn entered the house under the guise of needing a drink of water. And once in there, he started looking through the residence, claiming that she was trying to hide somebody inside the residence. Once they entered the master bedroom area of the residence, he tried to get into the bathroom to look inside. I don't know if she prohibited that or what she did, but he picked her up and threw her into the waterbed area that was in the bedroom. She said to me, 'The bruises you see on the hip there was where I landed on the frame of the waterbed.' The other bruising in the area kind of looks like fingerprints, stuff like that, where she was grabbed or struck maybe, or forced back."

It's unclear why Jiles himself didn't ask Downs to give details as to how Monica said the bruises had occurred and the possibility of fingerprints on Monica's skin. Had the juror not asked, this crucial information would have remained unknown. Defense attorneys later would bring up many instances of prosecutors not asking the right questions, performing a shoddy investigation and pursuing a case against all common sense.

"She described all this to you? Is that right?" juror Norris asked.

"Yes, sir."

At this, Jiles jumped in. "I'm afraid I need to advise you about that last answer, last two answers of Sergeant Downs. In a case like this, there is the opportunity for a great deal of hearsay evidence to be elicited, and this question and answer here, what we have is a situation where this is hearsay evidence, which means that this witness is telling you what someone else said happened. That other person being Monica Dunn. And, ordinarily, we must be somewhat cautious of that because, obviously, Monica Dunn will not be a witness in order to answer questions about that. Just so you know. But be cautious about that."

Jiles' reminder failed to intimidate juror Norris into silence. "I'm concerned whether or not she actually told him that Officer Dunn had injured her."

Jiles explained Downs wasn't in the room when the alleged abuse occurred, so Downs couldn't testify to the truth of her allegations—whether Paul had in fact abused Monica. But Norris hadn't asked whether Monica's accusations were true. He wanted to know if Monica had directly accused him or if she let Downs and others draw their own conclusions. Almost conveniently, Norris's real question was never answered.

Jiles invited other jurors' questions.

Paul Gordon asked, "When she was talking to you as a friend, did she ever mention to you that she would even be thinking about killing herself?"

"No, she did not."

Tim Ruare, a juror whose face bore an inscrutable look, leaned forward. "I would like to know if Mrs. Dunn ever indicated to you that her husband had abused her in the past or was this just a problem that was happening at the time?"

"If she was abused prior to this instance I'm relating here, she didn't tell me about it."

Frank Abutta asked Downs if he called Monica, as she asked, the Monday morning after he gave her the restraining order papers. He replied that his pager resounded at 7:09 A.M. Monica was already dead.

"Did Ms. Dunn die before the charges were filed against her husband?"

"It is my understanding that she did, yes."

"Were those charges that she was supposedly going to present against her husband, were they actually found?"

Downs said, "Officers found the unfiled documents in her purse. She never had the opportunity to file them Monday morning."

CHAPTER 13

BEARING WITNESS

The solemn, straight-backed investigator, Daryl Harris, showed a videotape of the blood-soaked walls and floor in the Dunns' home as if he were a realtor showing off a shined and polished new home for sale. As the video played, Harris, the district attorney's office's chief investigator, pointed out Paul's pick-up truck parked in the driveway and the open garage door.

"Located in the lower part of the picture is an area of blood that's at the entrance of the garage door itself. There's some debris around. This is—some of it's from the paramedics at the scene and the flash tape. A lot of it is small stuff on the driveway itself, some seeds that had blown in. Some of it, in the lower right-hand corner and the middle of the screen toward the left are two footprints that are on the driveway there, in blood. Panning around, looking at a doorway that leads from the living room of the residence into the garage area. This wall is the north wall of the garage and this is a large bloodstain with some blood running down the wall on the north wall of the garage. Now we're looking back down at the bloodstain at the entrance of the garage . . . In the center of the picture is a shoe that belonged to Monica Dunn. Now, we're looking at the driver's side of the van that she had been driving. This is another bloody area on the side of the van and there is her shoe again."

Harris paused for a breath and continued his narration. "Now we're looking at a closer view of some of the blood on the north wall. We're looking at the doorknob that goes from the garage into the living room of the house. There's some blood, I believe, on the side of the door. Now we're panning up and down the doorjamb itself. Now, we're getting a closer view of the blood that was on the wall on the north side of the garage. A large area and blood running off the wall and some drops of blood on the floor. And again, the shoe lying on the floor of the garage."

The camera operator entered the home through the front door.

"Just inside the door are some blood drops on the carpet leading from the living room to the garage," Harris continued. The camera moved slowly down the hall heading into the room of death. First, however, the camera captured a hallway bathroom and the little girls' bedroom, then the older daughter's bedroom.

Suspense in the courtroom built as the camera panned slowly to the right and Monica's bedroom came into full view. "Right here," Harris interjected, "about the center of the screen or on the left-hand side of the screen, is the shotgun. Here's an expended shotgun shell. And here's an area of blood in this Navajo rug. It's washed out a little bit, but right at the center bottom of the screen, you can see where the shotgun pellets and debris and tissue struck the wall.

"Panning around the east wall of the bedroom, the windows and drapes and now, we're looking at the headboard of the waterbed. It looks like an article of clothing, a remote control, a clothes hanger and another item on the waterbed itself."

The camera operator got a close-up of the dresser by the bedroom door and the walk-in closet, containing a gun case with weapons and ammunition. Harris pointed out to jurors that outside the closet, the wall was "loaded" with blood smears. Near the doorjamb, another blood smear darkened the picture. As the photographer left the bedroom, blood drops formed a path and he followed them. In the living room, more blood drenched one spot as if the person carrying Monica couldn't make up his mind where to take her.

"There are rubber gloves that were left by somebody," Harris pointed out.

As the camera moved back to Monica's bedroom, jurors saw state police officers sawing plasterboard from the wall containing evidence. "This is the area where the shot pellets struck the wall and also blood and fluid and tissue from the victim."

Juror Gallegos wondered if the pellets had traveled all the way through her body.

The witness peered at his notes. "Yes. That's what this is, the other part of the wall is . . . that's tissue, blood and fluid from the body that went out with the pellets."

Carnell asked if any other jurors had questions.

Leonard Gallegos asked, "Was that shotgun that was shown here an auto-loader?"

"Yes. It's a semi-automatic, Remington Model eleven hundred."

"Semi-automatic," Gallegos repeated. "Just to satisfy my curiosity, what was the barrel length?"

"I don't know that."

Carnell told Gallegos another witness would tell jurors the barrel length.

"Was the body found in the garage?" Tim Ruare asked.

"When paramedics and other police officers arrived, Paul Dunn and Monica were in the front of the garage, where the, the bloody spot was right on toward the front of the garage. That's where they were."

Another juror asked if Monica was dead when paramedics arrived.

Harris explained she was transported to San Juan Regional Hospital, where she was pronounced dead after intervention tactics were taken.

Juror Carol O'Day asked, "Is it believed that the gun came out of that bedroom?"

Harris said he thought the gun was taken from somewhere in the house but was interrupted by Harold Greenberg, another juror.

"Was there a shot round in the chamber when the gun was found?"

"Yes, there was."

Greenberg spoke up. "What size shot was in the shotgun, do you know?"

"Double ought buck."

Narrowing his eyes till they were just slits, juror Michael Roberts asked, "Was that shotgun shell we saw on the floor just a case that had been fired, or was it—"

"That was a shotgun shell that had been fired at that point."

"I have another question," Gallegos again piped up. "Being that you stated that this is a double ought, buckshot in twelve gauge, is that consistent with the numbers of pellets that were found in the wall that would be in double ought shot?"

"Yes. I believe there were one or two pellets that didn't exit and the others were accounted for in the wall. There's nine pellets of double ought buck and all nine were accounted for."

At this point, Carnell dismissed the jurors for the day, preparing them for some grueling testimony from upcoming experts like Chief Medical Investigator Patricia McFeeley, who'd supervised Monica's autopsy in the coroner's main office in Albuquerque.

At the hearing the next morning, Paul's words the day his wife died came to life through good-looking Farmington

Police Sergeant Mark "Hawk" Hawkinson, once a friend of the now beleaguered Paul. Hawkinson, who had dated Monica just prior to her affair with Paul, was preparing the briefing for the shift coming on duty at 7:00 A.M. Suddenly, the police radio screeched news of the shooting. Hawkinson raced to Sergeant Ken Walker's office. Walker was already on his way to the Dunn house. Hawkinson quickly followed after a dispatcher told him Paul specifically asked for him.

Uniform colors clashed as fire and ambulance staff performed cardiopulmonary resuscitation on Monica while police officers began their investigation. Neighbors gawked. The Dunn children stared in disbelief at the spectacle. Hawkinson met with an emotional Officer Cliff Ollum, who was tending to the children. Ollum said Paul was in the backyard with Walker. Hawkinson decided the best thing for Paul was to get him away from the house, from prying, accusing eyes. Paul grabbed his cigarettes and got into Hawkinson's police car. They drove to the police department, although Paul was not under arrest and wasn't handcuffed.

"He said he had made arrangements with Monica the day before to arrive at the residence about a quarter to seven or so. I believe Monica was scheduled to go into work at seven o'clock, earlier than usual, because of a shift adjustment or work detail of some kind. He said he entered through the front door of the residence and Monica passed by him in the living room. After she passed by, she glanced over at him and the first thing that she said to him was, 'By the way, Paul, I'm going to file charges on you for battery,' " Hawkinson recounted.

"Please go on," Jiles said.

"Paul said he was kind of stunned and he asked, he says, 'What battery, Monica? I've never hit you.' He said Monica just continued to walk toward the master bedroom."

"Did she make any reference at that time to, according to him, to any marks on her body?"

Hawkinson shook his head. "I don't remember."

The sergeant went on to say that Paul told him Monica kept walking into the master bedroom and shut the door. Paul stood outside the closed door. "He said, 'Come on, Monica, we have to talk this out. You know I've never hit you. Why are you doing this to me? Why are you doing this to me?"

Jiles asked him to continue.

"There was no response at the door for a period of time. He told me he walked back into the living room to check on the smaller children who were engaged in eating breakfast, a couple of bowls of cereal. And he remained there for a period of time."

Then Paul went back to the bedroom, Hawkinson recounted. He thought he heard the door latch unlock. He waited, thinking Monica might come out of the bedroom. After a moment when she didn't appear, Paul began talking to her again, telling her they needed to talk and he would never hurt her. Then he heard her say to come in.

"He said he opened the door to the master bedroom, saw Monica and this is, this is real unsure. I can't remember exactly. I thought he said that he saw Monica lying on the bed with the shotgun pressed up against her. And as he entered through the threshold of the doorway, the gun discharged." Hawkinson didn't say why he had trouble remembering this crucial piece of information.

"Then what did he say happened?"

"He saw Monica's body, or this is what he was describing to me, he used his own body as, uh, as a reference. He said that he saw her body jump as the gun went off."

Then, according to Hawkinson, Paul grabbed the shotgun from her and laid it on the floor. He tried to call 911 on the bedroom phone, but he didn't get a dial tone.

He began carrying his wife down the hall and yelled for the children to call 911. He carried Monica to the garage to put her in the van and take her to the hospital. But Paul couldn't put Monica in the van, he told Hawkinson.

"He had to release part of his grip on her to work the door of the van and she was becoming quite slippery in the blood and he couldn't pick her up and hold her anymore."

Instead, Paul laid her on the ground and began performing CPR on her until the paramedics arrived.

At Jiles' prompting, Hawkinson told jurors he and Paul were just talking at the station. This was not a formal interview. But it became central to the case since Paul had not told anyone except his attorney and polygrapher his story.

Jiles then asked if Paul indicated whether Monica kept loaded weapons in the house. Hawkinson replied that Paul packaged up all his guns when he moved out of the house. Monica had demanded he leave a shotgun for safety reasons, Paul told him. Hawkinson said he didn't know how Monica felt about weapons or if she'd ever fired a gun.

Two weeks before her death, Monica went to Las Vegas with someone, Hawkinson went on, relating what Paul had told him. She wouldn't tell Paul who had gone with her.

While Paul spoke, Hawkinson said he noticed blood smeared on Paul's white T-shirt. Blood had soaked through his blue jeans and turned his athletic shoes a reddish brown.

"Did you see any blood on any portion of his skin?"

"Yes, sir."

"Where did you notice that?"

"From about three to four inches above his wrists. All over his hands."

Juror Leonard Gallegos asked if it was normal police procedure to pick up an injured person and move them like Paul did. It's not, Hawkinson explained, but when police officers' family members get injured, training goes out the window. It's not uncommon for them to want to take matters into their own hands instead of waiting for help.

Craig Norris, another juror, wanted to know if Paul or Monica ever mentioned domestic abuse to Hawkinson, since he claimed to be a friend to both. Hawkinson said he knew Monica and Paul were having problems, but neither one had mentioned physical abuse to him.

"What would you say his demeanor was the morning of the shooting? Upset?" asked Carol O'Day intently.

"When I first saw him in the backyard of the house, he was sitting on the swing and basically in a just staring mode. Very stunned. And he remained that way or, you know, he would go in and out of the stunned stage. Staring off in the distance. When I told him that Monica had passed away, he broke down and cried."

Juror Frank Abutta asked if Hawkinson believed Monica could have reached the shotgun trigger in order to shoot herself. It was the million-dollar question in the case.

"The barrel of the shotgun is not the only length you have to consider," Hawkinson answered carefully. "You also have the length of the receiver and the trigger barrel, which is a third or quite a distance more. It could be done, but the person would have to be leaning over. It's not something I would relish doing in practice, but given the length of the barrel of the shotgun, the receiver and the trigger guard, you would have to, in my opinion, lean over to access the trigger."

"Okay and, as you say, you've known Paul Dunn for about twelve years. Did you ever observe that he was the type of person who would lose his control in that kind of situation?" Abutta continued.

"I've never seen Paul lose control. Either in the street or in the twelve years that I've known him," Hawkinson said firmly.

Jiles jumped in with a question next. "Let me follow up on that. Is it fair to say, Sergeant, that police officers who work the street are frequently confronted with tense situations that ordinarily might cause a person to lose control?"

"Yes, sir."

"And he was able to control himself under those circumstances?"

"Yes, sir."

Gallegos asked Hawkinson who he liked better, Paul or Monica Dunn. Despite the fact Hawkinson used to date Monica, he responded he liked both about the same.

Josie Frank, a juror, inclined her head and asked, "Do you feel like it would be possible for her to shoot herself if she was laying on the bed? She couldn't reach the trigger that way, could she?"

Hawkinson shook his head and then, looking straight ahead, replied, "I don't believe so, no." With these words, Paul Dunn's former friend, like so many others, deserted him.

Silence settled over the room briefly. Juror O'Day broke that silence by asking what happened to Paul after the interview.

"We were waiting for a paraffin test to be performed on his hands," Hawkinson said. "Normally, when someone discharges a firearm, there are powder residues left on their hands. I didn't know how effective the test would be because Paul's hands were saturated with blood. It was irritating to me to sit there with him and hold conversations, casual conversations for a period of two hours, waiting for a detective to get there and paraffin his hands." Hawkinson didn't explain whether it was "irritating" because he thought he was sitting there with a murderer or if he wanted the ordeal to be over for Paul. He also didn't describe how one can hold a "casual" conversation with someone whose wife had just died from a gunshot wound to the gut.

"At one point, Paul became quite agitated, saying, 'I've got to get her blood off of me. Off my hands. I'm starting to smell it.' He was becoming very upset. And I could not understand the delay."

A juror wanted to know if a state police officer had performed the paraffin test. Hawkinson said it was a Farmington police detective. Hawkinson told another juror he didn't know the results of the paraffin test because it takes longer than a month to get results back from the laboratory.

Juror Carol O'Day asked, "Since you've known Paul Dunn for so many years and you were with him for quite a period of time that morning, what was your feeling as to what he was telling you? Did you find him to be truthful?"

Jiles interrupted. "That is generally an improper question, because what is important is what you believe. However, I will permit the officer to answer the question, just keep in mind that you are the fact finders and not Sergeant Hawkinson."

Hawkinson shifted in his seat. "As to the information of the divorce, I was cautious on what to believe. Yeah, it could have been an act, but it could have been real. I just don't know. You know, maybe he was staring off into space, the blood that covered his hands, uh, your guess is as good as mine."

Paul spent another hour and a half in the interview room, according to Sergeant Hawkinson. Finally, he asked Hawk if he thought he should get a lawyer.

"I said, 'Paul, this is a very high, high-profile incident.' You know, because of past instances of domestic violence with police officers and their wives involved. I said, 'This is going to be investigated to the fullest.' I said, 'If I were you, I would get a lawyer working.'"

Hawkinson said Paul then called Victor Titus' office, but learned his friend was out of town. His associate, Steve Murphy, came to the station instead. Murphy and Paul met alone. When they were finished conferring, the state police investigator arrived. But Paul would not talk anymore.

Jiles interrupted Hawkinson again. "I must also caution you at this point that all persons have the right to remain silent and you should draw no interference from Mr.

Dunn's invoking that right. That should not be evidence of guilt or innocence. It's just an exercise of his right."

Despite Jiles' words, who knew what ran through the jurors' minds?

CHAPTER 14

DIAGNOSIS: MURDER

Chief Deputy Medical Investigator Dr. Patricia McFeeley entered the grand jury room. Her perfectly-coiffed, chin-length bleached blonde hair was unmoving. The blue-eyed, stylish, fortyish woman might have shocked anyone by her choice of a ghoulish job. Medical examiners solve death puzzles from the inside out. They dig organs out of bodies, evaluating injuries in a literally hands-on manner. Mc-Feeley obviously was no stranger to the courtroom as she politely answered both attorneys' questions and never lost her cool or air of elegance. It was hard for the casual observer to think of her sawing on a dead person's skull to inspect brain matter or making the typical V-cut down the front of the body to touch with gloved hands what most people refer to as "guts."

Sworn in, McFeeley said she had been a forensic pathologist for twenty years and was licensed in New Mexico and Colorado. She was licensed to practice general medicine. She had four years of college, four years of medical school and performed a four-year residency in forensic pathology. She'd been with the New Mexico office since 1977. She also was on the staff of the University of New Mexico Medical School, Department of Pathology.

Assistant District Attorney Kathleen Carnell asked McFeeley to explain her specialty.

She spoke almost like a professor lecturing students, none too intelligent. "It's forensic pathology. Pathology is the study of diseases and death and the process. A lot of pathology is really the study of the medical and legal and the interactions of those two. And essentially is coined— the medical examiner."

Board-certified in anatomic and forensic pathology, she had performed several thousand autopsies in her career. As assistant to the chief medical investigator, McFeeley's job entails performing autopsies, supervising investigators, writing autopsy reports, testifying in court and other administrative duties.

Her voice grew more serious, studious. "We usually have a profile that we use as far as the order that we bring in the body. Often, as in a case such as this, it would be in a sealed body bag. So we would break the seal . . . and then see the body just as it's received and then continue our examination. If we have clothing, we take off the clothing. Examine that. We examine the outside of the body as it is and then we would clean it up and examine the things that perhaps you couldn't see well because of blood or dirt of something else on it. Then we do a core examination, an initial examination of the outside of the body where we describe height and weight and other characteristics. Then we do a complete internal examination where we look at all the organs, the brain, all of the connections of those things. At that time, I take samples for toxicology, samples of histology using small slides you can look at microscopically and then we do dictation or description of all the internal organs. And then we put that all into the report."

Jiles scanned the jury. McFeeley was good. She was drawing them all in. In cold, clinical terms, McFeeley had just described a person's body being penetrated by saw, knife and gloved hands. A shell of a person lying on the table, pancreas here, liver there, body fluid everywhere. Someone must do this job and it must not be someone who has a queasy stomach or who can't eat a steak and French fries while riding on a roller coaster with two upside-down loops.

Carnell turned the doctor's attention away from general explanations and on to Monica Dunn. McFeeley began with the condition of Monica's body after the bag was opened. She failed to tell jurors that the seal had already been broken and resealed before it arrived at her offices. This is clearly against accepted procedure, but the pathologist didn't inform the jurors. Monica's clothing, the pathologist said, had been partly cut off, as is common when emergency staff try to revive someone. McFeeley described Monica's elegant, purple fitted dress with buttons up the front. McFeeley said something had been "partially cut," but she didn't say if it was a button or the dress itself. Carnell didn't press her for an answer. Specific questions about defects on the dress—and how this was handled in McFeeley's autopsy report—were not discussed. Of course, no defense lawyers were there to question her further about the matter.

"And then she had on several layers of underwear and pantyhose on the top. We examined the clothing and could detect that there were a series of defects in the middle of the abdomen area of the clothing, burnt with powder," McFeeley said. The slip, McFeeley told Carnell, was the type that had panties built into it—actually attached to the slip. She didn't bother to tell jurors that whoever broke the seal in Farmington before shipping Monica's body to Albuquerque also took Monica's pantyhose off and then put them back on the corpse.

McFeeley continued, "Portions of the purple fabric were missing on the dress and portions of those were found in the body wound."

Carnell asked her to continue describing Monica's clothing as McFeeley had found it in the Albuquerque office. The torn clothing made the wound visible although Monica's body was clothed when taken out of the body bag. Most of the buttons were off the dress, torn off during resuscitation, McFeeley surmised.

"Did you notice if Monica Dunn was wearing make-up or wasn't wearing make-up?" Carnell asked. This would later prove important in the jury trial, when prosecutors reminded jurors that Monica had her make-up on, her hair fixed and had taken the time to put on a dress, pantyhose and a slip. The prosecution surmised that someone who had planned to kill herself that morning wouldn't take too much time getting dolled up. But, as defense attorneys later argued, someone who set her husband up to take responsibility for her death, or someone who didn't want to die but just wanted attention, might put on a show, complete with costume and "stage" make-up.

"She was wearing make-up, yes," McFeeley answered.

"After you looked at the clothing, then what was the next step you did?"

"Then we went ahead and looked at the outside of the body and then examined that and did a full internal examination."

Carnell, moving closer to the rail, asked the obvious, "What was found?"

"The outside of the body, there was the most obvious injuries in the front middle. It was clearly a shotgun entrance wound. Around that were very, very tiny pellets of Styrofoam, very small pieces, and they were on the abdomen and were also on the inside of the clothing. Actually, there were a lot of these distributed particularly on the inside of the dress. The shotgun wound in the front was three-quarter inches in diameter. The edges were not round and smooth."

A series of "connecting half circles" gathered in a pattern around the edges, which is characteristic of shotgun wounds after the pellets start separating, McFeeley told the jurors.

Carnell approached the pathologist and showed her a picture of the wound made where the bullet entered Monica's body. A large amount of blood concealed the actual wound. The wound hadn't been cleaned when the investigator took the photo.

Carnell asked if pathologists can determine the distance of the gun from the victim through performing an autopsy. McFeeley explained that this is shown through the pattern of the wound on the body. With shotgun fire, it depends on whether one pellet hit the body or more than one. Besides the pellets, shotgun blasts contain the shotcup, which is Styrofoam wadding that holds the pellets in place as well as burned and unburned gunpowder. Where medical examiners find these items on the body also helps determine the distance of the gun to the victim.

Monica had one entrance wound to the abdomen and seven pellet exit wounds in the back of her body.

Carnell asked what McFeeley expected to see in a shotgun wound created when the gun was a distance away from the body. McFeeley explained that a very distant wound would cause fewer pellets to hit the body. Gravity would cause the shotcup petals to open, causing the wadding and gunpowder to fall from the shot before hitting the target. If the shotgun is closer to the target when shots are fired, the petals from the shotcup leave an imprint on the wound. If the shotgun makes contact with the person's skin or comes close to making contact, the shotcup, wadding and gunpowder will be found inside the wound. The pellets also might exit the body through one exit wound since the intact shot cup will keep the pellets together in the body.

A distant shot would be about five or six feet or more from the victim, depending on the type of weapon, the type of ammunition, the gauge and the choke of the shotgun.

Carnell asked the inevitable question next: Was Monica's wound in the distant range? McFeeley said her office determined it to be an intermediate shot, one having occurred with the shotgun between one and three feet from the body.

Carnell handed McFeeley autopsy photos so she could show jurors how she determined the distance of the barrel of the shotgun from the shape of the wound.

The courtroom was quiet.

McFeeley was quick to comply. "I can start and you can pass it around. If you look right at the body and you use a kind of clock face . . . at one o'clock there is kind of a squared-off, very distinct mark extending from the side of the wound and at seven o'clock approximately, there is another wound which is not quite as distinguished or squared off, but if you look at it, it would be a very similar kind of a mark at seven o'clock."

Carnell threw a quick glance to Jiles. She hoped the jurors would remain attentive through this technical testimony.

These marks, McFeeley told the jurors, were made by the petals of the shotcup opening up. The petals begin to open at one foot, unless an object—like a body—gets in the way of the shot. Had the gun been pressed to the body, no petal marks would show because the entire shotcup would enter the body before the petals had a chance to open. Forensic pathologists also would expect to see an imprint of the barrel of the gun on the wound if it was a contact shot. McFeeley didn't find this on Monica Dunn.

A contact wound would cause soot or gunpowder on the skin, but this wasn't found on Monica, McFeeley said. However, an internal examination of the wound found most of the contents of the shotcup inside, a finding experts would dispute in a distance shot because gravity quickly pulls the shotcup to the ground.

"We found the shotcup, we found what appeared to be pebbles that had broken off of the shotcup inside, we found the wadding material inside the body so that it had to have been propelled into the body along with the pellets, but the shotcup was open and some of the pieces were actually broken off."

McFeeley, with her nonchalance about the shotcup evidence, downplayed a piece of evidence defense attorneys and defense expert witnesses felt they could later use to their benefit.

Carnell interrupted the doctor's lengthy dialogue. "And in order for it to be opened up and propelled, does the entire missile have to leave the weapon . . . before it can . . ."

"Yes, the shotcup and wad have to leave the weapon, catch the air and have to open up, and then, as it's going into the body, actually hit the edges. . . . In order to leave those marks, it has to be open and hit the wound and then hit the edges of the wound and then be propelled into the body."

"Now, would the exit wound be different if it were a contact wound?"

McFeeley replied, "It may or may not be. It depends on what happens, the closer you are . . . you could generally expect the pellets to be grouped closer together and the farther they are apart when they come in, the farther they may spread in the body, but once they start hitting organs and other things in the body, they tend to spread."

Carnell asked McFeeley the reason she believed Monica's wound was not a contact wound.

"If it had been a contact wound," McFeeley said, "I would have expected the entrance wound to be rounder and not as scalloped. I would not have expected at all to see these markings from the shotcup. The shotcup would have immediately pushed into the body. We would have expected to see a great deal of soot and powder. Sometimes if it's a loose contact, the soot might actually be on the skin, otherwise it would be down into the wound and we would expect to see a lot of that because all of that powder makes it come out of the gun into the wound. Sometimes there is a pink discoloration."

Carbon dioxide causes the discoloration surrounding the wound. McFeeley didn't explain, for gun-illiterate jurors, this pink color or how carbon monoxide comes into play in shotgun wounds. The jurors listened on, none of them scientists or well-versed in death investigation, but all intent on doing a good job.

"Can you explain why there are just seven exit wounds if there were eight or nine . . ." Again, Carnell didn't get to finish her question.

McFeeley quickly responded that sometimes a second or third pellet enters the hole made by the first pellet.

"The track of the wound from entering the body to the exit, do you look at that, too?"

McFeeley had already explained that this was an important part of detecting if a wound was caused by a gun being pressed to the body. The shot entered Monica's abdomen just above her belly button, slightly to the left. It exited her body straight through her back. The shot didn't angle up or down but just went through level to the ground.

"Now, with that almost level track wound, can that . . . Would the shotgun have to be held in a certain way to get that tract wound?"

Monica must've been standing, McFeeley explained.

Carnell watched the jurors as McFeeley made her pronouncement, then turned back to her witness.

"Now, if the tract wound ended up being, instead of level, ended up going up or going down, would the gun have to be pointed at the body in a different way?" queried Carnell.

"You would expect that the body was in a different angle," McFeeley said and then elaborated.

The entrance wound, if Monica had been standing when she was shot, would have hit her body forty-two inches above the ground. The exit wound measured about forty inches above the ground. This difference in height can be explained because gravity would cause the pellets to drop somewhat before exiting or as they hit her organs. Monica's arm length measured twenty-seven and one-half inches from the tip of her extended forefinger to her shoulder.

"Now, as the pellets traveled through Monica's body, what did they strike?" Carnell asked.

The pellets ravaged Monica's bowel, the deputy medical examiner explained, detaching it from the blood vessels that go out of the bowel to the rest of the body. McFeeley didn't bat an eye as she described Monica's lacerated body. Pellets tore through her diaphragm and through the aorta, which is the main vessel that takes blood from the heart to the rest of the body. They tore through the vein that takes blood from the body back up to the heart and through the main artery that travels to the left leg. The pellets also went through muscle in the back of the abdomen and into the pelvis.

"And the fact that the pellets hit those organs and vessels, can you estimate within seconds and minutes, when Monica Dunn would have, what would have happened to her within seconds or minutes?" Carnell asked.

"Within a short period of time, she would have, one would have expected her to lose consciousness through standing up and opening up those vessels, which is really what you've done, opened the vessels from the heart going back. You lose blood pressure very quickly, so I would expect you would at least pass out and be unconscious pretty quickly, probably within a number of seconds, but certainly . . . I would expect her to pass out quickly."

McFeeley didn't explain the obvious to jurors, that a self-inflicted wound causes unconsciousness the same as one made by an assailant.

"Did you examine Monica's hands?"

"Well, we examined specifically for any soot on them. There is no evidence of soot or gunpowder."

"And why did you examine her hands for soot or gunpowder?"

"When someone shoots a gun, there may indeed be leakage from around the gun, sometimes around where the cases have been fired. There would also be any gunpowder that leaked out. If someone was holding a gun, if they were shooting themselves, they may indeed pull the barrel whether it's a shotgun or rifle or pistol and they may get a characteristic pattern of soot on the hands from holding it, because that comes out of the barrel even on the hands, so for both of those reasons, we do a visual examination to see if there's any soot or unburned powder or gunpowder."

"And you saw no soot . . . ?"

"We saw none on her hands."

"Another thing I wanted to talk to you about is, are you familiar with 'blowback'?" Carnell asked.

"Yes. If you have a gun that is in contact with the body, everything that comes out of the end of the gun, all of the things including the pellets, would be pushed into the body when the gun goes off. It's a very high pressure thing, in fact, sometimes you get a marking on the skin which is an impression of the end of the barrel, because all of those things push the skin back on the barrel of the gun in a way of really creating injury. Sometimes it's a marking, sometimes it actually tears the skin from all of the pressure coming back and what it can lead to is pushing blood and tissue out through the entrance wound. If the gun is in close contact, this tissue may be forced back on—or into—the inside of the barrel of the gun, that's called 'blowback,' when the tissue is pushed back into or on the gun." McFeeley stopped and took a breath.

"Were you able to, at the wound site, notice anything that would look like 'blowback' or starting 'blowback'?"

"You don't actually see that on the wound."

Carnell looked at the witness and framed her major question. "Okay, and based on our autopsy on Monica

Dunn, within the confines of reasonable medical certainty, did you reach a conclusion?"

McFeeley smoothed a non-existent stray lock from her perfectly groomed hair. Her voice no longer charming, hardened. "Cause of death was a shotgun wound to the abdomen and based on the investigative information from our own autopsy, our finding was that it was in intermediate range and was therefore not a self-inflicted wound and therefore—homicide."

Among other information McFeeley didn't tell jurors was that the "investigative information" from which she drew her conclusions came from police officers. She also had photographs of Monica's bruises and Downs' conversation with Monica naming Paul as her abuser. Because police investigations, after all, are meant to determine guilt or innocence, the information given to medical investigators becomes slanted—or at least tilted in one direction rather than another.

McFeeley continued. "Our conclusion was that the gun muzzle of the barrel had to be far enough away from her that she could not have fired it herself."

Carnell, surprisingly, since she had just gotten a much-desired response from the witness, interrupted. "Just a moment, I had it marked down, but I forgot to ask you. Did you notice any other types of trauma to the body, contusions or bruises?"

McFeeley described some bruises that were healing on Monica's right arm, left forearm and right hip. The bruises were a greenish color, indicating they were starting to dissolve and had been there for a few days before her death. Her knees had several smaller areas of bruising, with some on her lower leg, close to the ankle.

Carnell ended her questions for the doctor and opened up the floor for jurors' questions.

Gallegos waded in first. "I have several. Knowing that your findings would more than likely end up in a court of law, did you have the opportunity to, or need to, measure the barrel length of the shotgun that was used in this incident? Did you do that, do you know?"

"Yes," responded McFeeley. "We did not actually have the shotgun. Perhaps I should make it clearer. The autopsy was done on the fifth of April, but we didn't actually issue the death certificate until the eighteenth of April and we used that time to get much additional information. We didn't just jump to that conclusion. That's obviously a serious conclusion to make."

McFeeley didn't express what would be a more serious conclusion—that Paul killed his wife or that Monica devastated her family by killing herself.

"What was your finding as to the barrel length of that particular . . ." Gallegos began.

"Looking back on my notes, I see we got it verbally over the phone. The distance was such that someone couldn't pull it and fire."

Gallegos had another question. "I have a tape measure here. You say her arm measured twenty-seven and one-half inches from the point of the shoulder to right here. So my arm is . . . that is, I'm probably at least as tall as Monica and I can only reach twenty-seven inches, so is it your opinion with that arm length and the barrel length you described in your report, she would not have been able to do this?"

McFeeley told him that even if Monica could have reached farther, she couldn't have reached a trigger one to three feet from her body.

Another juror asked if McFeeley test-fired the gun to see at what range the shotcup would open.

This information, the prosecutor interjected, would be provided by another witness.

Juror Greenberg asked if Monica could have killed herself with the gun at the distance the medical investigator believed the shotgun was from her body when fired.

McFeeley explained again that she didn't believe it was possible without the use of some type of aid. "Someone could commit suicide like this from a distance. What they sometimes do is rig up something where they can then shoot the gun, possibly with a string or some sort of set-up to hold the gun."

Police, however, found no accoutrements in Monica's bedroom to indicate she could have pulled the trigger from a distance. Investigators also looked for signs that Monica might have used her toe to hit the trigger from a distance. But investigators were told she had high heels on at the time of the shooting, so this didn't fit the theory. Paul Dunn later said, however, that Monica's right leg was on the bed and her shoe was off when he opened the door.

Josie Frank asked if Monica was wearing pantyhose.

"Yes, she was," responded McFeeley.

"Any other members of the grand jury have questions?" asked Carnell.

Gail Davidos asked if the dress Monica wore looked like one a woman would wear to work.

"Yes, the dress is something she would have worn to work," McFeeley said.

"But the tears . . . were these normal tears?" Davidos pressed.

"One of them may have been kind of a split in a seam, but there could have been some sort of struggle that caused it. The tears were such that you would have expected them to be noticed."

Davidos' question still wasn't answered. "She wouldn't have worn the dress to work the way it was?"

"I see what you mean," McFeeley said. "You're right, the tears were something you would probably have realized were there and you wouldn't wear the dress to work without repairing them. I think that answers your question."

Carol O'Day spoke up. "If she leaned over and pulled the trigger, the wound would still be level if the gun was on the floor . . . I mean, it would still be level exiting her body, would it not?"

"It could be. Yes, it could be. It may not have been, but it could be. Yes, it's conceivable, but if you lean over and the angle is about the same with the body and it could have been a relatively level shot, the angle does not prove that she could have shot herself."

"You've said that you've performed thousands of autopsies," Tim Ruare said, gazing at the medical examiner.

"Uh-huh," McFeeley nodded.

"How many have been on female shotgun suicides?" Ruare asked a question that must have been forming in many jurors' minds.

"I could look it up," McFeeley offered. "I don't have the number. A shotgun suicide or shotgun wound is really not uncommon. In addition to the autopsies that I've actually performed myself, the staff and I meet every morning in our office. Every day I see the cases that everyone else is working on. We do approximately fourteen hundred autopsies a year in our office and we have a relatively large number of suicides."

McFeeley told jurors that a large number of the suicides in which her office performs autopsies are suicides with shotguns. "We also do homicides with shotguns, so we deal with gunshot and shotgun wounds frequently. I'm sure I have seen fifty to a hundred shotgun wounds myself."

Gallegos, clearly the most vocal juror, asked her about the tearing of Monica's dress near the entrance wound. "Those defects, I assume you mean they were perforations from the pellets entering her body. Am I understanding you correctly?"

"Yes," answered McFeeley, "when I was talking about the series, I was talking about the fact that there was a defect in the outer dress and then there was a defect in the waistband of her half-slip. That's what I meant when I said there were a series going inward from that. There was not a series in one piece of clothing."

"Okay, but the defects you were describing weren't spread out?" continued Gallegos.

"That's right," McFeeley said nodding her head. "They weren't spread out."

"Okay."

McFeeley reiterated that they had found a hole in the dress and a corresponding hole in the slip underneath.

"Okay," Gallegos said, "that was my question. I wasn't sure whether you meant the series of defects you described were in a wide pattern or in a close pattern."

Gallegos knew something about what gunfire does to clothing. It wasn't entirely clear, however, what point he was trying to make.

"There was actually a single defect in each of those pieces of clothing," McFeeley added.

"Okay." Gallegos nodded, seemingly content with her answer.

"How far do you feel the gun muzzle could be away from a human body," asked Frank Abutta, "and the shot cup still enter the body? It's an extremely light plastic. I don't see how it could enter the body with the muzzle very far away from the body." Abutta knew something about shotguns as well.

"Well, you could certainly be a couple of feet away," McFeeley said firmly. "It depends on the gun and the ammunition and the mount, the charge, the gauge of the gun based on the diameter and also the amount of powder. It really depends upon all of those things, but it's certainly conceivable that from a couple of feet away, those things could be and would be expected to be pushed into the body."

McFeeley told one juror who asked Monica's age and height that she was thirty-one and five feet seven inches tall.

"I would also like to know if she was wearing high heels at the time she was shot," the juror asked politely.

"Our understanding was that she wore high heels at the scene of the shooting. We did not receive the shoes ourselves, but that was the understanding that we had. It seems to me that I have seen a shot in one of the crime scene photos in which there is a high heel shown."

None of the jurors asked if it was office policy, in a shooting where a suicide was possible by using a toe to pull the trigger, to assume the deceased wore both shoes simply because a shoe appeared in a crime scene photograph. The significance of this seemed to be lost on the grand jurors and, evidently, Patricia McFeeley.

McFeeley's stubborn assurance that Monica couldn't possibly have killed herself would prove to be the state's main evidence, but her testimony made other experts call her a hired gun. When an attorney asks an expert if something is possible, they almost always have to say "Anything's possible." McFeeley's cocky self-assurance went beyond professionalism. To prosecutors, her testimony meant they had a solid case. But an expert in wound ballistics found McFeeley's behavior appalling and unethical. Later, this expert would point out crucial evidence McFeeley had overlooked. Rumors flew in the defense camp as to whether this was due to incompetence or because the truth didn't fit into her design.

After a break, Darrel Jiles took over for Carnell, turning to Firearms Tool Mark Examiner Larry P. Warehime of the New Mexico Department of Public Safety Crime Laboratory. At Jiles' request, Warehime rapidly recited his credentials for the jurors. Somehow he managed to condense a lengthy crime-fighting career—twenty years with the Wichita Police Department, training in firearms and powder residue at the FBI Academy, teacher and trainer in firearms, supervisor of the Firearms Division of the New Mexico Crime Laboratory and expert on firearms tool mark examining often called upon in federal and state trials for his expertise—into a brief, to-the-point, vocal résumé.

With prodding from Jiles, Warehime also told the jurors that he had taught the Kansas Bar Association at the Law School of Topeka, Kansas, and that his work had been published at the law school. He had worked for the state of New Mexico as the firearms and tool mark examiner and as the supervisor of the firearms division of the state crime lab for seven years.

The jurors looked impressed. Warehime would obviously be a strong witness for the prosecution.

Warehime told jurors he was at Monica Dunn's house around noon, five hours after the shooting. The New Mexico State Police had called him in.

"With the investigation of the crime scene, I always coordinate with the officers who secure the scene," he said in a firm, steady voice. "The first responsibility is to contact the investigator or the officer who is in charge of the scene and find out what happened and then walk through the area, determining what evidence there is and what sequence is needed to document and retrieve the evidence."

This is how he handled the scene at Monica's home, he said, which showed a trail of blood through the house and a lot of blood in the bedroom and on the portion of the wall where the pellets from the gun had entered. What Warehime didn't tell the grand jurors was that he didn't retrieve the wooden wall stud in which the pellets wound up after going through the wallboard. An expert for the defense would later show why this wooden stud was valuable evidence.

Warehime explained that he videotaped the blood on the walls, rugs and furniture in the house just as it had been left after the state police had secured the scene. Securing the scene means the state police leave everything the way it was found and keep family members, local police officers and others from entering and trampling or disturbing evidence. Warehime also took photographs using 35mm color film while another officer made a diagram of the house, measuring where evidence was found in relation to floors, walls and furniture and measuring the evidence itself. This is all done so a crime scene can be re-created later, if necessary. The "crime" scene at the Dunn home was re-created—in the main courtroom of the McKinley County District Court several months later.

Warehime recounted that he and his team collected a twelve gauge Remington 1100 semi-automatic shotgun and various types of ammunition. Part of collecting the ammunition involved removing part of the wall in the bedroom where the shooting occurred. Darrel Jiles went through all the procedural rules of asking Warehime about the serial number of the gun to ensure the gun the prosecution had as evidence in court was indeed the gun Warehime found in Monica's house. Each weapon has a serial number unique to it and is used in identifying lost or stolen guns or murder weapons in court cases.

Warehime explained to the jurors the workings of the gun. "A semi-automatic means that you must pull the trigger each time the weapon is fired. Each time you squeeze the trigger, it will fire one time, but the feeding injection mechanisms of the weapon will automatically work."

"Were there any expended cartridges in the area where you found the shotgun?" Jiles interrupted.

The witness replied he found one such cartridge along with the shotgun in the master bedroom of the house. The shotgun and cartridge remained in the exact same location in which they had been found, Warehime said and indicated he had seen no signs of a struggle in the room.

Jiles then asked what Warehime did with the shotgun and cartridge once the photographs were taken and it was safe to move them.

"The shotgun and the shotgun shell were packaged. The

shotgun was placed in paper bags and, due to the length of
the gun, we had to use a series of bags and staple them
together in order to cover and protect the shotgun. Now, I
did not completely unload the gun, but I removed one live
shotgun shell from the chamber of the weapon in order to
pull the bolt back. This same action caused another shell
to come out of the magazine. This was the one that would
next go into the chamber of the weapon in its normal function. I controlled this function, removed the shell from the
chamber, set it aside and physically removed the one next
in place in the chamber and marked them so I would know
which was which."

During his entire investigation and handling of the gun,
Warehime and his team wore gloves so they wouldn't leave
their own fingerprints on the weapon. The shotgun was
packaged so they could later test it for fingerprints and residue from the shooting.

"Are you also familiar with the methods by which someone might use some sort of mechanism or instrument to fire
a shotgun from a distance from one's person?" Jiles asked.

Warehime responded that he found nothing in the bedroom that might have been used to fire the shotgun from a
distance.

"Did you notice anywhere in the room a wire coat
hanger?" Jiles persisted.

"There was one on the other side of the bed."

"Did you have any reason to believe or suspect that the
coat hanger might have been used to operate the shotgun?"

"No," Warehime said shaking his head. "It was too far
away from the person who had just been shot. It wouldn't
have fallen clear over there."

That seemed to blow away the possible defense theory
that a clothes hanger could have been used by Monica to
trigger the shotgun. It seemed, one by one, the prosecution
was chipping away at Paul's defense.

• • •

A broken bathroom mirror and a hole in the wall of Monica's bedroom indicated violence to Warehime's trained eyes. "The holes were consistent with holes placed by putting a fist through a wall."

Warehime also photographed and examined the van parked in the garage, which contained a black leather coat, a black leather purse and keys in the ignition. Inside the purse, in an envelope, he found a handwritten document titled "Petition for Order Prohibiting Domestic Violence."

Warehime also collected six dress buttons, one in the house and the rest in the garage. He showed photographs of the bedroom to the jurors. One showed the scene of Monica's death, with pellet holes in the wall behind the waterbed, a football helmet–style telephone, bloodstains and a woman's high heel shoe on the floor.

After he bagged and tagged the shotgun, Warehime told the jurors, he sent it to Santa Fe for serologist and blood spatter analyst Larry Renner to examine. Warehime held up the shotgun for the jurors to look at, again showing the serial numbers on the gun to prove it was the same one he took from Monica's bedroom.

Warehime began the tedious act of explaining to the jurors the parts of the gun and how they work. "This is a Remington semi-automatic shotgun and a Model eleven hundred. The extra things this weapon is purchased with, that might be referred to as options, they are all factory options that Remington has made for this shotgun, including the length of the barrel and this extended magazine tool. The weapon is semi-automatic. This portion of the weapon is the bolt; this bolt will lock back in place. There are two ways to put a round in the chamber of this weapon. One is to open the bolt, as I have, and put a round into the chamber. Then you push this and let the bolt go forward, this lever here, then turn the shotgun upside down and physically put the other rounds in this tube. Or you can simply go ahead, place all your rounds in the tube, then bring this back. At this point, a round would come down through the tube, push this and you put it into the weapon.

"How this weapon functions is that a round is placed into the weapon, then you have to bring this bolt back—that cocks the weapon—and it's ready to fire. Like the rear portion of the trigger guard, here is the safety button, ON and OFF, right here. The safety must be on and, after the weapon is cocked and loaded, you simply pull the trigger and the weapon will fire. At the time of the weapon firing, when that firing pin strikes the shell of the primer of the shotgun shell and is discharged, the force of the shotgun discharging brings this bolt back. As it comes back, it's what we call an extracting, it's right here on this side of the weapon. Right here," Warehime repeated, indicating the spot on the shotgun, "over the left of the shotgun shell."

Warehime went on, "The shotgun shell is then extracted out and at the same time a round drops down right inside here. Then the weapon is automatically cocked again, it does not remain in the back position, the bolt comes forward and places a live shell into the chamber. At this time, the weapon is cocked and ready to be fired again. The shooter then has the option of shooting the weapon again, placing the safety on or whatever action he wants to do with it. But this is what happens automatically each time the weapon is fired."

Warehime explained that the diameter of the shotgun shell is twelve gauges, while the length of the shell is two and three-quarter inches. It is a federal twelve gauge double ought buckshot.

"The expended round you found on the floor near the shotgun and the other rounds that were inside the weapon, were they of the kind of caliber that you're describing right now?" Jiles inquired.

"Yes, sir."

Jiles next asked the witness to explain shotgun shells.

"A shotgun shell has red plastic and this brass." Warehime held up a shell for the jurors to see. "This is what is referred to as high brass and is used in magnum loads and other loads of shotgun shells. Low brass refers to one that is lower and manufacturers use that to save money and hold down the cost on shotgun shells. On the red plastic is the manufacturer's name and the size of the pellets that are in the shell. You'll see two flying objects in this plastic bag. That's what we refer to as the shotcup.

"The shotcup holds the pellets. As you can see in this particular round here, there are nine pellets. The pellets are referred to as double ought, which is the size of the shot. In this shotcup, you also can see some white granulated particles. The shotcup is loaded with these nine pellets and this white, granulated substance. The reason this is done is because these pellets are stacked on top of one another inside the cup. So what you have is nine round balls stacked on top of one another. Well, if you've played pool, you realize that when two round objects hit each other, they go in different directions. To eliminate that effect and to keep the pattern tighter, the manufacturer has placed this white substance in the cup to hold it together longer. The pellets will still scatter somewhat, but will do it at a farther distance. This next object is referred to in a few ways, as a spacer or a powder cup or a powder piston. It fits right up next to the shotcup. The function of this is to keep the powder down towards this in here, next to the primer and to fill up the space in the shotgun shell so it all fits compactly together.

"The next and very important item in the shotgun shell is at the base here in the center. This is the primer. This is what the firing pin strikes, causing the shotgun shell to discharge. This is done by setting off a small explosion in the primer. Actually, it is very minute, but it acts as the explosive. In a sense, all the fire or flame shoots it out, igniting this powder. The powder is burning rapidly and building up gases. As it builds up gases, it forces the powder piston and the cup and powder and all these pellets out the end of the barrel. This happens each time the shotgun is fired."

"Mr. Warehime, when a shotgun is fired, what comes out of the end of the barrel?" Jiles asked.

"The pellets, white powder, the plastic shotcup, the power piston, also called the spacer, flame, smoke, powder particles and expanding gases," the witness recited.

"When the shotcup and the pellets leave the barrel, extreme pressure propels them forward. The cup's petals expand as the cup leaves the barrel. The white polyester fill blows away and the pellets explode out. The shotcup and the fill drop to the ground quickly. The pellets can travel much farther if not obstructed by an object." Warehime said he examined the shotgun in the Dunn case and it worked exactly as the manufacturer expected.

The shotgun that killed Monica measured, from the tip of the barrel to the trigger, twenty-nine and three-eighths inches.

"Were you able to make any determination whether the expended round that you found on the floor near the shotgun at the residence was, in fact, fired from that shotgun?" Jiles asked.

Warehime explained how he did just that.

"As the weapon is manufactured in the plant, each component is made for that particular weapon. The breach face and the brace are made of lesser materials and marks or what we call striation ends up on them. Now, no two sets of striation are the same from weapon to weapon. So you might want to refer to this striation as the fingerprint of the weapon.

"Some of the things we look at when we're first starting our examination of a weapon is what we call class characteristics. With the firing pin, it could be the actual shape of the pin. Also, within that round firing pin, there will be little nicks, scrapes and scratches, again what we call striation, that we can use to identify this gun to the exclusion of all other guns. This also applies to the breach face. From this manufacturer, the breach face is fitted and polished, but with use, striations are formed there. It also has what we refer to as class characteristics, such as whether it is smooth, its lines are parallel—that sort of thing."

Jiles' next question—about Monica's dress and underwear—came out of the blue. A few of the jurors blinked in surprise.

Warehime described her form-fitting purple dress with missing buttons, her pantyhose and a pair of panties. He prepared to explain to jurors why his investigation included examination of her blood-covered intimate apparel. What could a firearms expert know about lingerie? At least, how could this man's knowledge of lingerie help a jury fathom evidence in a murder case?

Jiles calmly led him through his testimony. "Before beginning your examination of the actual shotgun itself, did you examine any items of clothing worn by Monica Dunn on the day of her death?"

"Yes, I did."

"What items did you look at?"

"I looked at the dress. It was a bluish purple dress, one piece, with buttons missing."

"Any other items?"

"Yes, sir. Pantyhose, a bra and a pair of panties."

"Now, if you're the gun guy, why are you looking at clothing?" Jiles asked the question on many jurors' minds.

"If you remember, I said the powder, the pellets and the shotgun wadding falls at the end of the barrel when the shotgun is fired. If the person shot is standing close enough to the end of the barrel, what we call a cone effect takes place. The cone effect varies at different distances. When the weapon is fired against a test item, it makes a nice, round hole, except when fired on cloth. When the weapon is fired against cloth, it just rips and tears the fabric, because of all the gases and all the pressure. Contact on a substance such as the human body forms a completely round hole with very round edges. Now, the farther back you move, the contact no longer tears and rips cloth, it simply puts a hole in the cloth. If you move back a little farther, the pellets start to spread and the pellets or fingers of the shot start to come out. When they come out and hit an object, they leave marks on the object. The farther you move back, the more the pellets start moving out and you see the shot-cup and the power piston start moving out to the side, one side or the other, in a cone-shape effect." Warehime's expression was intense as he did his best to explain the technical details to the jurors.

"What would you be looking for in examining the clothing?" Jiles prodded.

"Examining the clothing worn at the time a person is shot will tell me what type of pattern is displayed on that clothing. I can look at the powder, the type of hole that was made on contact, the pattern of the flakes of powder. Things of this nature will help me establish the distance on contact. Then I do a comparison. I try to duplicate what I see on the evidence."

Jiles asked Warehime if he had photographs of Monica's body and the wounds on it to help in his examination. Warehime said he had been given photos by Agent John Sides and had enlarged three of the photographs to the actual size of the body so he could check the shotgun's effect on the body.

"Is it possible," Jiles asked, "under the right circumstances, to make a determination or form an opinion as to the distance from which a shotgun is fired using this particular shotgun and this particular kind of ammunition by examining the clothing and the wound on the body?"

"Yes, it is," Warehime said firmly.

Jiles asked the witness to explain this procedure. Warehime told the grand jurors that he took a piece of the dress to clothing stores and purchased garments of the same type of material as the dress and slip. He used a monogahide material that is used in the laboratory to represent body tissue. He fired the shotgun from various distances, trying to duplicate the effects of the wound on Monica's body. This would determine how far away the shotgun was from her body when fired. He started the testing by pressing the gun to the cloth and ultimately backed away up to five feet, firing the gun at various distances. Behind the monogahide, Warehime placed a piece of poster board to hold everything together and, behind that, a piece of cardboard. He explained to the jurors that this is standard backing for firing tests. Through Warehime's testing, the holes in the clothing that most closely matched that of Monica's were formed by firing the shotgun at a distance of two feet. He explained this was not an exact number, but an estimate of a distance, because his test patterns showed the gun couldn't have been closer than one foot to her body. Warehime didn't explain what in the patterns made him determine this. He added that testing also showed the gun couldn't have been farther from her body than three feet, because of how the holes appeared in the tests.

"Based upon that information and the examination of the scene itself, is the information that you gained and the opinion that you formed consistent with Monica Dunn having fired the shot herself?" Jiles asked.

"No, it is not," Warehime replied.

"And once again, you found nothing at the scene that could have aided her in shooting herself?"

"No, I did not."

Jiles then asked Warehime if he was familiar with the paraffin test. Warehime said he was and that this test was used twenty or thirty years ago to determine who had fired a gun. It was not a reliable test then and it is not used anymore, he said.

"You had to literally put hot wax on a person's hand. The wax would adhere to any powder particles there. Then you would rip off the wax and look under a microscope to see if there were any flakes of powder embedded in the wax. Although it sounds good in theory, in practical use it was not effective," Warehime told the jury members.

A gun primer, powder, pattern and residue test replaced the paraffin test, he said. Jiles asked him to explain how this test works.

"When a test is performed on a person, you use a five percent nitric solution, you put the solution on two cotton swabs and place them in a bag or container. This is referred to as a "Crow's Law," or a control. We check for what is in the solution itself and the makeup of the cotton in the swabs. Then the same solution is applied to the same type of swabs. You swab the back of an individual's hand and the finger area, rotating the swabs and removing any foreign matter from the skin. You save these swabs in a container, then do the same thing to the palm of the hand with fresh swabs. The swabs are sent to whatever group is doing the analysis."

Warehime went on to explain that, while more accurate than the paraffin test, this test still doesn't always point to the shooter, because often anyone in the room where a shotgun is fired will have gunpowder residue on them. Blood on the hands of a person who is being tested for gunpowder residue further complicates the analysis, because the blood can mask the particles or cause them to be removed from the skin if the hands touch another surface, such as being placed inside a pocket or brushing against another object.

Jiles asked if the jurors had any questions.

Carol O'Day spoke up. "Earlier, you mentioned that you found some buttons or one button in the bedroom and then some buttons in the garage. Where were the buttons in the garage?"

"They were towards the front of the van and the side of the van in an area of a few feet. There was a pool of blood right out in the same area and this was also photographed and measured on the diameter."

The ever-curious juror Leonard Gallegos piped up next. "For the purposes of the clarification of the issues involving arm length and barrel length, could you stand up and take that weapon and hold it against your mid-section and demonstrate to the court whether or not you could reach the trigger?"

"Well, I could reach the trigger," Warehime said, demonstrating. "But in order to do so, the butt of the weapon comes up. Now, I can eliminate the idea of the gun being out a foot, because I cannot hold the gun out a foot and reach the trigger and, this is important to remember, keep the gun level."

Gallegos continued his questioning. "The barrel length of that weapon from the tip to the trigger is twenty-nine and three-eighths inches and, as I recall from previous testimony, the arm length of the victim was twenty-seven and one-half inches from the shoulder, so that would make it probably twenty-four inches from here to the tip of the fingers, is that . . ."

Warehime interrupted Gallegos, telling him that a person would have to bend over the gun in order to reach the trigger.

"But that creates a downward angle," Gallegos protested.

"That is correct, sir," Warehime replied.

Gallegos nodded and thanked the witness.

Paul Gordon raised a hand and asked, "In your test firing, how close did you have to be when you were test firing the monogahide and the materials in order for the shotcup itself to penetrate that?"

"I think it penetrated at five feet," Warehime responded.

"Thank you."

Another juror asked if Warehime knew if the shotgun came from the gun closet in the bedroom or from Paul's pick-up truck parked outside the house. Prosecutors interrupted to say that another witness would testify about this. Warehime said he was told where the gun had been, but hadn't seen the gun in the house.

"Mrs. Dunn—would she have had to be kinda sideways when she was shot?" asked juror Michael Roberts. "Was she sideways to the wall or was she straight at the wall? What do you believe?"

"She was probably fairly straight," Warehime replied. "I can't say that she was perfectly one hundred eighty degrees with the wall, of course."

To determine that, Warehime added, investigators would have to perform trajectory tests, lining up her body with the holes in the wall. But her body itself could have caused the shot to move about instead of going straight through the body. That means trajectory tests would be invalid in this case, he told the juror.

Later, an investigator for the defense would give another jury a whole new perspective on trajectory testing.

CHAPTER 15

MONICA'S DAUGHTER

Amanda Rose Cortez nervously stepped up to the microphone and recited the preliminary information asked of her: her age, address and the names of her parents. She told the jurors her stepfather, Paul Dunn, moved out of their house in March, after her mother found a letter he had written to Anita. She didn't specify who Anita was or what the note was about.

After the separation, Amanda explained, Paul began coming to the house to take care of Diane and Racquel when Monica was at work. There came a point, however, when her mother didn't want him around.

Amanda stressed that Paul gave Monica a shotgun to use for her protection after their separation. Her mother kept it in her bedroom near the waterbed. Amanda didn't know whether her mother kept it loaded.

"Do you know anything of your mom's feelings about firearms, guns?" Jiles asked.

"She never liked them."

"Did she ever go out with Paul and practice shooting?"

"No." The young girl shook her head slowly.

"Amanda, I know this is difficult, but I want to ask you to answer some questions about the day your mom died," Jiles said, then gently led her through his questioning.

Amanda remembered Monica's plan was to go to work early, dropping the younger kids off at their grandmother's house. Amanda was going to remain at the house, get dressed and take the bus to school. Paul was not expected to come over that morning. It had been about a week since he had come over in the morning to take care of the little girls. Since their break-up, her mother didn't let Paul into the house; she would go outside the house to talk to him. Monica had never given Amanda instructions about not letting Paul in the house, but Amanda said she wouldn't have let him in, because she never liked him.

Her mother told Amanda to close the garage door after she pulled the van out. As Amanda did so, she heard the van's horn honk. She saw Paul in the driveway. Paul, her mother, Diane and Racquel came back into the house. Amanda asked Monica if she wanted her to stay in the room while Paul was there, but Monica told her she would be fine.

"Now, why did you ask your mom if she wanted you to stay with her?" Jiles asked.

"She told me one time that she was afraid," Amanda replied.

Amanda left the room and began her shower. Suddenly, she heard a couple of thumps, followed by what sounded like a gunshot.

"What did you do then, after you heard the gun go off?" Jiles prompted.

"I, um, I jumped out of the shower real fast and grabbed my towel and I ran. I ran back in the hall. I looked in her room and he was holding her," Amanda said.

Paul yelled to her that Monica had shot herself and told her to call 911. Amanda ran to the kitchen and took the telephone away from Diane, who had learned to call 911 in school and was just beginning to punch in the numbers.

"What do you remember telling them?" Jiles asked.

"Hurry! My mom's been shot! Hurry, please!" the girl replied.

Then Amanda tried to calm her sobbing, hysterical sisters. Paul passed the girls, half-carrying, half-dragging her mother into the garage. Amanda stared at the blood-splotched trail and noticed how difficult the blood made it for Paul to carry her mother. She watched Paul through a window into the garage.

"Could you tell whether Paul was trying to give any kind of medical attention or perform CPR or anything?" Jiles asked.

"He wasn't," Amanda said firmly.

Jiles asked Amanda if Paul had ever behaved in a violent manner toward Monica in the weeks before her death. Amanda said they'd argued and he had grabbed her mother and pushed her around.

Amanda also described a night when Racquel slept in Amanda's bed with her and Paul came to the house. He and Monica argued and Monica locked herself in the master bedroom. Paul punched a hole in the bathroom door. Amanda ran to Monica's bedroom and found the two of them there.

"Go back to bed, Amanda. Everything's all right." Amanda recalled her mother's words, the tears in her eyes and the gaping hole in the door.

Amanda remembered another moment of violence that her mother had told her about. She was half-dressed and in her bedroom when Paul grabbed her by the arms and threw her around the bedroom, Monica had told her daughter. Amanda could hear their raised voices and the sound of thumps and bumps against the furniture when Monica and Paul argued, because her closet and her mother's closet were situated back to back. The sounds traveled. Amanda told jurors of another time when her mother showed her a bruise on her hip, a result, she said, of Paul's throwing her against the television.

Amanda didn't see Paul injure Monica, she just heard her mother's explanations for her bruises. "He'll never hit me again," Amanda recalled her mother's words shortly before her death.

Jiles felt the jury, leaning forward in their chairs, faces rapt, were with him now. "What was her mood? Emotionally, how was she when she was telling you about this?" he asked.

"She was crying. She would cry all the time."

"Did you notice anything, in the weeks leading up to your mom's death, that was different about her health or her eating or sleeping or anything like that?"

"She wasn't eating anything at all," the girl offered.

Amanda sometimes woke up late at night to her mother's sobs. Amanda had suggested counseling, but Monica refused.

"She laughed. She said, 'Everyone knows me and Paul around here.'"

Amanda, do you remember your mom ever talking to you about the possibility of her committing suicide?"

She did so once. Amanda asked her why she would kill herself. "Because he just hurt me so bad. He hurt me so bad," she quoted Monica as saying. But then Monica told Amanda she would never do it.

"I want you to graduate. You go and graduate. I want you to get married and lead a happy life." These were close to being the last words Monica spoke to her daughter.

Jiles asked the jurors if they had any questions.

The voluble juror, Leonard Gallegos, had no questions, but couldn't resist making a comment. Something similar was probably in the heart of every juror. "I commend you, Amanda, for your courage and what you had to go through."

Jiles had no more witnesses. The moment of reckoning had arrived.

. . .

After a short break, Jiles asked the grand jurors to consider finding for an open count of murder, which meant the trial jurors would ultimately make the decision as to what kind of act they thought had occurred. However, he told the men and women intently watching him that if they believed the evidence proved first-degree or second-degree murder, they must indict Paul on one of those charges. He added that if they thought the evidence supported probable cause of a lesser crime—like manslaughter—they also had the option of indicting Paul on that charge.

"For you to return a true bill as to the charge of first-degree murder by a deliberate killing, you must find probable cause as to each of the following elements of the crime: One, the subject killed Monica Dunn. Two, the killing was with the deliberate intention to take away the life of Monica Dunn or any other human being. Three, this happened in New Mexico on or about April 4, 1994. A deliberate intention refers to the state of mind of the subject. A deliberate intention may be inferred from all of the facts and circumstances of the killing. The word 'deliberate' means arrived at or determined upon as a result of careful thought in the weighing of the consideration for and against the proposed course of action. A calculated judgment and decision may be arrived at in a short period of time. A mere unconsidered and rash impulse, even though it includes an intent to kill, is not a deliberate intention to kill. To constitute a deliberate killing, the slayer must weigh and consider the question of killing and his reasons for and against such a choice."

Second-degree murder would mean Paul had known his acts created a strong possibility of Monica's death or great bodily harm to her, but Monica did nothing to provoke him into the act.

"Sufficient provocation," needed for second-degree murder means an action that arouses anger, rage, fear, sudden resentment or other strong emotions. Being provoked means that the person's ability to reason was temporarily affected and the person lost control in committing the act. Provocation isn't sufficient if a person would have had a chance to cool down before committing the crime.

"The cause of death is an act which, in a natural and continuous chain of events, produces the death and without which the death would not have occurred," continued Jiles. "There may be more than one cause of death. If the acts of two or more persons contribute to the cause of death, each such act is a cause of death. Also, I wish to advise you of the firearm enhancement instruction, which is not in your books, so I ask that you please listen to this. If you find probable cause that the subject committed the crime of murder or manslaughter, you must also determine if the crime was committed with the use of a firearm and report your determination."

Probable cause means a reasonable person would believe the subject committed an offense based on the facts heard in the proceedings. Jiles cautioned the jurors that probable cause doesn't require belief beyond reasonable doubt.

A solemn and somewhat confused grand jury returned shortly after Jiles released them to deliberate. Gallegos told Jiles that the jurors believed they should have an instruction for manslaughter along with instructions for first- and second-degree murder. The prosecutor told the jurors they have that option if at least eight of them agree manslaughter is the appropriate charge. Jiles prepared this instruction while the jurors continued their deliberations.

The grand jurors again returned without a decision almost an hour later. Gallegos reported that they wanted to know whether, if they found probable cause that Paul committed first-degree murder, the trial jurors could find him guilty of a lesser crime, like second-degree murder. Jiles told them it would depend upon the prosecutor, but many jurors are given the option of finding for a lesser charge. Gallegos asked for another explanation of an open count of murder. Jiles said this means the jurors are not specifying any particular degree of murder. An open count of murder could mean murder in the highest degree or the very lowest degree—manslaughter.

Ten minutes later, the jurors returned with a decision. First-degree murder. The jury members expressed concern that their decision would hit the media soon. Jiles said he couldn't control that, since indictments are public record. The jurors' names don't appear on the document, he added, just his name and that of the jury foreman.

Before the jurors filed out of the courtroom, a woman juror piped up. "We want a raise!"

"I'll bet you *do* want a raise," Jiles agreed. His mild attempt at humor was about as close to a joke as was possible for him.

When he heard the verdict, Paul's face was grim. For him, any comic relief was out of place. He now knew he would be tried for murder in the first degree.

CHAPTER 16

PSYCHIC DETECTIVE

The real work of piecing the clues and evidence together and creating a vital picture of what occurred at the Dunn house the morning Monica died began, for seasoned investigator Dave Pfeffer, with ghosts of the past.

No one, especially if they sized him up merely by his tall, brawny form, would call Pfeffer a clairvoyant. He would've liked the term, but he never would have told you so. Pfeffer was very in tune with emotions he sensed at every crime scene he'd ever investigated. It was no different with the Dunn house. In his heart, he felt the sadness still present in that shattered home. In his stomach, he sensed lingering anger. Besides being a keen observer, the light-brown-haired, brown-eyed, baby-faced cowboy had learned long ago to trust the emotions present at crime scenes. Many lawyers and other police officers think this is hocus-pocus and a lot of bunk, but then, they don't have Pfeffer's track record, either.

Before going to the Dunn home, detective Dave Pfeffer had bought a *Daily Times* from a small shop. Obviously a stranger to Farmington, Pfeffer found it no problem to nonchalantly ask the clerk what she thought of the case.

"That guilty son-of-a-bitch needs to fry!"

Her automatic response seemed to epitomize sentiments in the small town. No one in the community knew all the facts, yet no one seemed to be trying to be objective. Everyone deemed Paul a murderer.

To everyone's astonishment, it was sixteen-year-old Billy Pfeffer, Dave's son, who found the brass button missed by police in Monica Dunn's garage, where cardiopulmonary attempts to revive her were made by a distraught Paul. The defense team found it ironic that all the police, state crime investigators and district attorney's office employees missed the button, but young Billy found it on his first peek at the house. His father, private eye Dave, didn't find it unusual at all—he knew his son was smart and a natural for the business of detecting.

Later, the long-haired, dark-complected, half-Indian Billy spoke out about life with Dad and investigating his first case. Looking nothing like his father except perhaps in height, Billy's handsome features and style of getting off on life were his own.

Going into a crime scene and finding the button was no big deal according to Billy. He was "just doing nothing and decided to go." As Billy said, "snooping around" was the work he did for his father that day.

"The button was right there in plain daylight. Supposedly, it's where he [Paul] dragged her. It just popped off. I think I picked it up and I got in trouble for it."

Billy knew but temporarily forgot that you're never supposed to touch possible evidence with your bare hands. "What the hell is this button?" he asked before his father and police officers who let the investigative team in the house took custody of the small object.

Despite the small victory of finding the button, Dave Pfeffer didn't let it distract him from his work. He always took time alone at a crime scene before evidence gathering. It doesn't solve the case but it helps him piece puzzles together. Standing there he felt the energy in the Dunn house.

Death froze the garage in time. It came to him in a "sinking feeling" in the pit of his stomach. He knew Monica died there; he needed no proof.

As he walked into Diane and Racquel's room, Pfeffer felt tremendous sadness. He sensed more sadness there than he did in the master bedroom, despite the fact that the shooting occurred there. He believes their parents fought a lot and, of course, it affected the girls. Pfeffer even sensed that the girls intuitively knew something awful was going to happen, but they didn't know what. Paul and Monica didn't have this foresight. He attributed a lot of the sadness in the house to Monica. The energy suggested she was sorry for something she'd done—Pfeffer later determined she felt sorry for shooting herself, that she didn't intend to. But at the moment he first experienced Monica's sorrow, Pfeffer didn't yet know who had fired the trigger.

Paul believes Pfeffer's correct in sensing these emotions in the house. "There are lots of ghosts in that house, all of them are very sad—Monica, the girls and me. If truth be told, part of each one of us died that day. Can that still linger there in the house? I'm quite sure it does."

After he'd sensed the feelings left behind by its tragic occupants, Dave and his son, Billy, found pellet holes in the brick in the bedroom where the shooting occurred. State police officers had taken out the plasterboard wall with pellet holes but had ignored the holes in the brick.

At sixteen, Billy was about the same height and weight as Monica, so he and his dad did a demonstration with ropes and weights to check the trajectory angle and match it up with the gun. From the angle of the pellet holes in the brick, Pfeffer and his son used string to determine trajectory, or the path the pellets took before landing in that pattern.

The holes were too low if someone had been standing in the room. When his son sat on the bed, the trajectory fit perfectly with his back. The shotgun would have had to be on the floor or on the bed, pointing slightly upward. For Paul Dunn to have fired that shot, he would have had to be lying on the ground and Monica would have had to be on her knees, Pfeffer determined. It was a rather unlikely scenario.

Pfeffer passed this information on to firearms expert Nelson Welch of Cochito, New Mexico, who performed formal trajectory tests that weren't too different from what Pfeffer had done. Only with Welch's stamp of approval, they hoped the trajectory information could be shown to prosecutors to try to get them to drop the case. When this didn't work, they decided the trajectory expert testimony and demonstration could be used at the trial. Many, including more celebrated experts, would perform the same test but get more credit than Billy, who wasn't called to testify in any hearing about his makeshift trajectory test. Moreover, it was Pfeffer's son—not the police—who found the telltale button from Monica's dress in the garage, thus confirming part of Paul's story. "It was just some punk kid," some people said of Billy. But that punk kid outshone police officers in jazzy blue uniforms who couldn't collect all the evidence, and investigators for the prosecution who couldn't perform trajectory tests.

Most of the work in the case was first done by Pfeffer. He also was the first to press a shotgun to a piece of board and fire it to see if a petal could show at close contact.

"He's lucky the shotgun didn't explode." Paul didn't mince words when he found out about Pfeffer's dangerous experiment.

Luckily, Pfeffer wasn't blown sky-high and his experiment proved crucial. It *did* show that a petal mark could be seen. Pfeffer passed this on to Welch, who did more work on pigskin and other materials used to simulate human skin. Wound ballistics expert Dr. Martin Fackler of Florida later came up with a theory on this.

Of course, these important discoveries still didn't show who had pulled the trigger. But they were the first plusses on Paul's side. Pfeffer didn't take all the credit—he made sure his son got an equal amount of the glory! And, the proud papa said, his son was going to join his investigative practice, Shamus Investigations, as soon as he was ready.

Farmington police officers shunned Pfeffer, which he found odd, because he usually had a good rapport with cops, being one formerly. Pfeffer thought more people believed someone was innocent until proven guilty, but he soon learned he and Mitchell would have to prove Paul innocent.

Pfeffer often visited Paul at the jail. Paul always ended up crying during the interviews. Finally, Paul started crying when he saw Pfeffer coming. It was uncomfortable for the tough but softhearted investigator.

And Pfeffer kept on delving.

"Vic, when are we going to get the dress and the underwear?"

It was five months after Monica's death when the frazzled Pfeffer got an answer to that question. The damage to the dress could answer many questions. It immediately did for Pfeffer, whose lucky investigative hands were the first on the defense team to examine the gown, slip, bra and panties. The find chilled Pfeffer, who almost jumped through the ceiling when he saw them.

"This has to have occurred through a contact shot." Pfeffer's response was immediate, definite.

The investigator found grex, the white filling surrounding shotcups in a shotgun shell. The light, airy substance can only travel inches and drops like snowflakes when a shotgun is fired at distances. But the inside of Monica's dress was covered with the filling.

"Imagine, if you can, the Styrofoam stuffing that comes with boxes to protect their contents. It is light, it sticks to everything and is basically a pain in the rear. Now take that curly stuff and make a ball that is smaller than a BB. That's grex."

Again, Pfeffer passed along the dress and his find to expert Welch and wound ballistics expert Dr. Martin Fackler. Fackler received his MD from Yale University School of Medicine in 1959. He became certified as a general surgeon by the American Board of Surgery and is a fellow of the American College of Surgeons. In 1968, he served as a combat surgeon in Vietnam. From 1969 to 1971, he served as a surgeon in Japan during the war.

He studied the effects of penetrating projectiles on the human body as director of the Wound Ballistics Laboratory, Letterman Army Institute of Research, from 1981 to 1991. This occurred after he retired as a colonel in the Medical Corps in 1991, after giving thirty-one years of active service.

He is the author of over one hundred articles and chapters on wound ballistics, most notably, "Missile Caused Wounds" in the NATO Handbook *Emergency War Surgery*.

Fackler is a life member and technical advisor of the Association of Firearm and Tool Mark Examiners. He has been a member of the United States delegation to the United Nations Conference on Restrictions and Limitations of Conventional Weapons in Geneva, Switzerland. He was chairman of the section on body armor related to wound ballistics in the Eleventh International Symposium on Ballistics, Royal Military Academy in Brussels in 1989.

The busy doctor is a consultant to the United States Department of Defense and the Department of State, Forensic Science Criminalistics Laboratories Industry, the FBI and other law enforcement. He also reviews medical and forensic science journals.

A former rifle marksmanship instructor, competition rifle shooter and firearms technology experimenter, he is president of the International Wound Ballistics Association and editor of the Wound Ballistics Review. He was a member of the United States Office of Technology Assessment Advisory Panel on Soft Body Armor in 1991 and 1992.

Fackler received the Army Meritorious Service Medal in 1986 and the Legion of Merit in 1991 for wound ballistics research. He also is the honorary president of the French Wound Ballistics Society.

Since he returned from the wars, he has been a clinical instructor in plastic surgery at the University of Tennessee, an assistant professor of surgery at the Uniformed Services University of the Health Sciences in Bethesda, Maryland, and a visiting professor in wound ballistics at the University in Marseilles, France.

Fackler also has served as chief of several departments of surgery at hospitals in the United States and in Germany.

His list of accomplishments includes many professional and scientific society memberships as well as various awards for his work and special appointments.

Welch suggested the lawyers have the world-renowned Fackler take a look at the autopsy, photos and the garments.

"I got interested very rapidly." Fackler's first order of business was to look at all the autopsy and police photographs. He looked at the clothing the defense sent and inspected every inch he could find. The entrance wound didn't immediately suggest a contact wound. But he also didn't understand why only one petal mark would show. The other mark McFeeley identified in grand jury hearings as another petal mark wasn't in the same location as a petal mark would be found. Fackler matched it with the shotgun and found it to be an imprint of the muzzle.

When he noticed the grex littering the dress and on Mon-

Paul and Monica look lovingly into each other's eyes on the dance floor.

The only photo that Monica ever showed to others was this glamorous portrait.

Paul and Monica's two little girls, Racquel and Diane, shortly before their mother's death.

Officer Paul Dunn cruises down the highway on his motorcycle.

Paul Dunn shakes the hand of former Vice President Dan Quayle.

The home Paul and Monica once shared,
and the place where Monica died.

The shotgun that killed Monica Dunn.

Attorney Victor Titus was instrumental in defending Paul.
Photo by Olan Mills

Gary Mitchell, the primary defense attorney.
Photo by Olan Mills

ica's back, he knew it had to be a contact shot. As Pfeffer has described, the light substance would have fallen off early on, if it were a distance shot.

Fackler counted about two hundred specks of the Styrofoam grex on Monica's back and many on the dress.

"If it was a distance shot," Fackler explained, "I'd be surprised to see more than two or three pieces, not two hundred."

Pieces of the puzzle fell into place but nothing stirred Fackler more than the rather obscure bodily tissue known as the "greater omentum." Omentum is a fatty tissue that usually hangs about eight inches, like an apron, in front of the colon. In slim patients, you can see right through it. The omentum protects the organs of the lower body. No one knows how the omentum does this, but, for instance, it wraps itself around a ruptured appendix, possibly to ward off further infection.

Boring in a normal body, it was almost a medical miracle, had Monica not died. One and a half inches of the omentum stuck out of one of the half-inch exit wounds on Monica's back. It was like taking a vacuum cleaner and trying to suck up an entire glass without breaking it. In most circumstances, it was laughable. Yet here the substance stuck out of the holes.

Finding the omentum forced out of the exit holes posed another problem if the wound was caused by a distance shot. The omentum can easily travel around the bowel, but for it to travel through gunshot wounds out the back of the body, it must pass through the psoas muscle. This is a two-inch muscle in the back of the body that leads from the lower abdomen to the leg and moves the thigh. To penetrate it would require a lot of force. Like a shotgun being pressed to the body.

For the flimsy omentum to have traveled through two

inches of muscle and become lodged outside a half-inch hole, is like a man walking through a wall. It had to be the result of great force. The abdomen of an average woman who has had children can stretch to hold about two gallons of gas. But a shotgun burst contains about three or four gallons of gas. That is enough pressure to push tissue through muscle, although it's a sight rarely seen. Witnessing that would be similar to people involved in a tornado marveling at a straw penetrating a tree.

Fackler wished he had been at the autopsy to see the omentum sticking out of the exit holes—and then rifled through the wound. But the pathologists took a sharp instrument and sliced off the omentum in a clean cut from Monica's back. Fackler found this disturbing, as well as the fact that the tissue and the cutting weren't even mentioned in the autopsy. The pathologists might not have known what the tissue was, but they still had to report their findings.

"It would be an extremely remarkable finding at an autopsy," said Fackler, making it clear that although he's a surgeon, he's not a pathologist.

"I would've been very excited about this. I'd have called everybody and we'd all have been taking pictures. I've never seen anything like this. It would've been an event. This is not a tiny detail. This is a huge, very obvious thing."

If McFeeley or anyone else in the office noticed the omentum after that—and the fact that it was removed and not mentioned in the report—a corrected report would be difficult to make, Fackler noted.

"It's hard to amend an autopsy report to say, 'Oops, I forgot to report this big thing sticking across the belly and out the back.' "

Once the pathologist performing the autopsy decided the omentum wasn't relevant, she had to stick to her decision to give it no importance, as New Mexico Chief Medical Investigator Patricia McFeeley did in the trial.

But that's no excuse not to report it. "This is a major error. One of the worst I've ever seen in my life," Fackler said.

Fackler understood that another doctor, who was undergoing training after her pathology residency, might have completed the entire autopsy with McFeeley not overseeing any of it, but McFeeley denied this.

"The people running the program are irresponsible. I lost a great deal of respect for her," Fackler said of McFeeley. "The deficits in the autopsy were just definitely inexcusable."

He especially found this worrisome since McFeeley is the president of the American Academy of Forensic Pathologists, of which Fackler is also a member.

The issue of the omentum wasn't the autopsy report's only error, although it wasn't one that mattered as much to Fackler. An earlier draft noted that Monica's purple dress gaped open "as if the muzzle was pressed hard to her body." The final draft simply stated her dress was gaping open.

It appeared some pathologist believed early on that it was a contact shot. That belief was later silenced.

CHAPTER 17

A LOST MISSILE

Victor Titus couldn't stop thinking about his theory that Monica herself had chosen him as a pallbearer, but the how and when eluded him. Yet the thought that something existed to prove Monica's state of mind would not let him go. "I'm wondering if there could be a will or a letter," he finally said to Dave Pfeffer. "You have to check it out. Perhaps her family knows."

Pfeffer felt like he was not just stepping on eggshells but trampling whole eggs and smearing the sticky yolk all over disapproving Dora Sanchez's foyer when he walked in. That's as far as he got into the house. They also talked to him at his car as he left their house. They weren't about to be cooperative with the man who was going to help keep their daughter's killer out of jail. Dora's pursed lips and brooding eyes showed her disdain for Pfeffer's work better than any words could speak. Her severe, chin-length black hair was pulled back but it couldn't hide the fact that she must have been beautiful once. Perhaps could still be beautiful but for her obvious woe-stricken state.

Torry Sanchez's thick grayish-white hair and average height looked obscure near Pfeffer's massive body. Sanchez's form took on a firm stance as he told Pfeffer he had never seen Paul physically or verbally abuse Monica. Neither had Monica ever come to him and told him Paul was treating her poorly. Paul and Monica came to the Sanchez house on Sundays and on special occasions, and he never saw any arguments or fights between the couple. It was only after the break-up that Monica told her father about bruises. He assumed Paul gave her the bruise on her face, but she never came right out and told him that. He said he didn't remember what Amanda had told him about the bruise.

He admitted Paul did a lot for the Sanchez family, such as chopping wood for their fireplace.

"I can't say that I didn't like Paul; Monica loved Paul very much," Torry Sanchez told Pfeffer. He knew Paul did everything for Monica including cleaning and cooking.

On the day of the shooting, a police officer called and told him someone had been shot at the Dunn house. Torry Sanchez said he assumed Paul had shot Monica.

While Pfeffer and Sanchez spoke, a woman walked through a room adjacent to the foyer, momentarily interrupting their conversation. Though words weren't exchanged during the brief time she was in the nearby room, Pfeffer knew without being told that they would meet again later. And she had something she wanted—no, needed—to tell him. The "connection" between the two of them, as Pfeffer described it, almost frightened the tall, impervious detective. It was more psychokinetic than sexual. Just as quickly as she entered the room, the woman got what she came for and disappeared into another part of the house, allowing the two men to return to their discussion.

Sanchez, who obviously didn't want to give a lot of information, jumped from topic to topic as the tall investigator tried to quote him word for word. He told Pfeffer that he had noticed Monica was losing weight since the couple broke up. She had told him about finding the letter to Anita. In fact, she showed it to him. Sanchez said he tried to calm down his hysterical daughter.

Pfeffer asked him if he believed Monica wouldn't be in heaven if she had killed herself. Sanchez immediately responded that she was in heaven and he knew she hadn't committed suicide.

Finally, Pfeffer remembered Titus's suspicions when he was named a pallbearer, turned to the grieving older man and quietly asked, "What about the letter Monica wrote?"

Obviously thinking Pfeffer knew all about it, Sanchez replied that he saw the letter Monica wrote to Rick Jacquez the day she died. Sanchez had made the decision that the letter was private and chose to withhold it from everyone. What he didn't tell the detective but what later surfaced was that a law enforcement official had told Sanchez to destroy the letter.

Impartiality in jurors is difficult when a case has had as much publicity as Paul's had. Too much pre-trial publicity in Farmington caused District Judge Joseph Rich to move the trial to Gallup, a smaller town two hours south.

An *Albuquerque Tribune* series and *20/20* broadcast described Gallup as "Drunk Town USA" but failed to pick up on the raw beauty of the red rocks and other mountainous terrain surrounding the southwestern town twenty miles east of the Arizona border. The alcohol studies stemmed from numerous alcohol-related road accidents and deaths from people stumbling drunk in town and getting hit by cars or trains in the Gallup and McKinley County areas. Some people blame the alcohol problems on the town's numerous liquor establishments, which bring in a large portion of the town's cash value. Others blame the nearby "dry" Zuni and Navajo reservations, on which alcohol can't be sold. Also, voters determined alcohol could not be sold in Gallup on Sundays. Both situations cause some people to drive to Arizona to purchase alcohol on Sundays or to Gallup during the week if they live on the reservation.

Sometimes it's a two-hour drive back home to remote areas of the "rez," which is what the locals call the Indian reservations. Many of these drivers don't wait until they make the long drive home before they start drinking. Still other people argue that it's not the liquor inavailability on the reservation that causes the alcohol problems in Gallup. Instead, they say a high unemployment rate in the largely low-income town results in alcoholism. It seems people either rich or poor dominate the town's population of 22,000, with "middle class" being a small minority.

Beyond its problems, Gallup residents also thrive off tourists who visit the town's many Indian jewelry shops. Locals know to hang out at some of the restaurants or the flea markets to get the best deals on handmade jewelry in sterling silver. Locals also know how to tell sterling silver from nickel—and they might share the information with outsiders.

This town of 6,500 feet elevation has all four seasons and its nighttime weather is often the coldest in the nation. This belies the fact that the "Land of Enchantment" could also be described as the sunshine state. The National Weather Bureau describes southern portions as featuring more than 3,000 hours of sunshine a year.

Besides the Navajo reservation, the beautiful Zuni reservation is about an hour south of Gallup and also contains exquisite rock formations and sandstone mesas. Ancient Anasazi Indian ruins can be found on some of the land on both reservations, complete with priceless pieces of pottery and arrowheads left on the ground five hundred years ago or longer. Federal law forbids ravaging the ground of these relics, which makes it such a stunning sight for the average hiker to stumble upon the beautiful visions of past life. A hiker, however, can go quickly from heaven to hell on the reservation, as many people don't respect its beauty and use it as their dumping grounds. Beer cans here and there show how people use out-of-the-way sites as party spots.

Other places contain old, abandoned car parts, rusted almost beyond recognition, toilet seats, old clothing, chewed mattresses, broken bottles, dead animals—anything people want to just toss away. The area's designated garbage sites are often considered too far away for some people who live deep within the reservation. But that's no excuse for turning nature into trash.

Just east of Gallup, the sandstone formation known as "Church Rock" gained its name because it simply eroded away into the shape of a church, with its steeples and spires. Another small Indian community is called Church Rock after the formation. Just up the road from Church Rock is another semi-famous eroded rock formation that hasn't received notoriety in the form of a town named after it, but probably has had more than its share of gossip. Known as "Peter Rock," it looks like a giant penis, complete with a head and ridges above the ramrod-straight base. In fact, rumor has it that a Gallup resident called up some pornographic magazines and told them about the rock formation. As the story goes, one magazine set up a photo shoot using a helicopter to place a spread-eagle model atop the massive symbol of male virility. No one in Gallup seems to know which magazine took the shots, let alone has copies of them.

An area not far from Church Rock is known as Superman Canyon, because in the first Superman movie, with man-of-steel Christopher Reeve, some of the flying shots were taken over the rocky area. A McKinley County sheriff's investigator's claim to fame was meeting Reeve and co-star Margot Kidder, who played Lois Lane, while he worked at the motel where the stars stayed during the movie's filming. The deputy found Reeve, who had years to go before a catastrophic toss off a horse that would paralyze him and change him into a philanthropist for spine injury research, to be the kinder of the two actors.

If visitors to the Gallup area don't have enough to see

with all of its famous sites, they can still journey through canyons and pick up fossils like shark's teeth, stuck inside rocks. The teeth are testimony to the fact that New Mexico used to be under the ocean's water several thousand years ago.

A true joke for Gallup is the "Puerco River." Looking on a map at how the "river" twists and turns through Gallup, one might get the wrong impression. Hardly a river, it is bone dry most of the year, more of a meeting place or a thoroughfare for hikers to get to the red rocks or other sites. But during monsoon season, the "Perky," as it's called, can fill up with dangerous, rushing water. Some drivers have become trapped and died when their vehicles were carried off by roaring water or when they fell into the swirling abyss. Police officers and firefighters have earned medals of valor for saving residents caught in the usually dry ditches that fill almost to overflowing during flash floods.

Between Gallup and Farmington are various volcanic "plugs," extinct volcanoes which have eroded away leaving only the center. One such famous side is called "Shiprock," because the formation looks like a ship, complete with a huge sail. The Native American town there is called Shiprock. Other extinct volcanoes haven't acquired the popularity of Shiprock but can be seen popping up on the vast expanse of land between Gallup and Farmington.

So it was in Gallup that the attorneys called a special hearing just for the production of the letter written by Monica Dunn. It was then that Judge Rich ordered the letter produced and, suddenly, it appeared. It had been written March 11, 1994, just a few days after Monica found the letter Paul wrote Anita. Titus, Murphy and Mitchell were shocked at its contents.

"Help everyone get through this and remember, I will

never be totally gone, through my beautiful girls," wrote Monica to her sister's boyfriend, Rick.

The attorneys found the words rather strange, since Monica died right in front of those "beautiful girls." More than once someone would speculate as to just what kind of mother could shoot herself in front of her daughters. Others saw it as a sure sign that she didn't kill herself. Sure, Monica was in a back room, not directly in front of her daughters. But how could she believe the girls wouldn't know what happened, wouldn't see any blood and worst of all, wouldn't see their dying mother being hauled away?

"I am really sorry about this. I just don't have any more strength or power to go on. I'm tired," the sullen Monica admitted.

How could anyone know in advance that she was going to be murdered by her husband? And why would she apologize for it? The defense attorneys were more and more puzzled as to why Paul was being prosecuted.

The next words are sad to someone who knew what Paul was going through at the same time Monica penned the letter. It was almost as if they were both searching for the same things in other people. If they had just reached out to each other, they might have found it. Perhaps Paul and Monica should have refrained from their affairs and looked deep within their own relationship for answers to their needs.

"I was fighting so hard and struggling so hard for something that I know was never there or never would be there. But during the time I fought, I had no idea I was dead for him. If I had been told the truth, maybe I would have some strength left and an ounce of dignity."

Dramatic words. Intended to be her last on earth? Or part of some play, with her family to rescue her from deadly thoughts?

"I look in the mirror and I see nothing. I lost myself to someone who doesn't even care. I was led to believe he loved me in the same manner I loved him. How can a human lead another one for years and years to believe a lie? I don't understand. I have thought and tried to remember where I screwed up. I must have been so blind or lost, really stupid."

A psychologist might look at Monica's words and diagnose extreme depression, because she seems to have classic symptoms. Perhaps an antidepressant and a reality check would have been indicated, thought the attorneys. Her next words made the attorneys believe Monica wasn't just contemplating suicide—she meant to act on it.

"I know I must do what needs to be done."

But others would surmise she just meant to take some other kind of action, like somehow forcing herself out of her depression so she could care for herself and her children.

Her next words confused everyone.

"Don't mislead my girls. I could do that and be so dumb, never even realize it."

Mislead the girls about what? The attorneys wondered if she wasn't urging her family not to mislead the children into thinking Paul killed her. She also might not have wanted them to believe she was cowardly.

In the rest of her letter, Monica named pallbearers and honorary pallbearers. She wrote, "Paul (ha-ha) bearers." She suggested having a cheap funeral and to have her buried or cremated with that decision left up to her mother, Dora. She named who should take what furniture, which really went to Paul after her death, and asked her family to sell the house and put the money in trust for Amanda, Racquel and Diane.

Throughout the letter she bashed Paul, calling him a violent alcoholic who cared for no one but himself and who condoned drugs.

She asked for a closed coffin so people would remember

her as she used to be "when I had a face before Paul stripped that of me."

She asked the family to keep Paul away from the girls and to always remember he was violent and would try to manipulate them.

Her next words chilled the defense team. "When I am gone, the bruises on me will show."

Her death didn't come until a month later. How could Monica Dunn know she would have bruises a month in the future?

PART THREE

DEFENDING THE TRUTH

Lo, they lie in wait for my soul:
The mighty are gathered against me,
not for my transgression
nor for my sin, O Lord.
They run and prepare themselves
without my fault.

—Psalm 59: 3–4

CHAPTER 18

ON TRIAL

Despite the appearance of Monica's letter to Rick Jacquez and the defense team's certainty that it was a suicide note, Whitehead and others felt it wasn't. Whitehead decided to go on with his prosecution of Paul Dunn.

A group of attractive men seated at the defense table rose and looked with anticipation as the selected jurors entered the Gallup courtroom. There were five women and seven men. Some jurors looked too young to be on the jury. Others had the experience of age. None of them looked like ogres who intended to convict a police officer—or any man—simply because the man's wife lay dead. They didn't look scary at all, only a bit weary from the grueling jury selection process.

Paul Dunn's face remained expressionless as his eyes met the jurors'. The turquoise short-sleeved shirt he wore brought out the depth of those blue eyes. The debonair ex-cop stood ramrod-straight, not afraid to meet the stares of reporters and other people in the packed courtroom. Some of those people were his former in-laws, who glared back at him, daring to test whether looks could kill. Paul's handsome face remained composed as Eleventh Judicial District Judge Joseph Rich told the courtroom of spectators, jurors, lawyers—and the accused—to be seated.

Surrounding Paul like a football huddle were attorney Gary Mitchell, attorney Victor Titus and his partner as well as witness Steve Murphy and investigator Dave Pfeffer. Mitchell's country talk matched his apple-pie facial features, complete with large, hazel eyes, brown hair and a smile that said, *Trust me. Believe me. Would I lie to you?* Devilish green eyes and a come-hither smile combined Titus' well-built masculine strength. Murphy's dark good looks suggested mystery, like *You'd better not underestimate my innocent air*. Investigator Pfeffer's rugged cowboy toughness was tempered by a shy boyishness that didn't quite reveal his deadly on-target skill.

At the prosecution table, determination shone on the faces of Kathleen Carnell, whose hands shook, light brown hair pulled severely back from her attractive face, and Darrel Jiles, whose baldness and intelligent face behind glasses emanated a quiet sternness that should not be mistaken for gentleness. Jurors were to find very soon the prosecutors weren't going to buckle under in timidity. They meant business. The savvy defense attorneys, in turn, were equally determined despite the fact they had to overcome the average assumption that no woman could reach the trigger of a shotgun in order to kill herself with the weapon.

While tensions heightened in the courtroom, many throwing invisible daggers at each other for various reasons, Judge Joseph Rich told the jurors that prosecutors and defense would now give opening statements describing what they intended to prove. Anticipation reached its peak as Kathleen Carnell approached the podium placed several feet from jurors.

Carnell told jurors the case was pretty simple. As she explained, Paul Dunn had battered his wife. She was going to file battery charges against him, which would have cost him his job. She had the papers in her purse and was about to leave for work. Paul was not about to let her do this to him. So he killed her, not minding that the children were in the kitchen. He killed her with a shotgun, knowing, as any police officer would, that no one survived a shotgun wound. He followed her into the bedroom, grabbed the nearby shotgun and shot her as she stood against the wall, about two feet from the barrel of the shotgun. Then he carried her outside the room, not leaving her, as a police officer would be trained to do in an accidental shooting so paramedics would be able to treat her bleeding wounds before moving her and causing her to lose more blood.

According to Carnell, Paul carried his dying wife past the crying little girls on the couch to the garage door. He put her on the garage floor next to their vehicle. As if to make sure to finish her off if the shotgun wasn't enough, Paul pretended to do cardiopulmonary resuscitation on Monica. But really, he was pushing the life out of her with every pump of his arms. "Squish, squish," the blood left her body, Carnell said. She told jurors it was common sense that a woman of Monica's size couldn't kill herself with a shotgun because she couldn't reach the trigger from two feet away, which is where the medical investigator would testify the gun had to be based on the autopsy evidence.

Tension hung in the air as Carnell talked about a "will" Monica had written because she feared Paul and was afraid he would kill her. Carnell emphasized that Monica was wearing a purple dress for work, pantyhose, full makeup and had her hair done. No woman is going to go to this length before killing herself, she said. She was silent for a moment as if allowing this to sink in. Then, she added, when Paul arrived at the house, Monica was already backing out in the van. She pulled it back in when she saw him. She intended to take the girls to her mother's house, apparently, because they weren't ready to go to school. But Paul later said Monica had asked him to come over and watch them as he usually did on his days off.

A sick emptiness sat in the pit of Paul's stomach as he listened to the end of Carnell's diatribe. His emotions and thoughts were in a state of disorder. How could this be happening to him?

Gary Mitchell began his opening statement by pointing out a woman could use a hanger or other long object to hit the trigger of a shotgun if it were a few feet away from her body. A hanger was found on the bed. He presented a different picture of the morning Monica died. Mitchell explained as Paul had that Monica told him about the battery charges. He went to the house and begged her to talk; she wouldn't. He said Paul thought he heard the lock on the bedroom door click. Then he heard Monica say, "Come in."

Scenes flooded through Paul's mind as tears leapt to his eyes.

"What he hears and sees will never, for the rest of his life, leave his mind. He hears the gun go off . . . and he sees blood. He screams, 'Monica, no! Monica, no!'" Mitchell told jurors.

Paul stared up at the ceiling trying to regain his composure.

Mitchell told of Paul yelling at Amanda to call 911, how Paul carried his wife, who had lost so much blood from her abdominal gunshot wound that she slipped out of his grasp twice, to the van. Inside the garage, Paul realized he didn't have enough time to drive her to the emergency room. He put her on the garage floor and began CPR until emergency medical technicians arrived and forced him away from her. Immediately, Paul's former buddies at the Farmington Police Department treated him like a common criminal. They didn't let him wash Monica's blood from his hands. The hours passed, and her blood dried to a gruesome brown. Finally, gunpowder residue tests were performed on his and Monica's hands.

Mitchell scanned the jury box until he saw all riveted on him, waiting for his next words. He told the fourteen listeners that the test results showed residue on Monica's hands but none on Paul's hands. He explained whoever fired the gun would have residue on his hands.

Mitchell read from what he called Monica's suicide letter. "He doesn't want me, so now he must live without me. I'm really sorry about this; I just don't have any power or strength to go on. I'm tired."

According to her words, her alcoholic, estranged husband was not fit to raise their young daughters, Diane and Racquel. "I do understand they will grieve, a process everyone has to go through. But they're young, they'll move on."

Mitchell stressed that Paul took two polygraph tests, one for the prosecution and one for the defense. The tests showed him to be truthful. In fact, the prosecution's polygrapher would later be called by the defense to testify how well the defendant passed the test. Finally, Mitchell told jurors Paul never hit Monica. He described the one time Paul punched a hole in the wall. But he never hurt her. During an argument a few days before her death, Monica pushed open the bathroom door with her buttocks and the mirror attached to the door, which had become loose, crashed to the floor. This could account for the bruises to her thigh. Mitchell described Paul to jurors as a human being, capable of the same range of emotions as every juror in the box. Just like they could, Paul could display anger, but he would never hit his wife, just like any juror could display anger but knew they would never resort to violence. Mitchell spoke as if common sense said Paul couldn't have killed Monica. The only reasonable solution, then, was suicide. And it cannot be forgotten that reasonableness—whatever that meant to individual jurors—was the standard in trials. He had to put reasonable doubt in jurors' minds, so his entire presentation of the case would rise and set on what a reasonable person would do in the same situations Paul faced.

After opening statements, Carnell and Jiles brought in witnesses, one by one, to tell the tale of a gruesome crime scene. Paramedics described Monica's grim condition at the home and of her transport to the hospital. Titus watched with some disbelief at the parade of Farmington Police Department officers who testified. He couldn't believe it when he saw how the officers sided against Paul from the start. The small amount of officers who stuck up for Paul surprised Titus, too. It was hard to guess in advance who your friends would be in times of need.

Farmington Police Lieutenant Fred Frost testified in a mechanical voice that he found a large amount of blood on the driveway and a blood pool inside the garage as well as a bloodstain on the garage wall.

"There were buttons and I believe a high-heeled shoe in the area," Frost said.

The officer showed no emotion nor did he look at Paul as he described a blood trail leading from the garage through the indoor hallway to the master bedroom. He talked about finding cereal bowls on the kitchen table with milk-soaked cereal still in them. Farmington police officers were quick to turn the case over to the New Mexico State Police, because the main suspect was one of their own, Frost revealed, and now his voice held a tinge of disgust.

Young and grimacing a bit, Deputy Medical Investigator Renee Alford testified that it was her job to take photos and prepare Monica's body for transport to the Office of the Medical Investigator in Albuquerque, where an autopsy could be performed. Monica's dress and some of her underclothes had been cut off during the attempt to revive her. Alford said she took off Monica's bra and dress and put her in a body bag, placing the clothing in with her. She also removed Monica's earrings, a chain necklace and emergency room staff had already taken off her rings. The bag was sealed complete with Monica's belongings.

On cross-examination, she told the defense that she re-opened the sealed bag again at the morgue so state police officers could take photos. She also told Mitchell that forensic pathologists at the office of the medical investigator prefer deputy investigators to leave the clothing on. She didn't remember why the state police had removed Monica's dress and bra. Mitchell asked if it was unusual to break the seal on the bag for state police—for anyone.

"I've never done it before," admitted Alford.

It was the first example of procedures not being followed. It wouldn't be the last.

The trial wound on. In a dramatic oddity, as the police officers testified about the investigator they each stepped up to the witness stand by walking around Monica Dunn's waterbed covered with pillows and a sheet. It was an unusual sight for a courtroom. The attorneys had re-created the scene of the crime, which also included the headboard for the jurors' firsthand perusal. Farmington detective Jeff Miller testified he performed a gun residue test of Monica's hands and bagged her hands for further testing to be performed at her autopsy. He noticed a bruise on her right hip, which was evident through nylons and panties she was wearing.

At Mitchell's request, Miller explained to jurors that when a gun is shot, powder residue or gases land on the shooter's skin.

At this point, Judge Rich explained to the jurors that the defense and prosecution agreed to certain facts in the case to speed the trial along. In testing for gunshot residue, the results were inconclusive for Paul's left and right palm and negative for the back of his hands. The test for residue on Monica's hands was positive. Paul's test was taken prior to his being allowed to wash his hands and Monica's was taken prior to her body being cleansed. The attorneys agreed there was unburned black powder in the wound, and they agreed to the accuracy of a state police interview with Paul.

San Juan County District Attorney's Office Investigator Daryl Harris testified he took video of the death scene and of the state police while they drilled out sections of the wall where the pellets had entered before going through Monica's body. Rich let jurors go early for the weekend because the prosecution had no more witnesses to present that day.

On that Monday morning, the prosecution called defense attorney Steve Murphy to the stand. However, Murphy was there to testify more on behalf of his own client than for the prosecution. On cross-examination, he recalled taking the results of Paul's polygraph tests to District Attorney Alan Whitehead.

Murphy reported that Whitehead had said, "I don't care about that anymore. He's going to be charged."

Murphy explained Whitehead had a policy of dismissing cases if the defendant passes a polygraph test. Although Murphy and the defense couldn't tell this to jurors right then, Whitehead's statement to Murphy showed the impact of politics on Paul's prosecution.

As Jiles strode confidently into position, his next witness, Farmington Sergeant Mark Hawkinson was sworn in and testified that Paul gave him a statement at the shooting scene. According to it, Paul went to the home around 7:00 A.M. to take care of the children. Monica met him at the door. She told him, "By the way, Paul, I'm going to file charges against you for battery."

Relating Paul's words, Hawkinson said that according to Dunn, Monica continued to walk to the bedroom as Paul followed her. She closed and locked the bedroom door. Paul talked to her through the door: "Open the door. We need to talk about this. I never struck you."

She said nothing. After a long pause, she told him to come in. Paul said the shotgun went off as the door opened three-quarters of the way and he saw Monica fly backward from her sitting position and slump toward the floor. He picked up the shotgun and laid it on the floor.

He tried to use the bedroom phone to call 911, but the phone was dead. While giving his statement, Hawkinson said Paul's demeanor changed. "He started getting quite upset that her blood was still on his hands. He understood tests had to be taken, but he was angry it was taking so long," Hawkinson explained.

Later in his testimony, Hawkinson told the jurors he was the one who told Paul that Monica was dead. "He broke down crying. I held him for a little bit, patting him on the back, trying to keep him under control."

Under cross-examination, Hawkinson told Mitchell it was a traumatic event for him as well, because the Dunns were friends of his. He said they had a good relationship. He never knew them to be violent with each other. He said his conversation with Paul was not tape-recorded. Mitchell drew Hawkinson's attention back to Paul's comments about the blood on his hands.

"He was sitting there with his wife's blood on his hands, right?" Mitchell asked.

Hawkinson nodded. "I think it would traumatize anybody."

Hawkinson described Paul as a hard-working police officer and a dedicated one.

Courtroom murmur hushed moments later and spectators' faces gleamed with predatory excitement. All eyes were fixed on fresh-faced Anita Harris as she made her way to the front of the courtroom in a fashionable navy blue suit. Her fiery red hair, which usually hung naturally about her shoulders, was swept back into a French twist. Expressive crystal green eyes fixed on the jury as she took the stand to talk about the circumstances after Monica's death. Anita gave no appearance of being the femme fatale men would kill for. No sexy clothes, no sultry stares. She seemed a strong, sensible type, an independent woman who would disdain such behavior.

After being sworn in, the prosecutor looked at her with raised eyebrows and began his questioning about the day of Monica's death. In response, Anita said she had heard about the shooting and called Paul at his apartment to find out if it was true. Paul was devastated—in shock—when she spoke to him. Paul had told Anita a similar story to the one Hawkinson told jurors, of how Monica's body flew backward after she pulled the trigger on the shotgun pointed directly at her abdomen. Anita then told Jiles she and Paul were "close friends," admitting they were "intimate," but not openly saying they had had an affair. She said she knew he was married and had children. Jiles paused to let this sink in. Anita told Mitchell on cross-examination that she had met Paul when he worked security at a man's private ranch located near her small ranch. He talked to her about problems in his marriage, but never mentioned any moments of physical violence with Monica. The problem that troubled Paul most was how Monica treated April, Paul's daughter from his first marriage, who didn't feel welcome when she visited her father.

"Paul felt that no matter what he did . . . to make sure April was accepted, he was unable to accomplish that.

"It was very clear that his daughters were his life—he talked about them all the time and was very proud," Anita explained.

When Jiles with his sharp, hawk eyes not hidden by glasses probed as to where Anita was on the holiday weekend just prior to Monica's death, Anita responded with her usual clear frankness, "Easter weekend I was with Paul Friday night, Saturday night and all day Sunday. He was with me until 5:30 A.M. Monday."

She said she never received the fateful letter addressed to her that Monica found in Paul's truck. She believed it was written at the time the divorce papers were filed.

Though she did not lose her composure, her voice softened as Anita also reported that Paul had never been violent with her during their relationship. She told jurors she and Paul hadn't ended their relationship but had no plans for marriage. The courtroom again hushed as Anita calmly stood up and, with her head high, left the witness stand.

As the trial progressed, Victor Titus was finding not only his days but his nights consumed by it. The bars Titus used to frequent—and sometimes closed down—became battle zones to be avoided. Anonymous letters came to his office and his home. One letter which Titus saved and framed proclaimed, "Do you get a special thrill representing murderers or only cop killers? You have to know Paul Dunn killed his wife. You're not that dumb. Why do you want to get him off? God bless you in your quest for injustice."

Multiple calls threatened both Titus and his family. "One threatened to expose my wife's affair with Paul (untrue). Another, to expose my affair with Monica (also untrue). Several threatened to say my wife was habitually giving blow jobs in the parking lot of Clancy's, a local pub (also untrue). All of them strengthened my resolve to see that justice be done, despite any personal cost involved."

Titus wondered aloud if their business would survive the case. His wife, Debby, who he describes as "the finest woman I have ever known," wondered repeatedly if their family would survive the trial.

CHAPTER 19

THE MYSTERY WOMAN

It wasn't long after Pfeffer's search for evidence intensified that he met again the woman he'd encountered at the Sanchez house. She identified herself as a Sanchez family member. She didn't want anyone to know what she was about to tell him. She loved Monica and understood her relatives suffered much emotional pain before her death. She didn't want the family's wrath for having talked to the "enemy" and for admitting that Monica was hardly saintly. The investigator's ears perked as he waited for her to continue.

Monica was having an affair. She gave Pfeffer the man's name. She wasn't sure how long it had been going on. But Monica had gotten pregnant and had an abortion in Albuquerque. The woman gave Pfeffer the name of the doctor, who also asked to remain anonymous because of fear of what the Sanchez family might do if this event surfaced. The abortion occurred long after Paul's vasectomy, so Monica knew that the baby was her boyfriend's, the woman told Pfeffer.

Pfeffer could hardly conceal his excitement. Finally, there was some validation of his suspicions. Finding proof wouldn't be easy, but he had a lead and he had the name of the man who'd impregnated Monica.

Would this prove to be the first real piece of the Monica puzzle: Why a beautiful thirty-one-year-old woman with three children to raise would commit suicide? Depression over a broken marriage? Guilt over having aborted a baby?

A theory was forming in Pfeffer's head. A theory about what happened the day Monica died. He certainly didn't believe Paul shot her. He didn't believe Monica would kill herself. He didn't think they'd fought over the gun. Pfeffer wouldn't share his idea with anyone yet. Maybe it was too far-fetched. But then, Pfeffer was too much of a seasoned investigator to start distrusting his instincts now.

He will not identify the mysterious woman, he says, even if a judge throws him in jail for contempt of court. He'd take her name to the grave if he had to.

"It gives me chills because it was so special, this meeting . . . There was nothing sexual between us, just a connection that I will never forget." The doctor also asked for anonymity. He didn't realize then that he would meet a wonderful woman, eternally beautiful, inside and out, who would later become his wife, Carla.

With the revelations of the mystery woman in his thoughts, the determined Pfeffer kept searching. He found the doctor who performed the abortion. He obtained the record that showed Monica Dunn had the procedure done.

Then Pfeffer found the man with whom Monica had the affair. The man denied the affair and the pregnancy. Pfeffer's instincts told him the man was indeed the father of Monica's unborn child.

Paul wasn't happy when he heard this new information, even though it revealed secrets about Monica which cast light on her state of mind. Paul took out his anger on Pfeffer when the investigator gave Paul the news in jail.

"Prove it to me! You better damn well prove it to me!"

"Well, I have paperwork . . ."

Paul never asked to see it, never wanted to see it.

Monica's affair and abortion weren't allowed to be presented at trial. Judge Rich found them irrelevant. Pfeffer and the attorneys thought otherwise.

CHAPTER 20

THE CHILDREN'S NIGHTMARE MEMORIES

Court staff members pushed the microphone downward for the next witness for the prosecution. Paul's own flesh-and-blood, five-year-old Katie, swept into the courtroom to face her father and speak for the attorneys who wanted to see him in prison. Diane, her hair in a bow, appeared in a lovely blue velvet dress trimmed in white lace, looking less like a court witness than a princess about to attend a ball. Her daddy smiled at her as if he were the proud papa introducing her to the world: That's my girl.

Diane Dunn smiled back at her father, but in the hearing, she didn't call him "Daddy," she called him "Paul." Each time he heard it, Paul visibly stiffened, but he still smiled at his daughter as if reassuring her.

Jiles also had some trouble with names. He began calling his witness Racquel. Diane didn't hesitate to correct him. "My name ain't Racquel."

She explained that the morning of her mother's death, while she and Racquel ate Lucky Charms in the kitchen, she heard her parents arguing, saying "bad words and stuff." She heard a loud sound, which she thought was a dresser falling in her mother's bedroom. When she ran to the bedroom, her daddy told her to shut the door and call 911.

During her brief testimony, Mitchell asked her where she was staying while her father was in jail. She said she was staying with "Mommy and Daddy," who, at Mitchell's prompting, she explained were her Aunt Theresa and Uncle Rick.

On the rare occasions that Paul got to speak to his daughters from jail, Racquel always expressed her love, saying she couldn't wait to see her dad again. Diane, however, progressively turned away from Paul. As if hearing her call him by his first name in the courtroom wasn't evidence enough of the change in her attitude toward him, Paul received a shock during one telephone conversation. When he told Diane it would all be over soon and they'd be back together as a family, his daughter's response burned forever in his devastated heart.

"Let's wait and see what the jury does."

Diane's brainwashing shook Paul, although he understood a child her age could be made to believe just about anything. Still, he had a hard time putting the pain past him.

At the end of his questioning, Mitchell asked her to look at her father's smiling face in the courtroom.

"You don't get to see him, do you?" he asked.

"No," Diane almost whispered.

"Your new mommy and daddy don't let you see him, do they?" Mitchell asked again.

"No." The little girl shook her head and sighed.

After Diane stepped down from the witness stand, the court staff moved the microphone up as Diane's pretty older stepsister, Amanda, who was fifteen, took the stand. Amanda took a deep breath before she spoke of Monica's fear of Paul. According to Amanda, Monica's health declined after the couple separated. She didn't sleep, she didn't eat. Monica cowered into a prison in her mind as

Paul kept calling her, often showing up at their home without notice, Amanda said. Monica never would allow Amanda to step in and protect her mother; she always told her daughter she could handle it. However, after the separation, Amanda saw her mother's emotional state deteriorate as quickly as her rapid weight loss, turning her into a pale, gaunt, ghost-like skeleton with sinking self-esteem.

As Monica became more distraught, Amanda explained, "She always wanted to know where I was going . . . Sometimes, she'd say, 'Don't leave me.' "

Amanda felt that the morning of her mother's death, she didn't seem depressed. Her mother left before 7:00 A.M. to take the girls over to Grandma's house, where they would stay until they had to go to school. Monica was starting to work ten-hour days, four days a week, so she wouldn't be able to get the girls to school herself. Paul wasn't supposed to come over that morning, so Amanda was surprised when she heard her mother honk the horn just as Amanda was shutting the garage door after her mother's van pulled out of the driveway. Amanda watched while her mother pulled back into the garage and came into the house with Paul, who carried cereal and milk for his daughters. She asked her mom if she wanted her to hang around while Paul was there.

"No, everything is going to be fine. Go ahead; go take your shower. Get ready for school," Monica told Amanda. These words were the last Amanda ever heard her mother say.

While in the shower, Amanda heard loud thuds outside the bathroom, near the master bedroom. "I was scared. I was trying to hurry out of the shower and then a few minutes later, I heard the gun go off. I pulled the curtain back and I grabbed a towel. I took off toward the room, and I remember yelling, 'What did you do to my mom?' And she was just lying there."

"Amanda, who were you talking to when you said,

'What did you do to my mom?' " Jiles asked.

"Paul. I saw the way he treated her. I could tell she was afraid of him. She didn't want to be alone with him."

Amanda continued her narration. Paul yelled at her that Monica had shot herself and told her to call 911. Amanda testified that she ran to the phone and had to get little Diane off the phone, because she had learned how to call 911 in school and had dialed the number. Amanda hung up and redialed. "I said, 'Hurry, my mom just shot herself.' " She hung up on the dispatcher. Later, she said she realized Paul had killed Monica and wanted to make it look like an accident so he'd told Amanda she had shot herself. But at the time, she had trusted his words.

Jiles interrupted Amanda's account of the morning her mother died and tried to build on the tension that already permeated the courtroom. He asked Amanda if she'd ever seen Paul behave violently toward her mother. "Yes. She always had bruises all over her body. He used to grab her and I remember her once telling me, 'He'll never hit me again.' " She didn't remember when Monica had said that to her.

Jiles returned Amanda's attention back to the day the teen wished most to forget. After she called 911 that morning, she said she watched Paul in the garage. "He was just sitting there."

Her mother didn't like guns and would never have shot herself, Amanda claimed. They only had guns in the home at Paul's insistence and he made Monica learn how to shoot.

However, Amanda's last words on direct testimony for the prosecution gave the final sting. Instead of being the doting father to the abused, misunderstood April—who Anita had testified Monica mistreated—Amanda testified Paul would leave April alone with Monica and Amanda's sisters so he could go fishing whenever the girl came to visit.

Paul's eyes widened. He couldn't believe his ears. He

knew what really happened during April's visits, but would the jury be able to determine the truth from fiction?

During Amanda's teary description of how her mother's health—both emotional and physical—deteriorated during the split with Paul, she never mentioned any comments her mother made about suicide. It took Mitchell's careful cross-examination to bring out that, "Yes, my mother mentioned suicide but assured me she'd never do it." Amanda suggested her mother get some counseling, but Monica was too proud to ask for help. Amanda never considered Monica would kill herself because she loved Amanda, Racquel and Diane too much. She wouldn't do that to them.

Mitchell's questioning got Amanda to admit something she hadn't told before, that she had heard a scream after she heard the gunshot. She told the police she thought it was Paul.

Mitchell asked for more detail from Amanda. "He was holding her in his arms, wasn't he? He was holding her up? He was down on his hands and knees, and he was holding her up, wasn't he?"

"Yes."

"Was he crying?"

"I think he was."

In response to Mitchell's gentle probing Amanda admitted Paul never threatened her and she never heard him threaten her mother. She also said she never saw him hit her mother and that when Amanda had questioned her mother, she told her she got bruised on her face from falling, not from domestic abuse.

Mitchell asked her if it wasn't true that she told her friend, Jacob, that she knew her mother committed suicide, that she told him earlier that her mother wanted to kill herself. "And you told him you were worried about your mom because she was not eating and she was getting weak and she was falling down?" Mitchell asked.

"Yes."

Amanda agreed with Mitchell's characterization of the family as a happy one for many years before Paul and Monica separated.

"Do you remember telling Paul you know he didn't kill her and you still loved him?" Mitchell asked.

Amanda was stubborn. "I remember saying I still loved him, but not the other part."

Mitchell's cross-examination of Amanda also elicited that she participated in some talking on Monica's part two days before her death. Mother and daughter followed Paul to Anita's home. "She said she had to know the truth."

Mitchell looked at jurors as if to say he hoped they were going to look for the truth, too.

CHAPTER 21

TECHNICAL TENSION

The next expert to be sworn in, New Mexico Department of Public Safety Crime Lab serologist Larry Renner, testified similarly to the way he had testified in the grand jury hearing. He said that the shotgun couldn't have been tight to Monica's abdomen because the inside of the gun would have what's known in professional circles as "blowback"— blood particles or body tissue that flies back from a body onto the weapon after it is fired. This is expected in contact wounds. Renner told Mitchell that while the state's theory that Monica was standing against the wall when she was shot makes sense, she could have been sitting on the bed.

Distinguished-looking San Juan County Magistrate Terry L. Pearson, who had formally introduced Paul and Monica, testified he knew Monica thirteen years through her role with the City of Farmington. Monica was his grandson's aunt, he said. She was also his campaign treasurer and a trusted friend. Pearson spoke to her on Good Friday, three days before her death, because he needed her to sign some campaign reporting papers. They were to meet Monday for lunch to discuss the campaign. He noticed a bruise on her left cheek near her eye.

Victor Titus marched up to the podium to cross-examine Pearson. Pearson told him he was a motorcycle cop before he was a judge. He was around Paul and Monica often before they were married and often socialized with them. Pearson described Monica as "strong-willed, a dependent person. She was someone who needed to be with someone."

He said he had never known of any domestic violence or fighting between the couple.

Jiles asked Pearson during re-direct whether he would describe Monica as having a strong personality. "Yes," the judge responded.

Titus asked if Monica ever said Paul hit her.

"No," Pearson admitted.

Monica's cousin, Michael Martinez, swept past Paul as if he were invisible and took the stand to testify for the prosecution that he was at a barbecue with Monica on Easter Saturday. He said she was scared because earlier that morning, Paul showed up at her house and the two had an argument. Paul appeared in uniform and demanded to know if a man was in the house. Under the guise of needing a drink of water, Paul stormed into the house and searched it from top to bottom. Martinez testified that Paul threatened to kill Monica if he found a man in the house. He burst into a closed bathroom door, expecting to find a man hiding there. In the process, the bathroom mirror broke. It was later that night, as Amanda had testified, that Monica followed Paul to Anita's house.

Martinez inclined his head slightly in response to Jiles' query and admitted Monica spoke about suicide, but Martinez said he had talked her out of it. "Monica said she thought about killing herself with sleeping pills. I told her, 'Don't.' I had scars. I tried to kill myself in 1986. I told her my scars were outside; hers were inside. Later, she said she wouldn't let Paul have the satisfaction, have the girls and the house."

On Easter Sunday morning, Martinez said Monica called to tell him Paul was sitting outside her home. Paul went away when she didn't go out to greet him. Martinez saw her later, around 2:00 or 3:00 P.M. and she was still frightened. She told Martinez Paul had been following her. But, in a lighter moment, she also told Martinez she wanted him to teach her how to play golf.

On cross-examination, Titus asked Martinez if Monica told him about seeing the letter that revealed that Paul was seeing another woman. Martinez said she told him about it that Saturday night in Clancy's, a bar in Farmington. She said she couldn't take Paul back because of the affair.

"And you told her at Clancy's that she had nothing to worry about, because Paul was a gentle guy?" Titus probed.

"Yes."

"He'd never hurt her?"

"No."

Titus asked if Monica told Martinez she stalked Paul, following him to Anita's house. Martinez said she had not mentioned this.

Martinez exhibited a slightly mystified expression.

Titus, noticing it, went on. "She told you just the opposite? She told you Paul followed her instead of her following Paul?"

"Yes," Martinez quietly replied. Titus nodded his head in understanding and looked at the jury, his expression conveying more than words.

CHAPTER 22

SCIENCE AND OPINION

Gerald Gorley, a private firearms consultant who was a fifteen-year member of the Association of Firearms and Tool Examiners, took the stand. Again there were the routine preliminaries and Jiles sought to establish him as an expert. Through the association, he had been technical advisor to police examiners and the FBI throughout the world. He also had been chairman of the ammunition committee of the Association for Quality Control of the Sporting Arms and Ammunition Manufacturers' Institute and a member of the Institute for twenty years. Before becoming a private consultant, he worked as director of quality for twenty-four years for the Federal Cartridge Company in Minnesota. The company manufactures small arms ammunition, which includes shotgun shells. His job was to ensure that the design of the product will function and to test to ensure it's safe. He worked with twelve-gauge double ought buck, the same ammunition in the shotgun that killed Monica Dunn.

Gorley described that a wound made by pressing the gun to the skin leaves a round hole with a muzzle impression and a halo of black, burned gunpowder. The hole takes the round shape, because the entire shotcup goes into the body and it doesn't have a chance to open. He said a shot from a distance such as three feet will leave a jagged wound from the petals of the shotcup opening and will have unburned pieces of powder, known as stippling. Gorley then looked at a photograph of Monica's wound.

"The entrance wound itself has a very red bruise mark here," he said, indicating the spot on the photograph. "The beginning of some kind of bruise mark off on the side . . . it would be the one o'clock location. That particular red mark. And this one would be at a seven o'clock location. This has every appearance of the petal of a wad as if starting to open. This one down here has the appearance of maybe a partial start of the wad opening up, opposite that of the petal."

The petal wouldn't show on the wound had the gun been in contact with the skin when it was fired.

"Mr. Gorley, if the one o'clock position is in fact a petal . . . from the shotcup, could that have been, that mark in that place there, if it was a contact discharge of a firearm?" Jiles' question was a bit confusing, but Gorley seemed to understand it.

"No, it would not. It wouldn't show. It would be just a hole going in on a press contact."

Obviously dubious, Mitchell fidgeted and sucked his lower lip. Then, on cross-examination, Mitchell was able to get Gorley to admit that this was not an exact science. He conveyed that, from a wound made from a distance of two or three feet or so, he would expect to find stippling, gunpowder specks that can get imbedded into the skin. "The stippling, when it occurs, creates what looks like a rash, like you've got a bad rash." Gorley didn't see stippling in Monica's wound.

He also stated that prosecutors didn't ask him to examine Monica's dress and underclothing to check for stippling or gunpowder burns—or anything else. Mitchell asked if Monica's dress could have caused the petals of the shotcup to open if she pressed the gun to her body over the material.

"If it was a press contact shot, it would not open at that point, because there's just no room for anything to happen. It just blows on through, as I've described, like a slug."

"That's assuming that it's pressed all the way around. There's not any gap." Mitchell was not about to give up.

"I don't know that. I haven't run tests with just the angle of the shotgun."

Gorley also told Mitchell he didn't perform any trajectory studies at all in the case.

At his turn Jiles asked if stippling would show on a wound covered with material if the shotgun is two or three feet from the victim when fired. "I would say no. It doesn't take much to stop that from happening because it has no weight. Therefore, it doesn't blow through things the way the shot itself does."

But Mitchell wasn't finished questioning the meaning of Gorley's earlier testimony. He pressed the witness and Gorley contradicted himself, telling Mitchell that on a contact shot, he would expect to see stippling on the clothing.

Although jury members struggled to keep their attention from straying as the expert witnesses testified, one or two yawns could be heard. FBI firearms expert Gerald Wilkes of Washington testified that the muzzle of the gun must have been one to three feet away from Monica's body when it was fired, because of the test firings he'd done to try to re-create the same type of hole as Monica's entrance wound.

The wound most likely wasn't made by the gun making contact with Monica's body, because he didn't find any vaporous lead, which is what Wilkes said he looks for in determining distance of gun from target.

Wilkes explained that the term "vaporous lead" comes from the "vaporization of the primer residues, of lead, which usually coats the propellant charge in the shot shell as well as the vaporization of any lead deposits on the inside of the barrel of the weapon itself. And these vaporous lead deposits exit the muzzle in a cloud, like a ray. And at contact and near contact, deposit very heavily on the areas immediately adjacent to the shot pattern hole itself."

The "cloud" disperses rather quickly when a gun is fired at a distance.

Wilkes looked at Monica's dress while investigating the case and found no traces of vaporous lead. He also saw no vaporous lead deposits on the wound. These deposits are apparent to the naked eye, but Wilkes went further than that. He examined the wound with a microscope and he tested the area for chemical lead. He found nothing.

"But let me first say that if this is a cleaned-up version of the wound, it's not of any value to me. If it's been cleaned, the vaporous lead can certainly have been removed."

Before Jiles could interrupt or ask another question, Wilkes went on to explain that he also found what looked like the "buffer" or "filler" material, also known as "grex," around the wound. This material is present in the shotcup and prevents mutilation or change in shape of the shot pellets as they are fired.

Wilkes cautioned he did not see Monica's body itself, just photographs. But he thought he saw the filler in the wound. "Which tells me this buffer material escaped the muzzle at the time the shot was fired. And, if this buffer material is present, I should expect to see presence of vaporous lead as well, because it exits at the same time, and in a very intense cloud."

The filler, small white flakes of powder, fall to the ground relatively quickly in distance shots.

When asked by Jiles if this has any impact in determining whether it was a contact shot, Wilkes simply said he would expect it to be contact if he had seen vaporous lead. He offered no explanation as to why the filler would be seen there if the wound wasn't made by close contact range.

He added, as McFeeley and others had, that the presence of petal marks from the shotcup on the wound indicated to him that the wound was made from a distance.

Wilkes testified that trajectory tests would be fairly useless after a shot enters an object like the body because the pellets move around in the body in a random manner.

On cross-examination, Mitchell brought Wilkes back to the grex. "Something's troubling me with this thing. And, I suspect in the way you were talking, that it may have troubled you as well."

He asked Wilkes to step down to the jury box and show them a photograph of the wound. Wilkes pointed out the white powder in and around the wound. He said he couldn't explain why he didn't see vaporous lead when he saw filler.

"Did you have some difficulty in this case in trying to make some determinations?"

"That's correct."

"All these experts are going to come in here. There is a major dilemma as to what happened here," Mitchell commented.

During the cross-examination, Mitchell picked up the shotgun that had already been determined to be the one that killed Monica. While jurors leaned out of their chairs to watch, Mitchell showed them the gun was empty, sat on the edge of the bed in the courtroom and pointed the shotgun at his own abdomen, ready to fire.

"One can actually fire this without the shotgun actually touching the body, can't they?" As Mitchell asked his question, he leaned forward and pressed the shotgun's trigger.

"Yes, sir. You just showed me," Wilkes answered.

It wouldn't be the last demonstration of its kind in the trial.

Mitchell did other demonstrations for firearms examiner Larry Warehime of the New Mexico Department of Public

Safety Crime Laboratory in Santa Fe. Warehime also testified similarly to his grand jury testimony on direct examination by Jiles, that he determined the muzzle was two feet from the victim because of tests he did firing the weapon at different distances. At two feet, a hole in a cloth matched the pattern on Monica's wound. No one could reach the trigger himself if the gun's barrel was two feet away from him, Warehime said.

Mitchell picked up a clothes hanger resembling the one found on Monica's bed the morning she died, and held it up for the jurors to see. In a repeat performance of his demonstration for Wilkes, Mitchell held the shotgun a distance away from his body and used the hanger to press the trigger.

"As a matter of fact, you can get quite far away with the coat hanger, can't you?" Mitchell asked. "In fact, you can get eighteen inches, up to two feet away?" Warehime replied "yes" to this question made rhetorical by Mitchell's demonstration.

Mitchell asked if Warehime had tried firing the shotgun using a coat hanger, just to check if it could be done. Warehime hadn't tried that. "It didn't seem reasonable" for a hanger to be used when a gun was two feet from the body, Warehime said.

Warehime's testing also didn't show whose fingerprints were on the gun. Gunpowder residue on the shooter's hands wouldn't have helped anything because anyone in a room in which a shotgun is fired will have residue on their hands, he said. He would expect Paul and Monica to have had gunpowder residue on them. However, Paul had no gunpowder residue on his hands—which he wasn't allowed to wash for hours after the shooting—while Monica had residue all over her hands. Warehime had no explanation for this.

Warehime had a surprise for the defense. He said he

examined a piece of Sheetrock from the wall onto which pellets that exited Monica's body penetrated. After his examination of it, the piece of the wall was given to the defense for examination. Warehime said the pellet holes had been disturbed, altered from what they were like when Warehime had the wall. He said the holes were elongated, and parts of the plaster were pulled up around the holes. The way he talked, it sounded like the defense team had purposefully altered evidence.

As always, Mitchell had an answer. He asked Warehime if he'd ever heard of trajectory studies being done by a stick being inserted into holes to determine from which direction they came when they entered the object.

"Yes, that's done," was Warehime's reply. But in a shooting where bullets travel into a body, through a body, and then land on an object, trajectory studies are useless, the expert told the attorney. Once the bullets enter the body, there's no way to know which way they twisted and turned around or through organs before exiting. Mitchell had no response to that, but defense experts later would discuss the trajectory not through the body but from the back of her body to the wall. This would set up Monica's body position when she was shot.

Farmington policeman Neph Izatt put the technical mumbo-jumbo on the back burner as she told jurors some personal facts about Monica and spoke in some unfriendly terms about Paul. According to Izatt, Monica feared Paul. Izatt explained the often-told story of how one morning, Paul locked Monica, who was wearing only a slip and a blouse at the time, outside of their home. Monica told Izatt once that Paul said if he caught her looking at another man, he'd kill her. Standing near the jury box as was his wont during the trial, Mitchell asked Izatt why, if she believed Paul had threatened to kill his wife, she never told of it to the state police immediately after Paul's arrest. As a police officer, he said, Izatt would know homicide investigators need to know when death threats have been made against a murdered person.

"They never asked," was Izatt's cool response.

Izatt also never bothered to tell anyone Monica had talked about suicide when she and Paul separated and began preparing to file for divorce. "In fact, she told you she wanted to kill herself, that she couldn't live without him?" Mitchell asked.

It took Izatt a moment to answer that question, as she looked at a copy of the transcript of her recent discussion with state police officers.

"Yes, I made those statements."

But she said Monica had followed up her statements by saying she would never commit suicide because of Amanda, Diane and Racquel. Izatt didn't believe Monica wanted to kill herself, she felt Monica was just depressed because of the divorce. Izatt stated that many people talk crazily during divorces and even mention suicide, although few people follow through with it. Mitchell's narrowed eyes fixed on the jurors said a reasonable person could conclude that one who talks about killing oneself because he or she can't live without another person sometimes puts those words into action.

The next day brought a dramatic moment as handsome Farmington Police Sergeant Lawrence "Dusty" Downs, whose relationship with Monica was questioned by defense attorneys, took the stand. More marital woes were examined as Downs explained that Monica had come to see him and they had met several times, once for lunch, to discuss the violence Monica experienced at Paul's hands. Downs suggested she file charges against Paul, but she didn't listen.

Then, on April 3, the day before her death, she paged Downs.

"He hurt me again." Without a female officer present on a Sunday in his office, he photographed bruises on her hips, her pants pulled down to reveal the wounded skin. Monica's brother-in-law, Rick Jacquez, later would testify about Monica exiting Downs' office after a ten-minute photography session, fiddling with the zipper of her pants. Downs testified the drapes on the window to his office were open but couldn't explain the departure from police procedure of having a female officer present when a male photographs injuries to a woman's body. The question of the window curtains being opened or closed would arise again. Downs said he gave Monica domestic violence papers to fill out, not having to tell her how to do it, since municipal court clerks handle these papers daily. He told police how Paul had come over in uniform April 2 and searched the house frantically for signs of another man. During his mad dash, according to Monica, Paul came upon the closed bathroom door in the master bedroom. Monica tried to block the door, but Paul roughly pushed her aside and tore into the bathroom, breaking the mirror on the door.

"He told her if he found someone in the house, he would kill him and hide him, because he knew how to do that," Downs testified.

"Hide him?" prompted Jiles.

"Hide the body," Downs explained.

Downs, like most of Monica's trusted confidants, didn't know that the night of April 2, Monica and Amanda had driven to Paul's apartment and waited there to see if he had a woman with him.

Mitchell showed a bit of his country twang as he asked Downs about the Farmington Police Department's investigative policies. "Do y'all ever investigate these charges and make sure there's merit to it? Or do you just take one person's word for it?"

Downs coolly replied, "We can't investigate when charges aren't filed."

Whitehead's next witness, Municipal Judge William Liese, described Monica, who was clerk of the traffic bureau, as an "exemplary employee." He had just created a new community project that Monica would head. She knew about the program and was excited to handle it. She already began making referrals for the program. He also described the new hours for the court, to be open from 7:00 A.M. to 6:00 P.M. to help the community. Monica was excited about working four ten-hour days. Jiles was setting up for jurors the fact that Monica had made plans for her future—something suicidal people who know they are going to die don't do.

Liese told Titus he didn't know of any domestic violence problems between Monica and Paul.

Also testifying to the same information she gave grand jurors, Vicki Maestas, Monica's best friend and co-worker, testified Monica told her she was afraid of Paul and told her about the breaking of the bathroom mirror. "She was very afraid of what would happen when Paul was served with a restraining order."

She recognized Monica's handwriting on the domestic violence packet. Monica said Paul threatened her. "If she had anything to do with him losing his job, he'd kill her."

Monica didn't write about these threats on the domestic violence documents, which are forms to which she would have to swear the truth. On these, her most serious accusation against Paul was that he'd pushed her.

According to Maestas, Monica said she was going to take the girls to her mother's house on Monday. She never mentioned Paul taking the children anywhere.

On cross-examination, Mitchell asked if Maestas had ever described Paul and Monica's relationship as loving and "neat," to which Maestas answered she had. She also admitted that Monica never told her Paul had hit her, shoved her or pushed her. In fact, the first time she told Maestas about abuse was the day before her death. Furthermore, Maestas said she didn't know about any problems between Monica and Paul's daughter April.

"You never heard Paul Dunn say a bad word about Monica, did you?"

"No."

Testimony returned to the technical as Dr. Vincent DiMaio, Baird County, Texas, chief medical examiner, and director of the crime laboratory in San Antonio, took the stand. A forensic pathologist, he had performed more than 7,000 autopsies and written a book on gunshot wounds. He was asked to review the case and gave an opinion on the range of the muzzle of the gun to the victim. Basing his opinion on the autopsy report and photographs, he said the gun was between one and thee feet from Monica's body, most likely two feet. He noted the edges of the wound were scalloped and wavy instead of round. He said he noted no soot or carbon from the burning gunpowder around the edges. He explained that the shotcup petals had begun to spread, which would account for the shape.

"That indicates this is not a contact wound," he said. "It takes a while for the petals to open. The petals finally open up, but not before they travel a foot."

As if to sum up, he raised his eyes and said very succinctly looking directly at the prosecutor, "It's a very simple case." He didn't say whether he meant simply suicide or homicide.

The end of the day came, allowing the attorneys a break from the courtroom tension. But there was never a break from working on the case and fighting for Paul's freedom.

The defense team believed strongly and wholeheartedly in Paul's innocence, but they knew they had a tough battle on their hands. As Gary Mitchell explains, even on the days when the events in the courtroom seemed to go their way, "There wasn't a lot of back-slapping. It was very hard work. We weren't celebrating."

Mitchell spent the early evening driving around the streets of Gallup, the facts of the case swirling around in his mind. He felt certain Paul was innocent and found the idea of putting him through a trial cruel, not to mention a waste of time and money. Alan Whitehead's inability to see the pointlessness of the whole thing, and torturing Paul in the process, made Mitchell's blood boil. Then his thoughts turned to Paul's family. He felt bad for Paul's daughters. Within a very brief period of time, they lost their mother and, at least temporarily, their father. Paul's parents were stoic but Mitchell could tell they were suffering, too. The entire legal team spent a lot of time with Buzz Dunn, his wife Leslie and Paul's mother, Jane, reassuring them that everything would be okay. They tried to give the family peace of mind.

It's like being at war, Mitchell thought. *Thank God I'm on the side fighting the good fight.* Though Mitchell had always had great respect for his colleagues, now, after working so closely together for months, he got to know them personally. He met their wives, heard about their children's latest accomplishments and bonded with them through their mutual efforts to save Paul. In a way, they really felt like soldiers in battle. He just hoped they could win the war.

CHAPTER 23

A SUSPICIOUS MISTAKE OR TWO

Shakespeare might have said New Mexico Chief Medical Investigator Patricia McFeeley "doth protest too much" about Monica's death. She called the case a homicide, a homicide it would remain, no matter how much evidence to the contrary could be brought to light. Her testimony at the trial matched her grand jury testimony.

In her didactic way, McFeeley firmly stated that the shotgun had to have been one to three feet away from Monica's body to have made an impression of the shotgun petal on her abdomen. Petals don't open until they shoot a foot from the muzzle of the gun and, after three feet, the shells fall away. The shotcup, with white filler and packing, remained inside Monica's body while all nine pellets exited her back through seven exit wounds, the forensic doctor said. She said the shotcup and its contents show up in shotgun wounds at close distances, like one to three feet away, but wouldn't be seen at farther distances.

It was Kathleen Carnell's chance at a Broadway show. She picked up the unloaded shotgun and sat on the edge of the Dunn bed, holding a two-foot-long stick between her body and the shotgun. Leaning as far forward as she could, she showed jurors that she couldn't reach the trigger.

McFeeley picked up the cue saying a person cannot

commit suicide with a shotgun two feet away from his or her body.

But she quickly amended that statement when Mitchell took Carnell's place and pushed the shotgun's trigger with a hanger. "Oh, people can shoot themselves at a greater distance using something else," she said.

Mitchell pointed out a section in Stitz and Fisher's *Medicolegal Investigation of Death*, a widely used forensic book, in which the doctor authors discuss abdominal suicides where a toe is used. Paul stated Monica's high-heeled shoe was off when the shot occurred.

McFeeley still was not to be intimidated. "It doesn't always have to be suicide if one shoe is off and it's an abdominal shot." She added that while one couldn't immediately abandon the idea of suicide, the evidence in this case pointed to murder.

Mitchell asked her what she based her opinion of homicide on, other than her belief the shot was not made by the gun being pressed to Monica's body.

Dr. McFeeley was either stubborn or just believed in her own infallibility. She even had a pat answer as to why crucial words were removed from one paragraph of her autopsy report before it was "supposed" to be released to attorneys.

Either way, McFeeley had no qualms in reporting to attorneys on both sides of the case to destroy the early copy of the autopsy report and keep the later report. On May 23, 1994, she released a formal notice about the report to the district attorney's office, the San Juan Regional Medical Center, the Titus and Murphy law firm, Gary Mitchell's law firm and reporter Kelley Hatch at KOBF.

"This is to inform each of you that the autopsy report dated April 27, is the correct report and should be the copy you refer to in your files. All other copies, which were not distributed by this office, should be destroyed."

Destroy a written document that came from an investigative agency? The thought was unheard of. The request was unheard of. If defense attorneys hadn't caught on yet that the two copies of the report contained crucial differences, they had caught on now. The early copy of the report—dated a few days after Monica's death—had been faxed to the attorneys from the office of the medical investigator. The fax machines show on the tops of the pages that they were faxed from "OMI Albuquerque."

Why would McFeeley go to such lengths to get a document destroyed when her actions would obviously draw more attention to it?

The defense believes it was a last, desperate attempt to hide the damning evidence in both reports.

The first report noted Monica's fitted dress was "gaping open between the buttons, suggesting that the muzzle of the gun was inside the left side of the fabric." The second report simply noted the dress was gaping open. The second report indicated the gun had to be one to three feet from Monica's body when fired. An important difference, or "error," as McFeeley testified. The first report shows that the medical investigator also believed it was a contact shot. The second report—and the strange notice asking everyone to destroy the first report—made the defense believe McFeeley had been pressured by the prosecution to go along with their theory. Or, they asked themselves, was she a hired gun?

McFeeley simply testified it was a "mistake" that wasn't consistent with the wounds on the body, which is why the second report was changed. No one should get a copy of the autopsy report until the final draft is ready.

Mitchell wouldn't allow her to get away with testifying that it was only an examination of the body that led to the report being changed.

"When I read your report and you start to give an opinion, the opinion obviously includes materials received from somebody else. For example, from the police department you heard about marital problems."

"Yes, but that would be . . ." McFeeley trailed off.

"An implication."

"Yeah, that's certainly standard. We try and have as much information as we can at the time of autopsy, but we know that's often incomplete, and we don't complete the autopsy until we've had, you know, the ability to get whatever information we think is pertinent."

McFeeley said she did not have a suicide letter or any letter as part of the evidence she collected. Later, she did read the letter from Monica that provoked so many questions but McFeeley said she would not exactly call it a suicide note. She added she'd seen homicide cases where the victim wrote a letter.

Mitchell wondered out loud what other information McFeeley received in her investigation. She told him she knew Paul had passed polygraph tests. She didn't know Monica had told several people she wanted to commit suicide.

"Did you know that there had been started a transfer of life insurance policies? By Monica Dunn?"

"I don't think I knew that at the time of making the determination for the death certificate."

In a telling moment, McFeeley also said she wasn't aware that Farmington Deputy Medical Investigator Renee Alford had said Monica's body was taken out of the sealed body bag, undressed and then re-dressed before being sent to Albuquerque. Alford also admitted she'd never seen a seal removed on a body bag before it was sent.

"Well, I think there's going to be some evidence about the fact that the clothes and undergarments had been removed and then later on they were placed back," Mitchell drawled.

Mitchell explained that Alford told the defense she sealed the body and later, the bag was opened so Officer

Miller could undress the body and take more photos of the wound. Then the underwear was replaced.

"Frankly, that's a lot of manipulation of—"

McFeeley cut off Mitchell's words. "I'm not aware of that manipulation, no."

Mitchell moved on to the omentum sticking out of the exit wounds. McFeeley said she couldn't identify the tissue as omentum or some other type of body fat. She said she would expect tissue to come out of the exit wounds.

She readily admitted that the shotcup and its contents were found throughout the wound. McFeeley saw nothing unusual about the fact that the grex—the Styrofoam packing—was found through the wound, with most of it sticking to Monica's back on the inside of her clothing.

Mitchell asked how she discounted the nitrate tests, which showed no gunpowder residue on Paul's hands, while it was all over Monica's hands.

"The ballistics expert testified, and Larry Warehime testified, Doctor, that if you were in this room when that shotgun was fired, you'd have nitrate on your hands. You'd have it; it would show up on that test. And Paul Dunn is negative and inconclusive, Monica Dunn's positive. You would seem to think that you had to be in this room to shoot the shotgun."

"The tests aren't one hundred percent accurate," McFeeley said. She admitted her own findings weren't always one hundred percent accurate either when Mitchell questioned her on that, but she wouldn't admit the "possibility" of suicide.

Monica's brother-in-law, Rick Jacquez, added a personal aspect to the scrutiny of the letter held up by the prosecution as evidence Monica had been fearful for her life and the defense as proof of their case.

He reported Paul called him one day to ask about an alleged rape and beating of Monica. Paul hadn't concealed his rage.

"He wanted to know who the son of a bitch was who raped Monica. He wanted him bad. He said he wanted to fuck him up and if I tried to stand in his way, he was going to fuck me up, too."

He testified that it was he who had brought Monica to Dusty Downs' office but further said the blinds were closed, contradicting Downs, when she was photographed.

But Jacquez said the only person Monica ever named as an attacker was Paul. "She told me nobody really understood how violent Paul could get," Jacquez testified, although he later said he hadn't witnessed Paul ever being violent.

But since that statement was word-for-word what Monica wrote to Jacquez in her letter, it wasn't clear whether or not Monica also told Jacquez that or whether he was just quoting the letter.

The day before Monica died, she gave Jacquez the letter. She told Jacquez she planned to file battery charges against Paul on Monday and she wasn't sure how he would handle it.

As spectators quietly wept, a tearful Jacquez read the entire letter to eager jurors.

"Rick, I now realize life isn't fair, most of the time it seems very cruel. I have yet to understand why some people have to be so mean. What ever happened to kindness, honesty and caring? You know, Rick, it's all very inexpensive. Anyone can afford it and yet it is so rare."

She asked Jacquez to take care of the girls. "I do understand they will grieve, it is a process everyone must go through, but they are young, and they will learn to go on and live long, happy—God willing—healthy lives.

"Paul is not to get custody of the girls. He not only can't support them nor does he have the patience with them. Plus I now know he condones drugs. Dad has proof! He doesn't have it in him to care about anyone else but himself. He is honest with no one, so how can he even try to take care of them? He is a compulsive liar, not to mention an alcoholic, which he has admitted."

The letter went on to describe who should receive her belongings. She asked Jacquez to sell the house and put the proceeds in trust funds for the girls.

"Paul is to receive nothing. If he has any sense of dignity, he will abide by this. Don't let him manipulate you. He is a worthless piece for a man."

Jacquez continued on, reading Monica's endless attacks on Paul's character. He read her list of pallbearers. Sergeant Dusty Downs, who claimed earlier in the trial that he didn't know Monica until she came to his office and reported the abuse, was listed as a pallbearer. Then-Magistrate Terry Pearson, who was later shunned by the Sanchez family because his testimony didn't help Monica's case, also was a pallbearer. Titus' name was listed as a pallbearer. This might have been Monica's fatal error—had he not been asked to be a pallbearer, the defense might not have guessed she had written a letter.

He didn't skip over Monica's apology that she had no more strength to go on. He read how she had to take action.

Monica ended the letter by saying she hoped Jacquez wasn't bored by her depressing words.

Jacquez had initially refused to give the letter to state police investigators because Monica requested the letter remain in the family as private property.

Mitchell didn't buy that answer and he wanted to make sure jurors didn't, either.

"If you thought that letter pointed the finger at Paul Dunn, you would have turned it over immediately, wouldn't you?"

Jacquez said that wasn't true. The family didn't want to turn over a private, family letter. But when District Judge Joseph Rich ordered the letter not be destroyed, they decided they should turn it in.

In the trial the letter was private no longer and became part of the court record. It was often quoted from throughout the trial and in the newspapers, which couldn't seem to get enough of the lurid details of the case.

CHAPTER 24

THE RAZOR'S EDGE

Every evening during the trial, Paul took off his suit and exchanged it for an orange jail uniform as he returned to his seven-foot by eight-foot cell, toilet and bed only a foot apart. The brief glimpses and hugs from April only lifted his depression for a few moments as he stepped back into the jail routine. Nor did the brief wins his attorneys made in cross-examination of witnesses take away his humiliation. Were the tides turning in the case, were his attorneys proving his innocence? He prayed they were but neither he nor his legal team knew. It wasn't fair, having to prove your own innocence in the American justice system. Paul's belief in the justice system was losing strength every day. Paul knew that the district attorney's job was to seek justice. He wondered if Jiles, Carnell and their boss, Whitehead, knew that was their job, didn't care or were focused only on winning. Their win, his loss.

Back in the hole. Back to begging for a shower or a breath of fresh air. Paul fingered his razor. The trouble it took him to take apart the plastic razor they gave him, flush the plastic handle down the toilet and palm the razor tip was well worth it. The jailers never remembered when they gave him a razor. Nobody watched him use it. Paul saw the process go on for days, where he had to remind the jailer to take back the razor. Finally, he decided the razor was his own safety valve. One day, he didn't remind the jailer about the razor. That razor would be his best friend if he was convicted. He was not going to prison. No way. A cop in prison would suffer the worst death—or a living hell—from the torture of other inmates.

But for now, he was in solitary confinement, where there's plenty of time for the emptiness to set in. He remembered Monica's gorgeous brown eyes, her smile, how she turned her back on him in bed when she was mad. If only she could still be alive—even at her angriest! Her kind words, her caring, loving behavior. She could be so loving—when she wanted to be—and so terrible when she didn't. No, he wouldn't think of her that way. He focused on her smile, her eyes, her love for her daughters.

As always when he thought of Monica, the events of April 4—that last day of her life—invaded his mind. He would never forget that day.

Come in, reverberated Monica's voice in his head. He saw himself, as if from a distance, opening the bedroom door, the bedroom he used to share with Monica. The gun, pressed to her. Monica's eyes, locked to his. Her body, flying backwards, hitting the bed frame, falling off the bed. The shotgun, flying. Monica's body doubled over. Blood, soaking her purple dress. The bullet wound. So huge. She wasn't speaking. She couldn't speak. Her breathing, raspy and shallow. Someone screaming. It was him.

"Monica! No! No!"

Noise in the house. His sobbing voice. "Amanda! Call 911. Mom's shot herself. Keep the babies out of here!"

He could see her body in his mind, he remembered the gun, the blood. Everything was in slow motion. Him grabbing Monica, her slipping from his grasp. Too much blood. Picking her up again. The blood making her slip out of his grasp again. A third try. Finally, he is able to half-drag, half-carry her out the door, down the hall. The blood, dripping on the carpet. Not being able to keep the terrified little girls from seeing her, or him from seeing them. Diane's and Racquel's faces, horror so present. Amanda, her narrowed eyes staring accusingly.

Still struggling to get Monica out of the house, Paul envisioned the scene as he opened the garage door and carried her toward the van. Nearing the van, he felt her body shudder. He laid her down on the ground, realizing he didn't have the time to get her to a hospital.

Paul watched the scenes, frame by slow frame: Him doing CPR on her lifeless body. Blood spouting from her abdomen with every push of her chest. Forcing his breath into her mouth and again pushing down on her sternum. Someone pulling him away. Looking behind him and seeing the emergency medical technicians. Looking over his other shoulder and seeing the police, fellow Farmington police officers. Solemn faces looking back at him, then quickly looking away.

Paul remembered how he allowed himself to be led away from his wife so she could be placed on a gurney and hoisted into the ambulance. He watched while his friend, Officer Cliff Ollum, came up to him. "The shotgun's inside!" Paul heard his own words as if from a distance. "Please go to the babies," he told Ollum. The officer did as he asked.

Words buzzed as Paul waited. He could almost hear the voices, knew what they were saying. *If he'd hit her, he'd kill her. Monica was afraid of him.*

Sgt. Mark Hawkinson approached, asking Paul to explain what happened. Again, as if from a distance, he heard himself tell Hawk, another friend, how he found Monica with the gun pressed to her. He remembered looking at his friend's face, seeing doubt, disbelief. Then asking Hawk if he believed him and being shocked at the answer.

"I don't know, bud." And then, "You ought to talk to an attorney."

Next he remembered sitting with Ollum outside in the back yard, near the hot tub. Crying, dwelling on the fear, pain and disbelief that Monica had this big hole in her abdomen and he could do nothing to fix her.

And then the worst news: "I'm sorry, but she didn't make it. The family doesn't want you at the hospital."

The shame—how could anyone think he had something to do with her death? How could his friends, his comrades, believe it? Paul remembered looking into Ollum's eyes and saw the pain, but also the recognition that his friend didn't think he was a murderer. But he was the only one. He was the only one.

Paul remembered when he first talked to Steve Murphy. "I'm in some trouble," not knowing how this new attorney, green as he was, could help him while Victor Titus was out of town. Not knowing if anyone could help him. He would never get over that day, that sight of the shotgun, the body flying backwards. The accusing look in her face. The blood, sticky, slimy, forbidding him from picking her up to save her.

Paul sat on his bed in his cell, loneliness, memories and emptiness enveloping him. Would he ever recover from this terror? Certainly, being in a cell was hell. A hell Paul was getting used to. No, he'd never get used to it. But he was learning to live with it. Learning to wake up every day and beg for the ability to live. It was eight months in jail now. A sentence. He was paying for his affair. Paying for the comfort Anita afforded, even now. Paying for the pain he'd put his girls through, watching their mother die. Paying for the choices he'd made in life. Looking down at the razor in his palm, he clenched his jaw knowing he would always pay. He would always pay.

While Paul spent the night haunted by ghosts and sad memories, his attorneys worked feverishly, putting the final touches on their case. Tomorrow was their big day.

CHAPTER 25

THE DEFENSE BEGINS

Seven Gallup police officers surrounded the courtroom Thursday morning when the defense was to begin its case. Mitchell's standard defense move was to ask the judge to grant a directed verdict in the case. This happens infrequently when the judge agrees that the prosecution hasn't presented enough evidence to prove the crime beyond a reasonable doubt. Still, the verdict was a possibility, since Mitchell was able to use most of the prosecution witnesses to prove his own case. Nevertheless, Judge Rich didn't allow the verdict, so police officers began leaving the courtroom. Mitchell was told to proceed with his case.

Police investigators might not have believed Paul's story, but two polygraph experts' machines sure did.

Mitchell called famed Utah polygraph examiner David Raskin as his first witness.

Raskin, well known by psychologists and students of psychology, said not only that Paul didn't kill Monica, but Paul was a victim of trauma himself. Raskin gave jurors a gripping account of the case through Paul's eyes—exactly five days after Monica's death. He pressed the tape recorder play button, so the jurors and spectators could hear the proceedings of Paul's polygraph examination.

On the tape, Raskin introduced himself to Paul and told him, "An interview will precede the actual polygraph test." In response to preliminary questions so Raskin could adjust the machine, Paul said he had been living at 531 Peacock Drive in Farmington since he and Monica split up. He said he had never taken steroids despite the suggestions of Monica's family and the media. He began bodybuilding in his mid-twenties when he learned he had high blood pressure. His doctor also gave him an anti-anxiety pill, Halcion, that is known for lowering high blood pressure. Paul took it once, but didn't like the dry-mouth, "hangover" feeling it caused. According to Paul, he never used the pills again and just relied on exercise to lower his blood pressure. Blood tests police took the day after Monica's death showed he had no steroids or other drugs in his system.

When asked about his children, Paul told Raskin about his daughters, starting with Diane, whose beautiful smile and cheekbones, he said, made her a ghostly image of her mother. "Racquel's the little one and she is a daddy's girl." Paul's words on the tape brought a smile to his face in the courtroom.

A brief silence followed on the tape. The people in the courtroom leaned forward as if straining not to miss a word of Paul's tale of terror.

Paul began with Friday, April 1, when he stopped at Monica's office and told her he'd pick up the girls Monday morning. He also planned to cut the grass, clean out the hot tub and go grocery shopping for Monica, tasks he still did after moving out.

On Saturday, he had stopped by to drop off some Easter treats for the girls. He gave Diane and Racquel a dollar and Amanda five dollars.

Monica said she needed money also, so, without counting it, he handed her the rest of the cash from his wallet.

Later that evening, he stopped by and asked Monica what she was doing that evening. She said she was "going out." He didn't explain why he had stopped by or why he'd asked her what she was doing. He already had plans with Anita, a double date with another couple. Would he have canceled the date to be with Monica?

He and Anita had been dating for about fourteen months, Paul told Raskin. After their date that Saturday night, he spent the night at her small ranch. They spent Easter Sunday together. He slept there that night as well.

And then, in a quivering voice, Paul began to talk of the day of Monica's death. At 5:30 A.M., he left Anita's house and went to his apartment to change and get some cereal and milk for his daughters' breakfast. He arrived at his former home around 6:40 A.M., just as Monica was pulling out of the driveway with the younger girls in the van. Monica saw Paul and drove back into the driveway.

"What did you expect me to do with three dollars?" she demanded as she got out of the car, referring to the money Paul had given her at their last meeting. The girls remained inside the vehicle, Diane wearing her Catholic school uniform.

Paul said he didn't know he'd had only three dollars left when he handed her the cash. Monica told him she was taking the girls to their grandmother's house before she went to work. This puzzled Paul after the plans they'd agreed on.

He got the girls out of the van and they all followed Monica into the house. The girls started eating the cereal Paul poured for them. Monica asked Paul to dispose of some spoiled meat in the refrigerator.

"Monica had a real aversion to bloody things and to spiders," Paul's voice intoned.

Paul followed Monica into the living room and that was when she first accused him of abuse.

"By the way, I'm filing charges on you for battery," she told him.

"What?" The words stunned him. "Monica, what are you talking about?"

"You heard me. I'm filing charges on you for battery. You ought to see me. I'm bruised all over."

Paul interrupted his narrative to address Raskin. "I don't have a *clue* what she was talking about. I was raised never to strike a woman."

Of course, as a police officer, he dealt with domestic violence situations all the time. "But it's more moral to me than legal."

Monica walked down the hallway to the bedroom and shut the door in Paul's face. He heard a clicking sound that he thought was the door's lock.

Amanda came out of her bedroom and called to Monica through the door, asking if she needed her help. Monica told her daughter to go ahead, take her shower and get ready for school.

Soon Paul heard the sound of the shower running in the nearby bathroom as he spoke to Monica through the closed door.

"Monica, talk to me. What's going on? What have I done now? Babe, please talk to me."

Paul's version of the story didn't include the "bad words and stuff" that Diane testified she'd heard coming from her parents' mouths. He also didn't explain—nor was he asked—why he still referred to Monica as "Babe" when he was in love with another woman he had been dating for two years.

"I heard a click. I thought it was the unlocking of the door." Paul said he begged her to talk to him. "I heard her say 'Come here.' "

Paul's voice dropped to a whisper. Each word seemed an effort. "I put my hand on the doorknob and I turned it—to see if it was locked. It wasn't. The door sticks a little bit in the door jamb."

"Yeah." Raskin's voice could be heard on the tape prodding Paul.

". . . and I pushed on it and got it to open about two feet. I could see her on the bed. And the gun went off. I saw the gun fly down onto the bed and I saw her fly, not fly, but get thrown back against the headboard, then down on the bed."

A ghoulish silence followed as the tape droned on. A high-pitched, wailing sob broke through the stillness.

"And I ran to her and started screaming, 'Monica, no! Please, not this!' I put my arms under her and picked her up and looked at her. She was gasping for air."

Paul picked up the bedside telephone, but there was no dial tone.

"AMAAANDA!!!" The taped voice screamed the name, remembering.

"What've you done?" accused Amanda who had run from the shower at the sound of the gun firing. Clutching a towel around her body, water from her dripping hair mixing with the blood on the floor.

"Amanda, I haven't done anything. Mom shot herself. Don't let the babies back here!"

Meanwhile, Monica still lay gasping as Paul tried to pick her up.

Raskin asked if Monica always kept guns around the house. Paul stopped the narrative of Monica's death and explained he had packed all of his hunting guns when he moved out.

"I don't have anything to protect me and the babies. Leave me the shotgun," Monica had said.

"Monica, swear to God you won't do anything with it," Paul remembered saying.

Raskin interrupted. "Did you think she meant . . ."

"In the past, she'd said, 'I'll kill myself if you ever leave me.' "

This time she said, "Are you crazy? I have to take care of my babies."

Paul left her the four-inch Remington shotgun with double ought buckshot ammunition.

Raskin asked if Paul had shown Monica how to use the gun. "Many times," Paul responded, although he would later say she never used ammunition as deadly as double ought buckshot when she practiced shooting. But she knew how to work the gun.

"I'm assuming at this point in time," Paul's voice cracked and wavered, "that the click I heard . . . was her loading the gun." Explaining that the gun probably was loaded and ready, but that the slide has to be worked before shooting.

Raskin asked how far away Paul was when Monica shot herself. Paul replied that he was about ten feet away from her.

As a tearful Paul listened to the tape in the courtroom, his recorded narrative returned to seconds after the shooting.

"She was gasping so hard, I couldn't hold her. There was so much blood. She had on the most beautiful purple and black dress with brass buttons. Her hair was so pretty. Her makeup was on. She was so gorgeous."

He tried to pick her up. She slipped out of his grasp because of all the blood, but finally he managed to half-drag, half-carry her down the hall to the garage. He said he knew, because of his training, that you should never move a victim, but he thought he could get her to the hospital faster than if he waited for an ambulance.

"I know what double ought buckshot does to anyone," he said, later explaining it can slice someone in half.

In the garage, he realized he had no time left. "I felt her shudder. In my job, I'd held people and watched them die and I knew what that shudder meant. I put her on the ground and she wasn't breathing."

He leaned her head back and she gasped again. He grabbed the phone from Amanda and screamed at the dispatcher to get an ambulance. Paul began CPR. It did no good.

"I could hear the blood running out of her body. Squish, squish," he sobbed. "I knew if I stopped, her only chance had gone."

According to him, Paul never heard the sirens. He didn't see the uniformed personnel arrive until the paramedics pulled him off her and continued CPR. He finally saw his friend, Officer Cliff Ollum, and asked him to check on Diane and Racquel. He also informed Ollum the gun was in the bedroom.

Paul called Dora Sanchez, Monica's mother, and told her what had happened. He joined Ollum in the house. "I took my two babies and put them in my arms. It was two hours and forty minutes before they let me wash my hands. To this day, I can still see her blood on my hands."

Voices of other police officers drifted in and out of his hearing. After the ambulance left, he saw Sergeant Mark Hawkinson and told him the story of what had transpired.

Hawkinson spoke into his radio for a few minutes and returned to Paul.

"He told me she didn't make it," Paul said.

When Farmington officers took Paul's clothes, made him take a blood test and a breath test, Paul realized something was going on.

"Do they think I killed her?" he asked Hawkinson.

"I don't know, bud," Hawkinson replied. He suggested Paul get an attorney.

Paul told Raskin he had called Victor Titus' office, but his wracking sobs almost made the tape inaudible at that moment. "He loved us both. He loved us both," Paul repeated in a hoarse whisper.

After a break, Paul regained his composure and said he called Amanda later that day.

"You know, Mom and I saw you Saturday night. We watched you pick up Anita and go out. Mom was way upset. She was way upset at you," Amanda said to Paul.

"Was that the first time Monica had seen you with Anita?" Raskin asked.

"Yes," Paul replied and began sobbing again.

"If I had known, Doc . . . if I had only known. I didn't kill her. I didn't put the gun in her hand and I didn't pull the trigger. But I feel like she did what she did on account of seeing me with another woman, even though we had been separated and our divorce was filed and was in the works. I feel like she did what she did on account of me."

Then Paul said he wasn't sure if this mattered or not, but his friend, Officer Ollum, told him something Amanda had said that morning. "Mom said she was going to do this a whole bunch of times, but I never believed her."

Then Paul pointed blame back at himself. "I never should have left that shotgun there."

After another brief silence, Raskin began with questions that were tough and precise and Paul didn't dodge them.

"Did you touch the shotgun on April fourth?"

"No, I did not."

"Did Monica shoot herself while you were standing more than six feet away from her?"

"Yes, she did."

"Were you touching the gun when it fired the shot that killed Monica?"

"No."

"Did Monica commit suicide?"

"Yes, she did." Paul added, "I also didn't commit domestic battery on her."

Raskin asked about a four-inch bruise on the back of Monica's right thigh, possibly made by falling down.

"I never—you can ask me that one, too—I never hit her, smacked her, punched her, pushed her to the ground, hit her."

"What if I ask if you ever physically injured Monica?"

"There'd be times Monica and I got into pushing each other back and forth, playing. We were in love; we rough-housed. I have never, never hit her."

"Have you ever physically injured Monica?" persisted Raskin.

"I feel I harmed her by what I did."

"But I'm talking physically."

"*No.*" Paul's answer was definite, not defiant.

Raskin stopped the questions and explained he was placing wires on Paul's hands, preparing for the test.

"I just know in my heart and soul that this whole thing is going to turn out badly, because they're not letting me see my kids," Paul said.

"Now, I don't want you to think about that during the test," Raskin said. He would explain later that any strong emotion could cause a "false failure," meaning the person would fail the test for reasons other than untruthfulness.

"I know, that's going to make me all wacko," Paul said.

Then Raskin began the technical talk he gives people before administering an official test. Most of it, Paul already knew. But for polygraph examiners, the necessity of explaining the procedure is almost like a cop reading someone their Miranda rights.

"A lot of things go on inside your body that are controlled by the nervous system. Some of those things are under voluntary control—walking, talking—you do if you want to. Some things are controlled by a part of the nervous system you have no control over—the heart rate, blood pressure, perspiration. Generally, you're not aware of them. But when something happens that causes you concern, like a psychological or physical threat, your body reacts. You walk down the street and you hear something. Your heart speeds up, your blood pressure goes up, your hands start sweating a little bit—all of that is your body's way of getting ready to deal with that threat."

Raskin explained that this "fight-or-flight" reaction is used to determine deception in polygraphs. "If you know you're lying, you're going to be worried I'm going to find out and your body is going to give you away whether you want it to or not."

Raskin tested Paul's reaction by asking him to choose a number between one and ten and lie when Raskin reached his number. After doing this, Raskin asked about Paul's level of comfort when he lied. Paul said something inside of him was "screaming" that he had given an untruthful answer.

"Yeah," said Raskin, "there was a huge reaction on the polygraph there, in fact.

"The recordings are extremely clear. They're as clear as they ever get. That's good, because that means we shouldn't have any problem with the test as long as you're truthful. If not, there will be a big reaction on the machine."

To further check Paul's truthfulness or deception, Raskin asked Paul to say "no" to the following questions, to which no person over the age of twelve could truthfully answer "yes."

"Have you ever made even one mistake? Before 1994, did you ever violate one rule or regulation? Before 1994, did you ever do anything you later regretted?"

His pre-analysis complete, Raskin then began the real test, repeating each of the questions he had earlier asked Paul.

When the polygraph test was over, Paul didn't have to wait long before Raskin scored it and said to his emotional subject, who began to weep, "You passed with flying colors."

Polygraph skeptics abound, of course. Expert opinions and tests like this don't come cheap. Some argue that asking a hired expert's opinion about whether his or her client is lying is like asking a whore if the sex was good. However, David Raskin bears a distinguished reputation.

Now, as the tape recorder stopped, the jurors were brought back to the day the polygraph was administered. Mitchell asked Raskin to describe Paul's demeanor during the test.

"He was very emotional, very distressed. He had all the characteristics we see in victims," Raskin said.

It should be noted that Paul also passed a polygraph test—with a positive-nine—administered by Albuquerque polygraph examiner Jim Wilson, who was hired by the prosecution. The prosecutors hired Wilson, but never called him as a witness, presumably because he could help the defense more than the prosecution. Mitchell, in his ever-present attitude of reasonableness, made sure the jurors learned of this and caught the inference.

On her cross-examination of Raskin, Carnell brought up specific examples of people who had beaten polygraph machines. Raskin said this was possible, though rare.

Then Raskin gave the kind of odds any gambler would love. He said, "There's a one in four hundred chance that both polygraph tests done on Paul Dunn are wrong."

Mitchell didn't gloat. He just scanned the jury box and nodded sadly, as if to say, *See the unnecessary pain they've put my client through?*

CHAPTER 26

SPARRING MATCHES

The defense theory picked up momentum when Mitchell called Nelson Welch, a firearms examiner. Welch's recounting of his investigation explained why those holes in the Sheetrock of the wall behind Monica were slightly elongated when Larry Warehime received the section of wall back from the defense.

Welch used the sticks Mitchell asked Warehime about, the ones to help determine the trajectory of the bullets. But Welch also removed the stud in the wall of Monica's bedroom, which also had pellet holes but had been ignored by the state police. Welch connected the holes in the stud and wall with sticks to show the path the pellets made when they left Monica's body until they entered the wall. The seven sticks pointed slightly downward, just above the right edge of the bed. A mannequin was placed in a standing position in front of those sticks. The sticks pointed lower than the mannequin's back and would not correspond to where the pellets would end up if they shot out from the mannequin's lower back. Mitchell was trying to show that the prosecution's theory, that Monica stood near the wall when Paul shot her, couldn't have happened.

Welch moved beyond the mannequin, which was supposed to resemble Monica Dunn, and asked Victor Titus' wife, Debby, to step forward. A solid body-builder, Debby is the same height Monica was, five feet, seven inches tall, although thinner.

The next moments heightened the tension in the courtroom. In a dramatic reenactment, Debby lay on the bed in different positions, but none of these matched with the angles the sticks formed. Finally, she sat at the right edge of the bed. The sticks now pointed directly at her lower back. That, however, wasn't the only test required of the attorney's wife. Debby pressed the unloaded shotgun to her abdomen and leaned over it, easily hitting the trigger. Almost magically, the shotgun, held in this manner, lined up with the spot where the sticks pointed at the back of Debby's body. It was almost as if the shotgun and the sticks were one instrument, impaling her.

Then she moved the shotgun about a foot away and pressed the trigger with her toe, her high-heeled shoe lying on the floor. She pushed the shotgun about two feet away and used a hanger to push the trigger. At no time did she struggle to fire the weapon; it fired with ease.

Debby Titus was used as a stand-in for Monica to show that a woman can shoot herself in the abdomen with a shotgun, not only at close range, but up to two feet away. Debby's demonstration also showed the trajectory was right only if Monica had been seated on the bed with the shotgun in an upward angle, leaning on the bed's edge. When Debby sat on the bed with the gun pressed to her body and the sticks pointing upward from her lower back, it looked like the gun penetrated her abdomen and then split into the sticks behind her back.

While a stunning demonstration of what the defense team felt easily could have happened, Welch was not finished impressing the jury. He described tests he performed by pressing the shotgun against a cloth attached to a piece of wood. Tests performed with the muzzle pressing against the wood and cloth revealed a hole similar in appearance to that on Monica's purple and black dress. The hole in the cloth also contained gunpowder, which would be expected in a hole made when the gun is in contact with the person's skin, the expert explained. In three out of six test shots with the gun pressed to the cloth and board, Welch found a hole similar in shape to that of Monica's wound.

Welch said he found some evidence the prosecution failed to see. For instance, soot on the dress, which scientists would expect to find in a contact wound. "You can't get rid of it. It's embedded in the fibers. You can put water on it, blood on it, but you can't take it away."

Also damaging to the prosecution's case—and another example of shoddy investigative work or just plain carelessness—Welch found an imprint of the muzzle of the gun on Monica's wound. He showed where the barrel of the gun was on the wound, making a mark Monica's body would carry to the grave. Such an imprint doesn't fade on a dead body as it does on a living body. One can wear a tight belt or a tight skirt and find indentation markings on their abdomen at the end of the day. A few hours later, or by morning, those marks are gone. This doesn't happen on a lifeless body, because blood and oxygen are no longer circulating through the body and restoring the skin's texture. Without the skin's elasticity, any bruise or contact mark would leave a permanent marking. On a dead body, such markings may tell a tale. In Monica's case, the story told seemed to be that the gun muzzle was pressed against her body. Who pulled the trigger was another story, one the jurors would have to determine.

The angle of the trajectory, however, showed that if Paul had shot Monica, he would have had to have been lying on the floor with the gun angled upward. This is an awkward method of shooting someone, since the shooter, in a small bedroom with her, could have easily shot her while she stood or as he held her while she struggled to free herself from his grasp. To lie on the floor and angle the shotgun just right—assuming the victim would remain sitting on the bed while you were getting into this position—made no sense. Furthermore, a murderer would put himself in a vulnerable position lying on the floor where the victim could kick him or grab a weapon or object in self-defense. A drugged or otherwise incapacitated victim wouldn't be able to sit up by herself, which the killer would need her to do in order to set the shotgun up just right to coincide with the established trajectory of the bullet. If a drugged victim had slumped over to the side of the bed, the sticks showing the bullet trajectory would not have matched up.

As if giving the defense his stamp of approval, one of the jurors who was familiar with guns gave some suggestions on how the sticks should be attached to make a more accurate depiction of the path of the bullet from Monica's body. Defense attorneys gladly accepted the juror's suggestion, mentally high-fiving each other because they had a juror who understood what they were saying and one who, most likely, believed their theory.

On December 10, it was the prosecution's opportunity to turn around a defense witness for their own purposes. Jiles cross-examined Welch that morning in an exchange that turned into a battle of wills between the two men.

Welch agreed that experts can't tell who fired a weapon, they can only tell the distance from the wound. "We can't tell who pulled the trigger with a finger, toe, coat hanger, tree branch, barbed wire fence—we just can't tell," Welch said with a shrug.

Jiles was not intimidated by Welch's string of improbable methods of firing a weapon. "And among those possibilities is Paul Dunn's finger, is it not?" Jiles persisted.

Welch paused a moment. "That's correct," he said with his unfailing air of nonchalance.

It was Welch's turn to be stubborn when Jiles reminded him that no other experts saw soot around Monica's wound. Welch replied the soot ring was thin. He reiterated that the wound had a muzzle imprint around it. This means the gun was pressed very closely against the body.

"I have now seen a lot of people—including my wife—hold the shotgun to their abdomens and lean over to press the trigger. This posture causes a lot more than usual pressure," Welch said.

In his usual dry manner, Jiles asked, "Presumably this was during a test?"

"Yes," Welch said. He described again for Jiles how Monica's wound could have had a petal mark even though it was a contact wound. Through his testing, Welch showed that a hard contact shot can expand the shell's petals at the muzzle. Welch told Jiles the state's experts either misrepresented the truth or misinterpreted the facts before them.

Later, Dr. Martin Fackler of Florida, an expert in wound ballistics, backed up Nelson Welch's words. Fackler testified that the mark from the shell on Monica's wound indeed indicated the shotgun had been pressed to her body when fired. In a distance gunshot, air pressure causes the shell to open, he said.

"But something harder than air—like skin—also can open the flap," he said. The flap then breaks off. He pointed to Monica's autopsy report, which showed one flap broken off.

Fackler wasn't finished using the state's experts to prove his own points. He said prosecution experts' distance shots resulted in all flaps opening. According to the expert, had Monica's wound been caused by a distance shot, she would have had more than one flap mark on her body.

Next, the roles of physician and weapons expert converged in Fackler as he explained what happened inside

Monica's body at impact and how this proved without a doubt it was a contact shot. A fatty tissue called omentum, which extends across the front of the colon, was pushed through her body and out the exit holes. This might seem easy for the average person to understand, how tissue can be pushed through the body and out the holes caused by a gunshot. But Fackler explained that to make it out those exit holes, the omentum had to first travel through four inches of abdominal muscle. It is the same concept as when the force of a tornado causes hay to penetrate wood. Shotgun blasts explode into three gallons of gas at 1,500 degrees Fahrenheit. All that gas, plus the shotcup, enter the body when the shotgun muzzle is pressed against the skin.

"The abdominal cavity of a woman who's had children can hold four quarts—one gallon—of gas," Fackler explained.

The two other gallons of gas—more than the body can hold—blows everything out of its way and can force tissue through muscle.

Carnell, who was conducting the questioning, was not swayed by Fackler's words and reminded him that in the forensic literature, a distance shot can push ribs or arteries out of a wound. Fackler told her the circumstances were different in those studies.

Dr. Fackler also pointed out an injury on Monica's hand, one he would expect to find in a suicide with a shotgun. The hand pulling the trigger, in this case Monica's left hand, often bears a wound because the bolt slides back into the hand after the shot is released. The shooter is usually unconscious at this point and unable to withdraw the hand before the injury is inflicted.

"Research shows that a woman who commits suicide with a gun," Fackler told the jurors, "often shoots herself in the abdomen, so her face is not disfigured." A man, according to the expert, usually shoots himself in the head. An individual planning murder wouldn't shoot the victim in the abdomen, because there is a chance the person would survive. Police officers are trained to shoot for "center mass," the middle of the chest, because it's more likely to hit and kill the target. Few police officers would aim for a small target like the head, because the chances of missing are great.

Carnell still wouldn't give up. She asked why forensic experts didn't find soot in the wound if it was a contact shot.

"The dark red color of the blood," Fackler explained as if he were talking to a fifth grader, "masks the soot to the eye."

Tests, which state pathologists didn't take the fifteen seconds to do, would have determined soot was present. Not only wasn't that tested, but Monica's clothes and the wall behind her weren't tested for gunpowder, Fackler said, shaking his head in a mixture of irritation and disbelief. He placed the blame on the forensic pathologists.

"They saw that one flap and said, 'Oh, this indicates one to three feet' and they didn't bother to check for contact. They didn't look for searing of the wound under a microscope or use acetic acid to detect soot. They didn't look for these things, because they were already convinced it wasn't a contact wound." Fackler leaned back in the witness chair. "You're not going to find it if you're not looking for it."

Carnell asked Fackler why there was no blowback on the barrel of the shotgun. Blowback consists of blood and tissue that flies away from the body when contact with the bullet is made. Fackler responded that blood droplets on the shotgun were signs of blowback.

"If you have blowback, as you said you have here, you'd have blowback in the barrel. We don't have that," Carnell stated.

Fackler said to his knowledge, the prosecution didn't bother to examine the barrel of the shotgun for blowback, so he couldn't respond to the implied question.

When Carnell cross-examined him on the witness stand, it was obvious to discerning spectators that Fackler felt she knew nothing about guns. It showed on his face that she was asking the wrong questions. To Fackler, it was obvious she was in over her head.

At a break, Mitchell and Titus handed Fackler some notes they were passing around during Carnell's questioning. In law schools, attorneys learn to be careful when questioning experts if the attorneys don't know the subject matter well. They can get tripped up very easily. Attorneys call this being "caged."

The first note Fackler read said, "She's in the cage now." By the time Fackler stepped down from the witness stand, the final note Fackler was handed read, "There's nothing left but bones."

Fackler thought this was so funny he kept the notes.

Finally, the end of a long, grueling day of complicated testimony for jurors had come. Now Paul, his attorneys and the prosecutors discussed all weekend how well the doctor's theories had come across to the jurors. For Paul, it was forty-eight agonizing hours in which he lived and relived the murder scene.

Meanwhile, the attorneys prepared for their closing arguments which would occur after the last defense witness testified. While not considered part of the evidence, a poor closing argument could mean losing a case, while a good one could mean victory. Attorneys feel their cases ride on how the juries see them as people and how well they've researched their cases. Any sign of arrogance or excessive self-assurance can have a negative impact on jurors, who are human, after all. While arrogance can be viewed as a negative to jurors, attorneys must give the impression that they whole-heartedly believe in the innocence of their clients, if they expect the jurors to do so. Just as any human being brings their own biases to each of life's experiences and endeavors, jurors do the same. That's why twelve people come together to temper each other's excesses and make sure common sense measures are followed instead of emotions. Attorneys choose jurors with some of these ideas in mind. They're not always correct in their assumptions about jurors, which can lead to disastrous results, but at least they have the opportunity to make an attempt.

"Paul was a damn basket case that weekend," Titus said.

Who wouldn't be a basket case before having to testify in a trial in which he or she is charged with murder?

Titus had planned to put Paul on the stand and question him himself, but Paul's emotional state was making Titus uneasy. Mitchell thought it was a good idea, so the jurors could see the emotions between Paul and Titus. They were more than just friends; they were friends bound by the ordeal they were undergoing together. Paul kept saying he badly wanted to tell his story of what happened. He didn't want people to speculate that he had hidden behind his legal right not to testify.

Paul had the opportunity to proclaim his innocence in front of a jury of his peers but Titus was worried Paul might snap on the stand. And if he did, what would be the result in the minds of those deciding Paul's fate?

CHAPTER 27

ANOTHER THEORY OR TWO

Dave Pfeffer had come to believe, despite all the sweat and blood he'd put into the case, that Monica didn't commit suicide. He had his own theory.

"She was too vain. She just loved herself too much."

When he first met Monica, he had felt she wasn't the innocent, sweet wife everyone said she was. Pfeffer said she gave off an aura. This he noted when he met her at a party in 1992. He also remembered her "big boobs." Her breast implants were recent, but Pfeffer didn't know anything about them.

"She was sexy and she pushed it out. She strutted. She had real beautiful eyes. They spoke without her saying anything."

Smiling Eyes' vanity pointed out, Pfeffer also believed she loved her children and family too much to make them hurt in this way.

Listening to Pfeffer's theory, Paul wrestled with the idea that Monica wanted to hurt herself to get attention, that she didn't think she would die. He stopped believing this when he realized nobody could press a gun that big, loaded with double ought buckshot against their body and not expect to die. In fact, most people who shoot themselves with any gun expect to die. They don't shoot themselves so they can be vegetables for the rest of their lives.

Anita thought Monica wanted to injure herself, too, but didn't know how powerful double ought buckshot is.

What was the truth?

Pfeffer believes the shooting was accidental. Not the two of them fighting over the gun, or her cleaning the gun, or him trying to take it away from her, as many Farmington residents who knew little of the case had surmised. Pfeffer says that on April 4, 1994, Monica Dunn wanted to teach her husband a lesson he'd never forget. She wanted to control him the way a woman had never controlled a man before.

So she planned it. She would have the gun ready. She would sit on the bed. She had to have the safety off, or else Paul would know something was up.

"If she hadn't pulled the trigger, the next words he would have heard are, 'Paul, if you ever leave me, I'm going to kill myself, and this is how I'm going to do it. I'm going to kill myself and it'll be your fault.' "

A dramatic reunion would have followed, no matter how forced on Paul's part. Paul would be under Monica's thumb forever because of his guilt at her drastic action and what could have happened when he saw her holding a shotgun. Why Monica wanted to hang on puzzled Pfeffer. But he was sure she didn't mean to pull the trigger and never meant to die.

She didn't necessarily have to choose that day. She might not have chosen that day. She may have been hoping to get away from the house before he arrived because she was angry at seeing him with Anita on Saturday night. Carnell argued that she wouldn't wear a dress, pantyhose and put on makeup if she intended to shoot herself dead moments later. But it didn't matter that she had on a pretty dress or makeup if she had no intention of dying anyway. It also wasn't about a stupid woman who doesn't know how to use a gun. It was about a smart, controlling person who knew exactly what she was doing.

After all, weren't the little girls she loved so much in the nearby kitchen eating breakfast? Monica wouldn't chance them seeing the scary sight of their mom and a gun. Wasn't Amanda in the shower? Monica would have had Paul in the palm of her hand before Amanda even finished blow-drying her hair.

The more Pfeffer looked at the pieces of the puzzle, the more certain he became of his theory. It wasn't an exciting thought after months of the murder or suicide question and people taking one side or the other. But it was the only theory that made sense. Pfeffer didn't care if anyone believed him. He trusted his instincts.

Nevertheless, Pfeffer felt that without Gary Mitchell presenting the case to jurors and the talents of Nelson Welch, Martin Fackler, David Raskin and others, an innocent man might be found guilty. But he also felt Dr. McFeeley's mistakes were paramount. At the time of Monica's death, Pfeffer had been a deputy medical investigator. After he began investigating the Dunn case, he quit the OMI. Deputy medical investigators aren't doctors but are trained in pronouncing death and taking certain necessary fluids from a dead body before putting on the toe tag and shipping the body off in its body bag or sending it to a funeral home.

Although he let the experts and attorneys handle the case, for Pfeffer, one particular piece of evidence became extremely important, although the attorneys didn't see it that way.

It was a photo of Monica's hand with some kind of injury. Pfeffer didn't know why, but it bothered him. At the trial, the attorneys were trying to reduce the huge pile of photos. Welch kept saying Monica burned her hand on something before she died and it was insignificant to the case. The attorneys kept taking the photo of the hand out of the case files, and Pfeffer kept sticking it back in.

The attorneys found no significance to the hand injury,

even though a funeral home staff member had called Titus to report it.

It wasn't until Pfeffer showed Fackler the photo, and asked what he thought, that light was shed on the issue. Fackler examined the photo and said it could be a burn, but it was hard to tell. Pfeffer asked him if it was possible that the injury was caused by the extractor on the shotgun when she fired the trigger. She wouldn't have had time to move her hand before the slide hit it. Fackler studied the photo again and then looked at his own hand and how he would have fired the shotgun in the manner the defense surmised Monica did.

"Sure!" he cried. "It definitely could have happened that way!"

The stomping of feet probably rocked all of Gallup as the large Pfeffer marched up to the counselor's table. He slammed the photo down at astonished attorneys.

"I knew it!" Pfeffer explained what he and Fackler had just discussed.

"I was so angry. It was *that* important to me. But Gary totally missed it."

Welch had told Mitchell to ignore the burn because someone testified Monica was cooking tortillas earlier in the week and might have burned herself.

Pfeffer hoped he showed the attorneys they should trust his instincts. Mitchell made a big issue of the hand after Fackler verified Pfeffer's suspicion. The hand proved to be a big factor in the case.

CHAPTER 28

TO SPEAK OR NOT TO SPEAK

Monday morning, tension wafted around the hallway outside the courtroom as everyone debated and wondered if Paul Dunn would testify. Each lawyer has his or her own thoughts on putting defendants on the stand. Mitchell obviously believed in Paul's credibility and ability to reach into the souls of jurors, but he felt Paul's emotional state was tenuous. On the other hand, Mitchell was aware that jurors always wanted to hear from the accused, but by law, they are not supposed to hold it against the accused if he or she chooses not to testify. The right not to testify belongs to the defendant. Paul had made his feelings plain. He wanted to speak. Still there were several more witnesses before a decision had to be made.

Paul's stepmother, Leslie Dunn, testified after Fackler. She said she talked to the couple on the phone a lot. When Paul told her in February he was thinking of divorce, she was shocked. Then Monica kept calling.

"She said she loved him. She wanted him. She couldn't understand," Leslie said.

Carnell took an opportunity to use a defense witness for her own case when she asked Farmington Officer Rocky Falls why he didn't know the Dunns were considering getting a divorce. Falls explained Paul never seemed upset, that police officers learn not to show emotion after working for so long in a career that daily touches on tragedy.

"So, even though he was going through a traumatic event, he appeared normal?" Carnell asked.

"Yes."

Juliet Spackagna, who had been Paul's wife for four and a half years and was the mother to their daughter, April, testified she had known Paul since they were in the seventh grade. "I knew him when he was a Santa Fe policeman and then when he moved to Farmington." She knew Monica and said April would have a good visit followed by a "disastrous" visit with her stepmother. She wrote Paul a letter about not having April go there to visit. Monica was belligerent toward April at times.

"She would make comments within April's hearing that she wished April would go home," Juliet revealed.

Answering a telling question, Juliet testified Paul was never violent. "If we did have an argument, he would walk out of the room."

April Dunn followed her mother in testimony, pausing to beam at her father before taking her oath. She told jurors, "Monica was never nice to me.

"She would say things to hurt my feelings. She would give me ugly looks. She'd embarrass me in front of other people."

April, although she never told her father, overheard her father and Monica argue about her and felt like she wasn't wanted at their house. After her father separated from Monica, she visited Paul at his apartment. Then Monica was nice to her, telling her she was welcome at the house and to come over any time or to call. Monica called Paul every night the week before her death.

· · ·

Adding a twist to the morning tension was the testimony of Jinx Finch of Farmington, a friend of the Dunns. She recalled Monica's chilling words in a moment of despair and a glimpse of vengeance. "If Paul ever were to leave me, I'd do everything I could to destroy him and then I'd kill myself."

Tensions heightened in the courtroom as it became obvious that the only defense witness left was Paul himself—if Mitchell chose to call him. A trick in defense, which attorneys don't like to admit, is that when an attorney believes the defendant is guilty, they don't have them testify. Of course, there are other reasons not to have the defendant testify, such as it the person has been convicted of a crime. No matter how innocent of the current charge the defendant is, when jurors hear the person is a felon, the theory is, they will believe the person would commit the current crime, too. But Paul had no prior arrests; his clean slate was almost virginal.

Suddenly, the question all of the spectators had been asking was answered. A shaken Paul took the stand in his own defense, fully aware of how prosecutors would badger him. A police officer, Paul knew this was the prosecution's last chance to get a defendant to break down or accidentally make an admission. Nevertheless, as he had said from the beginning, Paul wanted to testify.

As he had on the polygraph examiner's tape, an emotional Paul described the morning's events when he went to pick up his daughters and his wife threatened to file battery charges. He tearfully recalled seeing her alive for the last time—that last microsecond before she pulled the shotgun trigger and flew backward.

Paul's cries of "No, Babe. Please no!" went unheard, as

the blast caused Monica to immediately lose consciousness. As Paul spoke in a hoarse emotional tone, tears fell down his cheeks. He was not the only one crying. Victor Titus also openly wept. Later he said, "For the first time since my own father's funeral, I cried. I cried watching the pain of my old friend describing holding his wife as she died."

Paul continued telling the story through his tears. Monica was dying, but not dead. She had no time for last words. Paul recalled Amanda's accusation and his screams for her to call 911. Paul prepared to move the slippery, blood-soaked Monica. As a police officer, he should have known to leave Monica as she was until emergency medical technicians arrived. He didn't.

"I know I've had all this training, but I just panicked," he said. His testimony with Mitchell asking questions seemed to fly by, leaving him as prey in front of a tiger while Carnell took her place behind the podium and prepared to delve into cross-examination.

Carnell was quite brutal in her interrogation of Paul, who looked at the ceiling above the jurors while he spoke, rarely meeting Carnell's eyes. In a dry tone, Carnell congratulated Paul on being such a good actor. She asked him if it didn't follow that since he'd deceived Monica for a year about his relationship with Anita Harris that it would be easy for him to be deceiving jurors all along. Paul insisted, "I'm not acting."

Carnell used his police training to try to nail Paul as a cool killer who must maintain control at all costs. She said that police officers are trained not to show emotions at traumatic crime scenes and to detach themselves personally from cases. Paul agreed. Carnell pressed on. Being in control and using force—wrestling with suspects, striking fighting suspects with a baton or the ultimate, shooting someone—are parts of police training. Paul again agreed.

Carnell wasn't finished. She asked Paul why in the world he would give a suicidal woman a shotgun and teach her

how to use it. Paul said he didn't know Monica was suicidal. "If any of those people Monica talked to had just
whispered to me, I would've taken it back," he said, his
voice breaking from the strain.

The prosecutor's aggression increased as she slowly
stepped closer to the witness box where Paul sat. With each
step, she asked a different, more burning question. "On
April four, when you entered that house, you took your
jealousy with you, didn't you?"

"No," Paul replied.

"And when you entered that house, you took your
threats of harm with you, didn't you?"

"No."

"You took your loss of control with you, didn't you?"

"No, I just took cereal and milk for the girls," Paul responded. The comment would have been humorous had the
circumstances not been so serious.

Carnell certainly didn't laugh. "And when you pushed
her, she fell, didn't she? Did you push her a second time?"

Paul reminded Carnell that he wasn't in the room before
Monica shot herself. Carnell turned away from the witness
stand for a moment to show the jurors her disgust. She
quickly turned back.

"Then you shot her, didn't you?"

"No."

"Then after you shot her, Diane came to the door and
you said, 'Call 911,' didn't you?"

"I never shot her," Paul said firmly, his head down.

"You decided to hide what you'd done and claim it was
a suicide, didn't you?" Carnell persisted, seemingly oblivious to each denial.

"I think we're all victims in this," Paul said. "I'd never
seen anything so horrible in my life. If I see it again, I'll
start crying. This will be with me for the rest of my life."

Carnell continued, unabashed, as if she hadn't heard
Paul or somehow wasn't listening. She plunged on as if she

were driving at something besides an answer. "You are capable of bluffing, aren't you?"

Paul raised his head, his eyes alone reflecting the depth of his pain.

"We are all capable of bluffing, Miss Carnell," was Paul's quiet response.

Mitchell rested his case as an emotionally battered Paul slowly left the witness box. It was 2:15 P.M., December 13. Judge Rich took a break. As everyone in the courtroom shuffled about nervously, Paul's family members expressed confidence in Mitchell's work to reporters outside the courtroom. But still, the lingering doubt was obvious in their nervous glances at watches on quivering wrists.

CHAPTER 29

HOMICIDE OR SUICIDE?

It was now time for closing arguments, the attorneys' last opportunity to get their points across. Jiles' stern face somberly gazed at jurors as he prepared to make his last, probably most important argument. He made the case sound like one end-of-season cliffhanger on a nighttime soap opera. The courtroom was quiet. In the jury box, heads were moving, alert.

"Who fired the shotgun that killed Monica Dunn?"

Paul Dunn's face was pale. He sat rigidly as the prosecutor spoke.

Jiles described the murder as a deliberate intent to take away Monica Dunn's life. "So what happened in that room?" he asked rhetorically. Jiles first attacked Paul's story on the witness stand, saying that it didn't match all the facts. He reminded jurors of Rick Jacquez's words spoken to him by Monica herself—that nobody knew how violent Paul could get. He talked about Paul's need for control and that it was all right for him to have a girlfriend, but when he thought Monica had a man in the house, he stormed through the house searching for him and broke the bathroom mirror. "He could file for divorce, but she could not file against him for domestic violence."

He threatened to kill or "kick the shit" out of any man

she was with. "He stalked her," Jiles hissed at the jurors, not mentioning Monica's own stalking as testified by her daughter, Amanda. "Then there's the bizarre rape incident." Paul knew Monica had gone to Las Vegas and he'd pumped her friends to find out who she went with. While his jealousy raged on, Monica found the letter to Anita Harris in his truck. "She was crushed. She was hurt. She was not angry . . . but she had to know the truth."

Jiles talked about Monica's bruises and her pat answer that she had fallen. According to Jiles, despite her job where she saw domestic violence petitions and knew the consequences of unreported violence, Monica still didn't want anyone to know it was happening to her. "Domestic violence is a very, very private affair. Monica Dunn was a very private person," Jiles said. His voice rose ominously. "And she was afraid of Paul Dunn. He had not only psychological control but he certainly had the means to have physical control over Monica Dunn . . . This domestic violence ended with the death of Monica Dunn."

What couldn't happen, Jiles explained to the jurors, was for Monica to appear before jurors and explain her death. "When the floodgates finally opened on her willingness to tell people what was going on in her life . . . she described the violence the defendant had perpetrated on her that very afternoon."

Jiles said that Paul had to explain the bruises, so he told Vicki Maestas that Monica had told him she was raped. "He was aware there was evidence of what he had done to her." He had to take action before she showed that evidence to anyone. Everyone asks themselves why women involved in domestic violence don't leave, Jiles said—but Monica was trying to do that, trying to get on with her life even as she grieved for the loss of Paul. He wouldn't let her move on.

"Had she considered suicide?" Jiles asked. He reminded jurors how stressed out Monica was. Separation and divorce are some of life's biggest stressors and adding violence to the picture must have seemed horrible to Monica. "The most important fact is, upon writing the letter, what did she do? Did she write the letter and go kill herself? No. She writes it and puts it aside." She had moments of despair but never acted on them. Paul used those moments for his own devices, to make murder look like suicide. After putting aside the letter, she goes to Las Vegas with friends. Jiles pointed out this is not generally something someone who is planning suicide does. The letter was more a will because she fears something might happen to her—she never says in the letter she plans to kill herself. " 'Now I've thought about it and I'm going to kill myself tomorrow morning right when I'm supposed to go to work.' No, that's not what happened." She gave that letter to Jacquez with the fear that "something" might happen to her. Jiles also pointed out that when she talked to Michael Martinez about killing herself, she said she was going to take a bottle of pills. She wouldn't shoot herself.

Jiles cleared his throat and assumed an air of Lincolnesque studiousness. "Monica Dunn hated the sight of blood, remember? She asked the defendant to take spoiled meat out of the refrigerator. If she were going to kill herself, why would she care about the inside of her refrigerator? It doesn't make sense."

According to Jiles, ego was behind Paul Dunn's motive for murder. "Paul told Monica he would kill her if she ever did anything to make him lose his job. She was going to file domestic violence papers." Jiles paused. Tension hung in the air. Then, with a glance first at the jury and then at the defendant, he said, "This enraged Paul," so he plowed down the hall after her, trying to follow her into her bedroom. "He follows her into the bedroom and grabs the shotgun," Jiles explained, setting up the scene for jurors. "She falls, grabs for the gun . . . he takes the gun away from her and he shoots her . . . from about two feet away."

Sighing distastefully, Jiles showed his disdain for poly-graph tests, reminding jurors that if they were as reliable as everyone seems to think, there would be no jury system. Why have juries if polygraph tests are proof-positive of innocence? Jiles mentioned the other so-called evidence the defense presented, expert witnesses testifying about trajec-tory tests that Jiles claimed aren't possible because the bul-let went through Monica before winding up on the wall. He asked jurors if they didn't find it curious that this case should create a new "phenomena" never seen before—that petals of a shotcup can open when the shotgun is making contact with the body. "Monica Dunn is not going to be written up in medical journals. Monica Dunn will be just as dead. He'll be just as guilty."

Jiles kept coming back to the letter Monica wrote before her death. He told jurors she gave it to Jacquez because of her fear of Paul Dunn and her confusion—she didn't know what he was going to do to her. "She had immediate future plans," he said.

Jiles made his own plea to jurors in case they found Paul a likeable person. "Sometimes nice guys do terrible things, things they regret. This happens in life." Giving Paul a hard-eyed stare, he asked jurors to remember Monica's words about him: "He's a worthless piece for a man."

Gary Mitchell's hazel eyes regarded each juror separately as he made his dramatic, cowboy-like strut to the podium. All of the attorney arrogance was in his gait, yet he spoke to jurors as if they were neighbors from up the street, re-laxed, forthright and sincere. Monica Dunn killed herself, he simply said. Adrenaline rushed through Mitchell's veins and into his voice as he continued.

"Frankly, if you missed that, I'll have to live with that; Paul will have to live with that." He told jurors a person didn't have to be a rocket scientist to figure out that she killed herself when it says so in her own words in the suicide letter. It's "ridiculous" to try to bring evidence to the contrary. He pointed out how unfair the justice system is to the average, poor defendant who doesn't have the almost limitless resources of the prosecution. After all, the prosecution has the office of the medical investigators with its forensic pathologists, serologists and the state police crime lab with its experts. The state pays for experts to be brought in. The average defendant doesn't have the money to provide all of this evidence for the jury.

During the rest of the trial, Mitchell and the other attorneys had made it a point never to speak disrespectfully of Monica. All the trial attorneys did their best to keep Monica's dignity intact. The defense did, however, try to get evidence of her abortion presented to jurors, but Judge Rich wouldn't allow it because he found the facts irrelevant to the charges against Paul. All the trial attorneys did their best to keep Monica's dignity intact.

It was only during closing arguments that Mitchell almost regrettably brought up the "real vengeance" in the case, which he said Monica showed. Whether she meant it at the time or not, Monica told a couple of people, including Paul, that if he left her, she'd destroy him and kill herself. And it was Monica who went to Anita's office and confronted her about "ruining" Monica's marriage, despite the fact that Monica had already aborted a baby conceived by another man. The letter, given to Jacquez the day before her death and her visits to Downs, especially the one on Sunday where she showed the bruises, made it seem Monica might have been setting up Paul to take the fall for her death. Some people bruise easily. A husband for eight years, Paul knew Monica did so even when she barely touched something.

After a dramatic pause Mitchell said fiercely, "That man sitting right next to me during most of the trial is an innocent man." His voice dropped. "None of us wants to speak ill of someone who died. We don't want to speak the truth. The truth of it is, doggone it, Monica Dunn committed suicide."

Although Mitchell said Paul had suffered more victimization than most, the lawyer also reminded jurors the four children were victims. "I'm not here to say Paul didn't sin." But he cautioned jurors not to ignore the law because of the lost morality. "Sure he made a mistake. He'll live in hell for the rest of his life."

As he watched Mitchell giving his summation, Victor Titus, once known for his cool composure, wept again.

Mitchell's eyes narrowed, focusing on the ever-alert jurors, who followed his every move as he began slowly pacing in the courtroom, as if gathering his thoughts. When he spoke, the words were completely focused, flowing from thought into speech. He reminded jurors of Monica's stalking Paul after she learned of his affair. He reminded them that no one can corroborate what most of the witnesses said Monica told them. He reminded jurors of the evidence. "I think we've shown a lot more than reasonable doubt. I think we've shown this was a suicide."

Now Mitchell began attacking the prosecution's case. "When has the state ever placed that shotgun in Paul's hands?" Mitchell spoke about the gunpowder, none found on Paul's hands while it was found all over Monica's. He brought up a problem he had with the suicide letter. "It says something like, 'The bruises will show,' or words to that effect. On March eleven . . . there were no bruises." She was setting him up, setting the stage for her last, dramatic exit. "No one wants to speak the truth about the vengeance in this case. Finally, the prosecutors had no evidence to show it was not a suicide; the district attorneys were just trying to show how far the gun was from Monica's body when she was shot: 'If you don't believe this is a contact wound, then you must convict Paul Dunn.' That's what they're really saying."

Mitchell didn't ignore the implications that Paul was an angry, explosive man after Paul and Monica's separation. However, he recalled the testimony of his first wife, Juliet. "She experienced no violence from him even during and after their divorce."

Finally, Mitchell reached the crescendo of his remarks. He inhaled deeply and looked in the jurors' eyes, one by one. "Paul Dunn is innocent—dead innocent—and he has been all the way through."

For a heartbeat, there was utter silence, then Mitchell dramatically strode to his seat next to Paul. Jiles had one last shot at the jury, during the rebuttal, which is given to prosecutors, because they have the burden of proof in trials. In these final moments, Jiles reiterated most of what he told jurors in his closing argument, reminding them of the evidence on the dress and on the wound, of the fact that the shotgun was two feet from Monica Dunn's body when fired. He touched on the quality of Paul's responses to Carnell's on-the-stand interrogation of the defendant.

"Don't ever lose sight of the fact that the real victim is a dead victim," were his parting words. The dramatics of summation were over.

The judge began to give his final charge in a quiet monotone while the jury struggled to keep their attention on him. His last instruction concerned that jurors must be convinced of Paul Dunn's guilt beyond a reasonable doubt to find him guilty. It was 4:51 P.M. as jurors slowly left the courtroom to deliberate. The minutes inched by as Paul, his family, Monica's family, friends on both sides, police officers and other spectators waited for the verdict. No one could really be sure what the jury would do until the twelve people returned with their finding.

The defense prepared and Paul agonized for what could be a long wait. But less than an hour later, at 5:49 P.M., a court clerk announced the verdict was in. Silently, everyone filed serious-faced into the McKinley County courtroom as if their lives depended on it. Indeed, many lives did. After the jury entered, and in response to the judge's command, Paul rose, fear evident in his eyes.

The bailiff took a slip of paper from the jury foreperson and handed it to the judge. When Judge Rich unfolded the paper and read the verdict of "not guilty," Paul exploded into a cheer and a prayer. Dora Sanchez cried loudly in the front row of the courtroom as family members bent around her in gestures of comfort. "Thank you, thank you!" Paul called to the jurors, tears streaming, voice choking. "God bless all of you. Merry Christmas." Some jurors wiped their eyes while others smiled openly at Paul, who was about to be swept out of the courtroom by deputies. Deputies were to take on the role of protectors now, with the job of making sure Paul made it to a location in Albuquerque without any of the death threats being carried out. Then they were supposed to stand outside the courtroom doors to prevent everyone else from leaving until Paul had a good head start out of town.

Before Paul was whisked away, Mitchell turned to his client and asked what he wanted to do with his freedom first. Paul smiled. "I just want to hold my kids."

Jurors later reported to the defense that they immediately voted "not guilty" in the jury room. They knocked on the door, but reportedly the judge had left the building expecting a long wait. Another juror said they voted right away but waited forty-five minutes so Judge Rich wouldn't get angry with them thinking they didn't ponder all the evidence thoroughly. A third juror reported that they all agreed they could have made the same vote seconds earlier in the jury box. They socialized for the rest of the forty-five minutes until they returned with their special Christmas-present victory to Paul. In an after-trial survey, one juror, a Gallup dentist, went one step further writing to defense attorneys his belief that the hotly debated injury to Mon-

ica's hand only made sense if she had just pulled the trigger
and killed herself with the shotgun. The juror surmised that
the case was only prosecuted because of politics and that
Paul should sue the town.

PART FOUR

TRIUMPH AND REPROACH

We are born, we suffer,
we love, we die,
but the waves continue
to beat upon the rocks.
The seed time and the harvest
come and go,
but the earth remains.

—Victoria Holt
Mistress of Mellyn

CHAPTER 30

LAWSUITS AD INFINITUM

Victor Titus wasted no time filing notices of potential lawsuits asking the bearers to contact him to financially compensate Paul Dunn for their wrongdoing instead of going to court. He sued San Juan County. Titus wrote because during the trial it had come to light that a law enforcement official had engaged in misconduct by advising Monica Dunn's family to destroy her suicide letter and promised he'd do everything in his power to put Paul away.

Titus sent notices to the City of Farmington, the office of the medical investigator, the New Mexico State Police, the New Mexico Department of Public Safety Crime Laboratory and privately to Dr. Patricia McFeeley and Larry Warehime.

The City of Farmington quietly settled for $30,000 and gave Paul his job back under the condition that he would resign immediately. Paul did so with no hassles. He had no desire to work for a system that was supposed to consider those accused innocent until proven guilty and hadn't.

One by one, the district court dismissed the lawsuits. Not that the attorneys didn't expect it. It's pretty customary. The law protects district attorneys, law enforcement officers and other agents of the state from prosecution if they are acting within the duties of their jobs. Unless they flagrantly step out of line, and even sometimes when they do, recompense is difficult. Of course, anyone who examined Paul's case could see serious problems with the way the state agents handled the case, but allowing a civil lawsuit against a police officer or medical examiner is so rare, most district judges just dismiss them, passing them along to appeals judges to evaluate. Usually, the Court of Appeals agrees with the lower court. At any rate, such an examination can take years. Sometimes the defendant dies before the process is over—or just quits caring. Or, his funds exhausted, he stops paying his defense attorney.

In his brief to the New Mexico Supreme Court justices, Titus didn't break the news about the state employees gently.

"The negligent (and/or conspiracy to alter the evidence) investigation by OMI, McFeeley, Warehime and the State Crime Lab is the lynchpin of wrongful arrest, false imprisonment, slander, defamation of character and constitutional deprivations of Plaintiff.

"Put another way, but for the investigation and opinions of McFeeley, OMI, Warehime and the State Crime Lab, Galvan and the State Police would not have had evidence to arrest Plaintiff. The findings of McFeeley, OMI, Warehime and the State Crime Lab combined hand-in-hand with the negligence of Defendant Galvan and the State Police to secure the arrest warrant. Without this evidence, no warrant could have been secured and no tort claims violation would have occurred."

Immunity to being sued on the job is granted to law enforcement in general. The Appeal listed exceptions to this as being when officers cause injury or property damage during false arrest, malicious prosecution, abuse of judicial process, libel, slander or violations of constitutional rights. This is why Whitehead, Jiles and Carnell couldn't be sued. They had the evidence and information gathered by McFeeley, Warehime and Galvan—they had the probable cause to make the arrest. Under the color of the law, you can't go after the district attorney when the police or medical investigator make gross errors.

However, in Paul's case, he got some good news in 1999. Ironically, it came in April, the same month Monica died. The New Mexico Court of Appeals overturned some of the lower court's decisions and was allowing civil trials to be held. In a lengthy document full of legalese, the judges made it clear Paul was not only a victim, but the justice system had been tangled around him like a vine during prosecution. The appeals court determined Paul could sue Dr. McFeeley and Warehime individually.

The high court dismissed the civil rights claims against the experts but reversed the lower court's determination that Paul couldn't sue McFeeley and Warehime as individuals.

"As we read Plaintiff's amended complaint, it encompasses allegations that the Individual Defendants (McFeeley and Warehime) acted recklessly and with willful disregard of Plaintiff's rights in providing inaccurate information that contributed to the arrest, prosecution and incarceration of Plaintiff," wrote Justice Harris L. Hartz.

A 1985 New Mexico case found that "state officials could be held liable . . . for conspiring to procure groundless state indictments and charges based upon fabricated evidence of false, distorted, perjurious testimony presented to official bodies in order to maliciously bring about a citizen's trial or conviction."

This prior ruling helped the justices make their decision in 1999.

In an accompanying opinion, Judge Michael D. Bustamente wrote that he agreed with Hartz's conclusions but also thought they should have allowed the civil rights issues, which were thrown out because according to case law, if you aren't considered law enforcement officials, you're exempt from civil rights issues. For all practical purposes, the judges decided McFeeley and Warehime weren't law enforcement officials because they didn't have the power to make arrests or maintain public order. Bustamente disagreed.

"Our case law reflects an outdated model of the law enforcement officer as the 'cop on the beat'.... Focusing too narrowly on the activities of commissioned officers on the street creates the risk of missing a large portion of the law enforcement function today. The business of solving and proving crime is increasingly a technical pursuit. Mrs. Dunn's death is a case in point.

"The decision to arrest and prosecute had little to do with the activities one normally imagines with pursuit and arrest on the street. Rather, it turned largely on the result of a scientific evaluation of technical aspects of the body and the death scene. If a technical investigation is handled recklessly—or is wantonly perverted—an improper prosecution can ensue as surely as if an officer on the street chooses to arrest and prosecute without reasonable suspicion or probable cause. There is no reason why the concept of 'law enforcement officer' under the Tort Claims Act should not reach the technical, investigatory side of the law enforcement house."

The Court of Appeals decided that, based on the evidence Mitchell's team produced, they proved more than just negligence—they proved conspiracy.

"How Warehime's conclusion of one to three feet caused Dr. McFeeley to change her autopsy report has yet to be fully explained, but certainly smells of conspiracy to 'make things fit.' When combined with Warehime's failure to do trajectory analysis, McFeeley's failure to identify soot in the wound, consider the omentum and the grex that extended through the exit wounds and Galvan's failure to question these inconsistencies and not require the family to produce the suicide letter, the smell at least suggests something is wrong here."

The Court left McFeeley and Warehime open for career-busting lawsuits that would be hard for them to win.

CHAPTER 31

BITTERSWEET AFTERMATH

All of those who believe in Paul and those who didn't were forever touched by Monica's death and its aftermath.

Unless you've been there, you can't understand the pain of having a child locked up in jail. Many parents believe—whether true or not—that their flesh and blood can do no wrong and is unjustly accused. But others just know. That's how Harvey "Buzz" Dunn described his feelings after the trial of his son, Paul Dunn. Buzz had given his life savings to prove his son innocent, even though he didn't like the fact that Paul was still seeing Anita. Nevertheless, he never stopped loving his son and believing in his innocence.

"You know he's not guilty," he said in explanation of his devotion. "That's not his nature. He was taught you never hit a woman. It's been a real tragic chain of events that's affected everybody."

He recalled his son lost his wife, his career and his livelihood. "We have heard all about the victim. The question is, who is the true victim here? I think it's Paul Dunn."

There was a time, Buzz said, when he and Monica were like father and daughter. That changed to a point where Harvey could almost predict trouble in her and Paul's marriage. "I began to see her controlling nature—something you just couldn't put your finger on, yet you felt it was there." Living in Florida, Buzz didn't have enough day-to-day contact to be sure. Still, he never thought she would kill herself and set Paul up to take the fall.

Paul's stepmother, Leslie Dunn, said she felt a mixture of relief and anger. She was relieved at the jury's findings and angered that it took eight months for Paul to be found innocent.

"Paul's life was ruined," she lamented.

The day of Paul's acquittal, his mother, Jane, thought for a moment about what Paul would want to say if he hadn't been sped away by the deputies.

"I think he would want to ask the Sanchez family to try to start to heal. He would want to thank the friends who stuck by him. He wants his children back. He wants to get on with his life."

Shortly thereafter, his mother ran a full-page advertisement in the newspaper declaring Paul had been a political prisoner. He was a pawn in a cruel game where his friends abandoned him, his department condemned him, his state's crime laboratory and medical investigator did a sloppy job and changed documents to fit a theory and the district attorney and governor used his case to run for reelection.

Defense attorneys felt triumph after Paul's verdict, although they adopted somber attitudes concentrating on the pain and suffering Paul experienced. "This innocent man has been in pure agony and hell for seven months," Gary Mitchell said as reporters sought to interview him. "People jumped to conclusions." He called freedom for Paul Dunn a blessing.

"It's one thing to have your wife die in your arms. It's another thing to be accused of something you never did."

Mitchell's attention turned to the aftermath of the trial, as family members prepared for the trek back to Farmington and the semblance of some normalcy in their lives. "I hope for all these people's sakes everyone remembers those children. They all need to work to the betterment of those children. We don't need any more feuding and fighting. There are good people on both sides."

The next order of business for Paul would be to get his job back and get custody of his young daughters. Mitchell said thoughts of vengeance needed to be abandoned along with threats against Paul's life. "We just need time to heal," he said.

Attorney Steve Murphy, who stayed behind the scenes during most of the trial except when he testified about the disturbing words of District Attorney Alan Whitehead that he would pursue the case despite his policy of dismissing charges against people who passed polygraph tests, now voiced a few insightful thoughts. "Justice has been done. I'm sorry it wasn't done eight months ago."

Titus praised the work of Gary Mitchell and the loyalty of Paul's father, Harvey Dunn. Without the support of Paul's father, who had spent his life savings defending his son, the awesome power of the state would have overcome Paul. "So an innocent man got blasted by the system and we have a prosecutor who could have dismissed the case."

Titus said that without Buzz Dunn's retirement fund and Paul's other financial resources, Paul would probably be in prison. Or, most likely, dead, since Paul had his trusty razor. His lawyer, Mitchell, added that the case was a classic example of the difference between a defendant with money and one without.

After the trial, Victor Titus' outlook on life changed mightily. "Mitchell taught me it was okay to care. In fact, it was not only okay but essential. Partial justice is no justice at all. And to achieve full justice takes all your heart, all your soul, all your guts. In Paul Dunn's trial, for the first time since my father's funeral, I cried. I cried watching the pain of my old friend describing holding his wife as she died. And as I watched Mitchell deliver his summation, he too cried. And so did I.

"Those who knew me or my reputation probably didn't

believe or understand the metamorphosis. Probably thought it an act. But it was oh, so much more. An awakening.

"For the accused, 'presumed innocent until proven guilty' sounds like hollow words, the platitudes of a government which crushes the little people in the system and makes those on the outside feel safe enough to leave the system alone as it slowly imposes the strength, the power and the money the government has at its disposal when its representatives and prosecutors choose to spotlight a single individual."

Titus' feelings echoed Mitchell's on the advantages of those who can afford to seek help from a qualified counselor. "Too often, that individual does not have the resources, can't afford the lawyers or the experts to fight back. Paul Dunn was one of the lucky ones. He had a father who loved him enough to give up his retirement—cash in a life savings account and his 401(k) to hire me, Mitchell, expert reconstructionist Nelson Welch and ballistics expert Dr. Martin Fackler. Would the same result have come from a public defender receiving $375 to try his case?"

At the start of the trial, Gary Mitchell had told Titus there was a skunk in the courtroom and it was their job to make sure the jury smelled it. But first, Titus said he had to smell the skunk. He had forgotten that it takes more than your nose to "smell the roses." Life is not made that way. Rather, it takes your heart and soul. You don't just smell it with your nose but all the way to the bottom of your feet.

Titus went on, "So it was that Agent Wilkes' 'dilemma' allowed me to solve my own dilemma. Paul Dunn is an innocent man. The jury said so in less than one hour. But I ask myself, is he truly free? Will he ever be truly free?"

The trial, which began on December 1, 1994, ended on December 12. Yet for Paul Dunn and Victor Titus, it continued with trial after trial, appeal after appeal. Of particular importance to both Titus and Paul, was regaining custody of the girls. "Christmas passed without Paul ever seeing his children. When Valentine's Day, 1995, came and Monica's parents still withheld his children from him, we called a press conference." The nationally syndicated television show, *A Current Affair*, did a piece in early 1995, yet Paul continued without his kids until a second trial was held on May 2 of that year. Titus stood by Paul's side, fighting for his client's rights, throughout the ordeal.

In Titus' wallet, he carries three quotes by which he has dedicated his professional life:

> *Justice, sir, is the greatest calling on earth.*
> —Daniel Webster

> *The rights of every man are diminished when the rights of one man are threatened.*
> —John F. Kennedy

> *Keep your eyes on the dream: Justice and equality for all.*
> —Dr. Martin Luther King, Jr.

"With much soul searching after this case I have decided only one thing: I can never quit being a trial lawyer. It is my calling."

With the trial ended, Paul got rid of the razor he had carried throughout his ordeal, his last resort. He hadn't had to use it. "I wasn't going to prison if they convicted me. Cops don't survive." Asked later about Paul's suicide plan if convicted, Anita's eyes teared over as she said that only she knew about it.

Despite their immediate joy and relief, everyone concerned about Paul would soon learn that getting out of jail and being clear of guilt didn't mean smooth sailing. Not by a long shot.

. . .

No one's life was the same after the trial. Not even Paul's victory could take away the pain of Monica's violent death and the subsequent humiliation of jail time and proving his innocence.

"When she killed herself that morning, she killed me too. The only difference is she died and I have to stay alive." Paul's eyes clouded at times while he relayed the pain.

Not only did he have to fight City Hall about their error in firing him, but he had to win back his daughters. The Sanchezes refused to let him see them and Social Services became involved. Richard Gerding, a Farmington attorney, was assigned to protect the interests of the children as Paul and Titus went to battle in Farmington Court with the Sanchezes and Marie Geer, an Albuquerque attorney who fought for the Sanchezes to get custody.

It was as if the judgment of a jury of Paul's peers wasn't enough for Social Services. He had to prove his innocence again. He had to prove that he was a fit father. Paul didn't get to have Racquel and Diane for Christmas, two weeks after the verdict, and he also didn't get to spend that Valentine's Day with them. Two months after his acquittal, he still didn't have custody of his two young daughters! Titus had never heard of this type of courtroom sanction of injustice. By then, the courts allowed Paul to see the girls every other weekend and on Wednesdays. But the Sanchezes maintained temporary custody. And the girls weren't even living in the same house. The Sanchez family never had to answer for this inexcusable decision. Why did they separate two traumatized children so close in age who depended on each other? The civil judges didn't seem to care. Social Services' staff didn't care enough to force the family to keep the girls together. Did Gerding, who was supposed to represent their best interests, even care?

Gerding, who is a friend of Paul's, explained in the hearings that since the girls were so attached to the Sanchez family, he had to make sure custody was given to the appropriate adults. Paul eventually got custody, but with the stipulation that the Sanchezes would get to see them every other weekend and on Wednesdays. Paul always maintained that he would let the girls see their grandparents whenever they wanted. He never would have refused, hearing or no hearing.

The early weeks after the custody hearing passed fairly smoothly, with the girls trading homes on the weekends. Problems arose only when Diane was sent back one day wearing a T-shirt with Monica's photo and a slogan speaking out against domestic violence. It was the first time since the trial and custody battle that Paul realized the vengeful feelings the Sanchezes had were still alive. During the trial, he knew they had somehow gotten to Diane, especially when she called Aunt Theresa and Uncle Rick "Mommy and Daddy" and called her own father "Paul."

Between the acquittal and the Court of Appeals reversal, under the severe strain of all they had endured, Paul and Anita broke up and got back together several times. Then Paul made a wise decision. He moved to Albuquerque and shared a house with his sister, Robin. Everyone told Paul he needed to get out of Farmington. He seemed to blossom in Albuquerque. But he still longed for Farmington, which he always saw as home.

For Titus, Paul's incident and the way Farmington residents handled it changed the way he lived. He used to stay out late at bars with friends drinking and talking. After Paul's trial, he felt like a walking target in Farmington. If he wanted to socialize and have fun, he would have to go out of town. He just made that a policy.

Pfeffer decided the golfing was better in Farmington than Ruidoso, so he moved up north and put his office in Titus' building. A few years later, he moved Shamus Investigations to a larger building with more space. Sometimes, his beautiful golden retriever, Sherlock Holmes, runs around his office. Pfeffer hopes his son will one day join him and eventually take over his business.

Paul's daughter April began living on her own in Albuquerque while her overprotective father tried to let her live her own life.

After years of silence between Paul and Amanda, his stepdaughter, he finally had breakfast with her in 1998. She called him because she was in town and wanted to visit the girls. Married and pregnant, Amanda confessed she never believed Paul shot her mother. But, like Paul, she blamed him for her mother's depressed state that led to the shooting. Amanda and Paul remained friends until the Court of Appeals overturned the District Court's decision about the civil lawsuit. She begged Paul not to sue anyone and bring more pain to the family. She went a step further and said if he went through with the lawsuits, she'd never speak to him again. She hasn't.

Torry Sanchez slammed his front door on the opportunity to talk about his daughter and give his family's point of view on the subject. Paul said he and Dora Sanchez have an uncomfortable but cordial relationship. By court order, they must see each other every week when the children visit.

The cases continued to drag on, past the Millennium. Paul waited in the sidelines. But he knew it would never be over for him and he was exhausted financially and emotionally waiting for vindication. Paul decided it was time to put the past behind him. He chose to end the legal wrangling.

In early 2000, Paul returned to Farmington with daughters Racquel, ten, and Diane, eleven. Anita still lived on her ranch with her son, Josh, now twenty-one and handsome as ever, if still a bit on the shy side. Paul still believed Anita walked in his soul.

Anita, while being open and knowledgeable about emotional issues, was conversely more reticent to talk about matters of the heart. She had a "deep and abiding affection" for Paul. "I feel a whole lot of responsibility for the welfare of those girls," she added.

The girls love Anita and see her as part of the family. They say they couldn't see their family without Anita being there.

And for Anita's part, relationships are hard enough, but when you've left an abusive one, beginning any new one is even tougher. Pile on top of that Paul's unbelievable incident and it's amazing Anita's optimism and will survived.

"It cost me my uterus. I had a hysterectomy in January 1995 because of massive tumors, probably stress-induced. One was the size of a Nerf football; two were the size of goose eggs. They were all benign, fibroids."

Emotionally, she didn't want to let Paul out of her life. Paul came to a point where he told her he needed more than just friendship and if she couldn't give that to him, he needed to get out of the relationship. That woke Anita up and she told him she definitely wanted him.

"It's so complex, I spend so much time pondering the situation."

Anita feels that Paul has the type of insecurity now that requires so much affirmation it's hard for a woman to handle. Nevertheless in her usual upbeat way, Anita takes life one day at a time, knows that she loves Paul and believes that should be enough for now.

"It was the most devastating emotional experience I've ever had. It still is. It's still going on. What happens is your coping skills get better."

After Paul stopped having to cut his hair regularly for police uniform, he just let it grow. He keeps his honey-brown, thick locks captured in a ponytail that extends about halfway down his back. Even on his most moody days when his memories overcome him, he walks tall, his mustache nicely trimmed and his cowboy hat neatly perched on his head. The pain which never goes away hides deep inside.

Since Monica's death, Paul has never shirked from owning up to his responsibility in Monica's unhappiness because of the affair Monica learned about from the letter she found in Paul's truck. He paid for his sin.

"I still love her. I miss her and I weep for her. My heart aches all the time."

Paul still talks about how much he needed the strength Anita provided when Monica died. Anita kept Paul alive. "She carried me. I couldn't walk. I know God sent her to me. It's like 'Footprints in the Sand.' "

Paul walks on his own now, but he hopes Anita will always be by his side as his girls grow up. He still wonders how he can ever repay someone who has become a part of his entire life, a muscle he didn't know he had until he needed to flex it. She fits so closely into his life. She is his life. Six years after his trial, Paul, Anita and the girls have decided to live together. And so Paul's spiritual bond with Anita continues. The years have seasoned it, perhaps changed it, but never dissolved it.

AUTHORS' NOTES

When I first set out as a police reporter to cover the trial of Paul Dunn, I had no clue what I was getting into. In fact, it was just a normal day for me, dropping in at District Court to check the schedule. Clerk Tina Yepez looked at me with wide eyes and asked, "Aren't you going to cover the big trial? Gary Mitchell's here!"

Stunned, because Gary is the most well-known defense lawyer in New Mexico and other states as well, I asked what the case concerned.

"You know, it's that cop who killed his wife in Farmington. The one where they have some kind of suicide theory. Yeah, right!"

We laughed about it and I offered my own piece of wisdom to the clerks—"If a man will hit his wife, he'll kill her." (I still believe that. In Paul's case, I know now he never punched Monica and he certainly didn't kill her.)

I regret to admit my own human weakness of believing someone guilty until proven innocent.

In this case, it took me only the first day of court to change my mind. Murdered people don't usually leave suicide letters behind. Gary Mitchell began reading Monica's words, "I can't go on . . ." and "I know I must do what I have to." I kept looking at the prosecution team, wondering if this letter was a trick of the defense and wasn't real. But the district attorneys didn't argue about the letter's validity.

I took careful notes on Monica's supposed words while I wondered, *Why are we here?*

Hopefully, readers have had the opportunity to judge for themselves what happened in Paul's case. In the following appendices, I will allow readers to continue to draw their own conclusions by including notes from Paul, Monica's suicide/will letter and a host of letters citizens of Farmington wrote in praise of fifteen-year veteran officer Paul Charles Dunn.

I've come to know and love Paul like a brother. He's such a special person. Imagine going through what he's gone through and then being able to lift *my* spirits when I'm down.

Another example of this kind of selflessness is my Uncle Richard A. Coyle, known to most as Dick Coyle, who was a United States Army prisoner-of-war with famed author Kurt Vonnegut after being captured during the Battle of the Bulge in World War II. Both spent time at Slaughterhouse Five in Dresden, Germany. Mr. Vonnegut's 1991 autobiographical book, *Fates Worse Than Death*, contains a photograph of my Uncle Dick driving a horse and buggy containing the prisoners, with Mr. Vonnegut in the back. In 1993, Mr. Vonnegut sent my uncle the photograph with the inscription: "Dick: You've never been anything but honorable, courageous and kind."

Although losing all of his teeth was, I'm sure, the least of my uncle's memories of war, he never seemed to let the horror of it all affect his positive outlook on life. He always had the sweetest disposition when I knew him as a child. Like Paul, he was another person whose jokes and precious attitude could uplift the most depressed mood.

Politics can make us all prisoners-of-war when sanity is overlooked. What's amazing is that while warriors like my uncle spit teeth to keep our great country intact and help other nations in danger of destruction, politics internally rot our country through the justice system. How do veterans of political wars survive the justice system? Without the great lawyers and back-up Paul had, he would almost surely be in prison right now. Actually, he'd probably be dead, as he told me he was able to keep a razor given to him in Gallup's jail in 1994. No one bothered to collect the razor after he had shaved one morning. Paul had no intention of being a policeman at risk in prison.

Perhaps through this book, some people in their community will change their attitudes toward Paul and Anita and be more welcoming. Anita has an aura about her that makes people feel good whenever they're near her. It's hard to describe on the page. I wish the Sanchez family spent some time talking with Anita and Paul, really getting to know them. If only Farmington residents who condemned Paul without knowing his side of the events would learn from this horrible true story that they should never, ever make assumptions. A lot of people have missed out on two friends I would never trade for a million dollars.

I believe Dave Pfeffer's version of Monica's death. I think she was just trying to scare Paul with the gun and didn't intend to fire it. It's the only thing that makes sense. My own instincts about Monica have changed over the course of the years I've worked on stories for the Gallup *Independent* and on the book. At first, I had such a sense of evil about the woman. How could she set up her husband like that? Writing the letter a month before, giving it to Rick Jacquez the day before her death. It *had* to be planned, I thought. She knew everyone would blame Paul for her death and she wanted him charged with murder. I couldn't get away from the revulsion of the evil involved in someone doing that. I now see her as a depressed, desperate woman who loved Paul in more of a childlike, dependent way than in an adult manner. She couldn't see her life without him and the discovery of the affair made her certain he'd leave permanently. But if she could play upon his sense of guilt . . . That's what I think was behind the chilling suicide "performance," which is all she meant it to be.

Dave Pfeffer never got the credit he deserved for basically single-handedly solving the case, determining the wound was made by a contact shot and, along with his son, Billy, being the first to show the trajectory of the shot. That meant that they knew the gun had to have been pressed to Monica's abdomen and that the angle of the gun had to be upward, making it almost impossible for Paul to be the shooter.

I trust my instincts that evil touched Monica's life in some way. I believe she really did tell Paul she was sexually abused in her childhood. I hope her abuser comes to light and faces the tornado of grief he caused in so many lives. The film *It's a Wonderful Life* taught through Jimmy Stewart's character that each of us touches so many lives. That, if we were never born, life would be phenomenally different. An act of abuse touches lives the same way. Not just the victim's, but so many more. In a very real way, Monica's victimization as a child may have caused the whirlwind in her husband's, children's, parents', brothers', sisters' and other relatives' lives as well as bringing together a group of strangers who would never have met had it not been for that tragic day when Monica died.

—Andrea Egger

I had been a police officer for nearly sixteen years and I had always believed in "the system." I had believed that district attorneys and their agents were supposed to search for and vehemently pursue the *truth*. In my particular case, I found this was not so. State police investigators, district attorneys and medical investigators acquired tunnel vision and once they locked into this mindset, they all refused to look at anything else or consider another way. Then they set about trying to make the evidence fit their scenario. It didn't matter if it was the truth or not. They had to make it fit, regardless of the fact that it was a strong example of the "square peg, round hole" syndrome. Thank God a jury was able to see the truth and recognize it as such. The district attorney and his agents never cared about the truth. Even when they realized the truth, they shied away from it, because they refused to admit or even acknowledge that they had made a mistake and that the mistake should be righted. Instead they perpetrated the worst form of injustice imaginable. With this act, self-centered greed and ego, they took away my belief in our justice system, which is why I am not nor ever will again be a police officer, the job that I loved.

Surely, I didn't get justice, nor did my children or anybody at all, for that matter. I used to believe in the adage "innocent until proven guilty." This is not what our legal system has now become. In reality, our legal system is now "guilty until proven innocent." Thanks to my attorneys and the experts—Dave Pfeffer, Nelson Welch, Dr. Martin Fackler and Dr. David Raskin—my innocence was proven. It's a sad state of affairs that our legal system has come to. I was the square peg they were trying to pound into a round hole, fully knowing it wouldn't fit, but beating the peg in anyway, switching to a bigger hammer. Big Brother (the state of New Mexico) and his endless resources were the bigger hammer, in my case.

I have never denied I made a mistake, nor have I shirked the responsibility that my actions (my affair) caused. I bear the responsibility for Monica's death and will continue to do so for the remainder of my life, a very real and painful reminder of the hurt and irreparable damage an affair can cause. Some say I bear too much of the responsibility, some think not enough, but to me, it is something I am responsible for and have to live with. So if you're ever thinking of cheating, *don't*. You will not like the price that may be attached to your actions, as I so painfully learned.

The cost was too high. I lost my self-respect, job, friends, family, retirement, home and, at the age of forty-one, I'm having to start from scratch again. But my children and I are on our feet again and while we're not off and running, we're at least walking down a path toward a good place. Running will come later. I believe and have faith in this. I learned my lesson and changed my life behavior. We all can, if we want to badly enough.

As my attorney, Vic Titus, said, I fear this is far from over. His words spoke volumes. After my acquittal, I was sued for custody of my children, Diane and Racquel, and it was months after my acquittal before I was deemed a fit father and my children were returned to me.

Two years after Monica's death, I was forced through a bizarre divorce trial (a new state law required a divorce trial to divide property and debt in a pending case, even when one of the spouses died before the proceedings) by her parents. It was the strangest proceeding that I and my attorney had ever seen, much less heard of. "We're plowing new ground here," my attorney said. How true it was. My former in-laws are basically good, decent people. I understand their grief and their need to make someone (me) pay, but not their actions. After many years, my former mother-in-law, Dora, and I have come to a good place and an understanding of sorts, based on love, concern and what is in the best interests of Diane and Racquel.

The rest of my in-laws believe what they want to believe and I don't begrudge them that. They are entitled to their beliefs, even if they are wrong. My stepdaughter, Amanda, has grown into a beautiful woman. I'm proud of her and I know her mother would be also. She is married and has a child of her own. I love her dearly, miss her deeply and wish that someday our relationship can be reestablished in some way, shape or form.

I would like to express my deepest gratitude to Andrea. I could never have written this book on my own, as it is/

was too close and painful for me. Without Andrea, the *truth* would have been glossed over into the realm of obscurity. Andrea didn't know me prior to my criminal trial. She was a newspaper reporter who covered the trial. After hearing the evidence, she became vehemently convinced that I was an innocent man being falsely accused. She took up my cause. For this and her ceaseless pursuit of the truth, I thank her and I will always be indebted to her. I love you, Andrea.

I would also like to thank the following people who believed in me and stood by and with me when doing so was very unpopular. Andy and Margaret, Bob and Nancy, Kim Shirer (I love you, wherever you are), Madrina, Rocky, Cliff and Kathy, Larry and Sharon and the boys, Elaine, Nancy and Kelly, Bill Morgan (thanks for being just plain kind to me in a bad situation), Richard, Jan, Elaine, Dennis, Ron and Sandy, Mike and Nancy, Mike and Stacy, Jack and his wife, Mark and Georgeann, Tom and Suzanne, Rosie, Bill Anamosa, Kelley and Brett, JeriSue, Dr. J. W. Ragsdale, Josh and my family.

Anita, I couldn't have survived it without your support and faith. You are my soul mate and I will always be in love with you. I know not what the future holds for us, but I do believe that hope floats and just maybe, someday our love will rise to the top.

Vic Titus is not only a great man and a fantastic attorney, but he's a man I am privileged to call my friend. I could live a thousand years and never be able to tell him enough or repay him enough for the belief, compassion and generosity he's shown me and my children. Gary Mitchell and his investigator, Dave Pfeffer, are two of the most unique individuals I have ever had the pleasure of meeting. Thank you both for putting up with me, listening to me and comforting me during my eight months of living hell. God will remember and reward you both when your time comes, because you took it upon yourselves to stand in the void and say "This isn't right," no matter what the personal, professional and monetary cost. I love, admire and respect you both.

To April, Diane and Racquel, my children, your daddy wants you to know that you and you alone are the main reasons that I get up every morning, go to work and draw breath. You three are the joy and loves of my life and I thank my Creator every day that he chose to bless this lonely sinner with your beautiful smiles, warm hugs and "I love you." I am far from being wealthy by any stretch of the imagination, but I am the richest man in the world because of your love.

Thank you, God, for showing me the errors of my ways and for showing me what matters most in this world is generally free: honor, self-respect and love. I won't forget!

This book is about truth. You decide. I know the truth. Monica knows the truth. God knows the truth. When my time comes, I know that I'll have to answer for some things. But Monica's death won't be one of them and my punishment shouldn't be too severe, because I've already been to hell, right here on earth.

Whatever cocky, arrogant attitude I had died the day Monica died, as well as thirty-five years' worth of life as I knew it. I like myself now and I like who I am. Even though I realize I've got a long way to go I can now look in the mirror in the morning and like what I see looking back at me.

Prosecutors and police should remember before counting someone "guilty until proven innocent," that once someone is accused of a felony, it stays on his or her record forever. Whenever I apply for a job, a background check will show I was arrested for murder. I'll never get away from that.

Finally, I'd like to say to anyone who is even thinking about suicide: *Please, please don't do it*. Get help, tell someone, talk to somebody, think about what you will leave behind. Monica wasn't the only one who died on April 4, 1994. However, she was the only one who did not have to suffer through the aftermath of her actions, as the rest of us were forced to do. It's a daily thing—it never leaves, it never ends. It will be with all of us for the remainder of our lives. We all still suffer from it and I personally will be haunted by it until the day I die. So please, don't even allow the thought of suicide to enter your mind. The survivors you leave behind will be just that. Survivors who have been forced against their will, ghostly shells of what they once used to be, to walk through the fires of hell and back.

—Paul Dunn

APPENDIX 1

MONICA'S LETTER
(edited for spelling and grammar)

3-11-94

My friend Rick,

I am writing you this letter because I know I can trust you.

First of all, thank you for all your kind words, friendship and your ear for listening to all my depressing words.

Rick, I now realize life isn't fair, most of the time it seems very cruel. I have yet to understand why some people have to be so mean. What ever happened to kindness, honesty and caring? You know, Rick, it's all very inexpensive, anyone can afford it and yet it is so rare.

I have a few things for you to please try and take care of for me.

The girls, please tell them I love them very much. All I ever wanted is what was best for them. I do understand they will grieve, it is a process everyone must go through, but they're young and they will learn to go on and live long, happy, healthy—God willing—lives.

Paul is not to get custody of the girls. He not only can't support them, plus I know he condones drugs. Dad has proof! He doesn't have it in him to care about anyone else but himself. He is honest with no one, so how can he even try to take care of them? He is a compulsive liar, not to mention an alcoholic, which he has admitted, any questions there, ask Tom Bolack. The girls need stability in their lives. He has none. He's lost himself.

Trying to think of everything right now is hard, but I will try:

1. Insurance policies are to be turned over to my mother to be put in trust funds for Amanda, Diane and Racquel—only—until they are either in college or twenty-one years of age. Paul is not to receive a cent. He has made a decision, he wanted out, he's out. He has no conscience, so do not let him get to you. Be strong.

2. My personal stuff give to Amanda first, then save some for Diane and Racquel. Then let Teresa, Diane and Mom see what they want. My rings belong to Diane and Racquel. My bedroom set—Amanda. Sell the van and fix Amanda's car. Make it supreme for her. She is a beautiful girl who needs a beautiful car.

3. The house: I want it sold and any extra money put it in the trust funds for the girls. Paul is to receive nothing. If he has any sense of dignity, he will abide by this. Don't let him manipulate you. He is a worthless piece for a man. I hope he doesn't ever get the opportunity to ever hurt anyone else. He has hurt so many people in his life that I don't want him around the girls without supervision so he won't hurt them also. He can be very violent, he's only concerned about himself and no one else. When I am gone, the bruises on me will show. He also has a sharp tongue!

4. The funeral: Please help with the arrangements. Go as cheap as possible—nothing expensive—save the money for the girls. I don't care if you bury or cremate me, whatever Mom wants. There is to be no viewing, i.e., family only—immediate—except Paul. No one else is to see me, let them if they choose to remember me the way I used to be, when I had a face, before Paul stripped that from me.

Choose a jumpsuit for me to wear. I used to look good in them when I was a whole person. I am now a nothing. Paul managed to strip me of me.

Paul (ha-ha) bearers:
1. Nathan Lovato
2. Rick Jacquez
3. Terry Pearson
4. Sgt. Dusty Downs
5. Allen Ehney
6. Victor Titus

Honorary:
1. Sonny Martinez
2. Judge Bill Luise
3. Michael Cortez
4. Nestor C. Cortez
5. Nick Sanchez
6. Co-workers—except Lucila Nent

Eulogy
Vicki Maestas, Judge Byrd

Family car
Dad, Mom, girls, anyone else Mom needs. Not Paul.

Honestly, truthfully, he doesn't need to be anywhere near me. I don't ever want him there. He wants out, remember. I don't want him there. He has made his choice. He doesn't want me, so now he must learn to live with it. I'm sure he will be fine since he has no conscience, no feelings for anyone else but himself. He says he is sorry a lot. Don't believe him. To him it's just another word like *and, the, a* . . . It is a common word. To him it means nothing.

5. My last wish: I want you to receive some money to help you and Teresa. Please, I ask this of you. Mom is to give you what you need. I will rest if you are taken care of. You are very special, you never judged me. All you ever asked for was friendship and I do admire your friendship. Thank you. You were the one who always called just to say hi, how are you and I appreciated you for that.

Again, thank you and I trust you will do your best and keep an eye on my girls. Between you, Mom, Teresa, my girls will be in good hands. You are an honest man with good moral values. You will do right by my girls.

Help everyone get through this and remember I will never be totally gone, through my beautiful girls. I am really sorry about this. I just don't have any more strength or power to go on. I'm tired. I was fighting so hard and struggling so hard for something that I now know was never there or never would be there. But during the time I fought, I had no idea I was dead for him. If I had been told the truth maybe I would have some strength left and an ounce of dignity. I look in the mirror and see nothing. I lost myself to someone who doesn't even care. I was led to believe he loved me in the same manner I loved him. How can a human lead another one for years and years to

believe a lie? I don't understand. I have thought and tried
to remember where I screwed up. I must have been so blind
or just really stupid. I know I must do what needs to be
done. Don't mislead my girls. I could do that and be so
dumb, never even realize it. They need strong people in
their lives. You, Mom, Dad, Tea . . . Tell the boys I love
them and I am very proud of them. They're good boys. I
have faith in them.

You must be bored now, but I hope you do understand.

Thank you!

> Respectfully!!
>
> [Signed:] Monica E. _ _ _ _ _ _.

APPENDIX 2

INTERVIEW WITH ALAN WHITEHEAD

Alan Whitehead looked uncomfortable as he leaned on the counter at his Farmington law office, where he was a partner in 2000, having lost the race for district attorney after the Dunn victory. His untamed gray hair and forty-ish face still were handsome, despite the fact that he looked tired. Although he had a definite opinion on the Dunn case even then, he didn't deliver it with gusto. Perhaps the years of looking at the law from the other side, as a defense attorney, caused him to soften his view of prosecution. Or else he just decided it wouldn't matter anyway if he spilled his guts about Paul's misery—he didn't directly prosecute the case and he could always fall on faulty memory if the questions got too intense.

But memory shouldn't have been a problem with questions about the Court of Appeals case, which he said he'd never read. In fact, he didn't even know the court reversed the District Court's decision about Paul's suing the Office of the Medical Examiner, state crime laboratory and the New Mexico State Police for malicious prosecution. He had never read the reversal judgment, never read the words "conspiracy" and "negligence" in black and white, appearing several times in the court's brief to explain its decision.

He never read this by February 2000, several months

after the judgment. At least, that's what he said. The information about the appeal court was big news in Farmington. It made the Farmington *Times* a couple of days in a row. The television stations played it up big. Judges rarely declare that a medical investigator, a police officer and a firearms specialist conspired to wrongfully arrest a man. In fact, it might have been the first time in history—at least, the first time judges used such strong language. Appeals briefs are usually rather "lawyerly" or "boring" to anyone who chooses to read them. Most people probably have never read a judge's brief unless they are lawyers, investigators or writers researching a case.

As if the media coverage of the appeal wasn't enough, the New Mexico Bar Association's bulletin ran part of the judgment. Every other attorney in town had read the case or learned about it on the news. Lawyers have to keep up on all case reversals and new laws so they can use them in their own defense cases if they come across a case where the reversal or new law applies.

Whitehead had more reason than the average Joe Lawyer to be a little bit curious about the Court of Appeal's decision. He graciously agreed to review the decision and see if his opinion on the case changed after checking out the reasons behind their words.

Lawyers' and judges' briefs are written like college papers, complete with title pages and tables of contents. They are very detailed. Appeals judges don't sit on a trial; they review the trial's court tapes and transcripts as well as the evidence presented in the case before making their decisions.

When he agreed to an interview, February 17, 2000, he didn't recall much of the occurrences in the case—such as the fact that two autopsy reports were issued and the final one was significantly altered—but he had very strong opinions about what happened on the day of Monica's death.

Whitehead moved from his stance at the front desk of

his office into a conference room just off the waiting area. He sat at the head of the table, chair pushed back. Leaning back, he crossed his legs, resting an ankle on the opposite knee.

"I think Paul Dunn was on the end of that gun and pulled the trigger," he said.

Whitehead was in California on vacation the week Monica died. He got a phone call from officials the day of the shooting. He remained on vacation and allowed his Deputy District Attorney, Darrel Jiles, and Assistant District Attorney, Kathleen Carnell, to take on the legal headache.

Whitehead made no bones about his own personal verdict in the 2000 interview. He stated this was the only "murder" case in his career in office in which he didn't personally attend the crime scene.

Despite Governor Bruce King's and Lieutenant Governor Casey Luna's presence in Farmington and their visits to the Sanchez family, Whitehead maintains his office received no political pressure to prosecute Paul. Monica's family members called his office daily while Whitehead was sunning in California—but nobody in his office received a telephone call from the governor or lieutenant governor. He said if either politician had called Jiles or Carnell, they would have immediately called and informed Whitehead.

Whitehead didn't believe Paul went to Monica's home that morning with the intent of shooting her, but when she said she planned to file battery charges against him, Paul became enraged. He grabbed the gun and shot her. Whitehead didn't believe Monica struggled with Paul over the gun. He didn't believe Monica even touched the shotgun. Asked about all the trajectory evidence, Welch's graphic depiction in the courtroom with the bed, shotgun and the wall containing Monica's blood, Fackler's information and Paul's passing two polygraph tests, Whitehead had only one thing to say:

"It sounds like a story prepared for trial."

Whitehead didn't care that Paul's story of how Monica shot herself never changed from the day of the shooting to the Millennium and beyond. Whitehead countered that with the fact that many killers stick to the same story until their deaths post-prison, in the penitentiary or by lethal injection, New Mexico's form of the death penalty.

Whitehead gave in slightly by saying that a defendant's behavior does not affect jurors. And whether or not someone truly pulled a trigger, sliced a throat or pulled a cord around someone's neck, jurors decide whether that person legally is responsible. That's why verdicts are determined "beyond a reasonable doubt." It's not possible for anyone who wasn't a witness to an incident to know what happened beyond all doubt.

"Juries don't like stories changing over time," Whitehead said. He couldn't remember one "not guilty" finding in one of his cases where the accused's story changed over time. But he remembers many cases where a defendant's story remained the same and jurors found the person innocent even though Whitehead thought that person was guilty.

Regarding Paul, Whitehead carefully explained the "probability" that a killer was loose on the streets of Farmington. "I wouldn't invite him over for coffee at my house."

Whitehead knew Paul through the years while Paul was a cop and he was the District Attorney.

"He was a nice guy, a good cop. He did good work."

It was evidence, not Paul's personality, that led Whitehead to his conclusion of guilt.

Paul and Whitehead also had attorney friends in common. They'd see each other often at parties attorneys gave.

In fact, it's a Farmington attorney who has Whitehead

convinced Paul killed Monica for fear of losing his job. Whitehead said he heard at the time of the shooting, Paul was being investigated for covering up for an attorney friend who had an accident while intoxicated.

Paul was livid when he heard Whitehead brought this up. Although Paul didn't volunteer information about this situation during five years of interviews, he said the DWI occurred in 1989 or 1990 and he was suspended for three days. Case closed. "Nobody was hurt. I made a mistake. I got caught," Paul explained the years-old incident. Besides, that wouldn't have come into play had Monica filed battery charges. And a battery conviction against a police officer didn't mean firing in 1994. A few years later, the legislature passed a law that anyone convicted of battery could not possess a gun, so cops would have to be fired if convicted.

Whitehead said although he was the district attorney, boss of the office, most of what he heard about Paul's case—the office's most high-profile one—came via periodic updates from his staff attorneys and information reported in the media. At the time of Monica's death, the media immediately pointed to murder without spelling it out. This isn't the media's fault entirely. When someone is arrested, the arrest documents, court file and police reports become public record. Sometimes they have the defendant's statement so reporters can write balanced stories. Usually the defendant takes the Fifth Amendment right to silence until an attorney can be sought. The attorney usually tells the defendant not to talk to the cops and definitely not to the media.

So, it isn't until the trial that the defense case reveals itself.

But Whitehead had more access than media accounts. He had access to the evidence, if he chose to explore it.

Mitchell made a big deal about the two autopsy reports, one saying the gun must have been pressed to her skin, the final one saying the gun was one to three feet away from Monica's body when fired.

"I only know of one autopsy report. I don't know anything about the muzzles being pressed up against the skin." Whitehead's explanation just didn't ring true.

How could he not know?

He adamantly explained he would question the two reports if he'd seen them. "That would be one factor we'd use in determining whether or not to prosecute the case."

Of course, people kill others by pressing a gun to their skin, but either way, Whitehead said he remembered the evidence indicated a distance shot because of the markings on Monica's skin. He said he's not sure anything would have changed in the prosecution had he known about the two reports.

"A medical examiner can tell if a shotgun is close as opposed to other distances," he said.

Then why have a ballistics expert work to determine what the wound would look like if the medical investigator can do it all?

Whitehead qualified his statement by saying a medical investigator can tell a contact wound from that made by a gun held at some distance. Besides that, prosecutors don't hire ballistics experts; it's routine in gun killings for the state experts to be involved.

Experts also are supposed to test their theories for fallacies. Science requires trying to disprove a theory. In disproving scenarios, the right one unfolds. But, as Welch and Fackler wrote in their journal article for the International Wound Ballistics Association, police officers and prosecutors often suffer from tunnel vision, focusing in on one suspect or one theory and not letting go despite new information or evidence that indicates a different scenario is possible or even likely.

The damning evidence in the medical investigator's final report, the state police report, the ballistics report and his knowledge of Monica through her job as a municipal court clerk were the main reasons Whitehead felt Paul killed her. He knew she and Paul were having marital problems. Someone told Whitehead that Monica was afraid Paul would "do something."

Whitehead had no knowledge that Monica told anyone suicide plagued her mind.

He also didn't remember telling attorney Steve Murphy that he didn't care about the polygraph tests. Whitehead denied it was office policy to dismiss cases after a defendant passes a polygraph test. New Mexico is the only state that allows polygraph test results as evidence.

He added he understands from a professor at the University of Utah in Salt Lake City that David Raskin is a hired gun, his results therefore a bunch of "bull." Whitehead had no explanation for why the state's own polygrapher, Jim Wilson, also found Paul to be truthful.

In the final analysis, Whitehead admitted something Dr. McFeeley wouldn't do while under oath. He admitted it's "possible" Paul's story is true, but called it unlikely.

"Would someone inconvenience herself to do it that way?"

Rather than taking a bottle of pills or using a smaller gun and another part of the body, Whitehead found it strange anyone would sit on a bed, point a shotgun at her abdomen, lean over it and fire the trigger. And to do this with kids in the house? It could happen, but it was unlikely. As far as Whitehead was concerned, it was more likely a human being would react to bad news by flying into a rage and killing another person.

Whitehead, unlike state firearms examiner Warehime, wasn't bothered by Welch's description of trajectory. Warehime didn't even try trajectory tests because he said they couldn't be considered in a shooting since the pellets move in different directions in the body.

"I don't believe you can *never* determine trajectory—if the pellets travel through soft tissue, there might be a path straight through."

Again, one might wonder why so-called state "experts" were needed when the district attorney himself knew this. Why didn't his office ensure Warehime conducted trajectory tests if Whitehead himself knew they could be used? And why couldn't Jiles and Carnell see that Nelson's description of the trajectory had to be right, based on how the holes in the wall and brick lined up toward the lower back of someone sitting on the waterbed?

Whitehead had no problem with Monica wearing a beautiful, probably expensive, dress, her face fully made up and hair perfectly coiffed if she planned suicide. Carnell found this off, but in Whitehead's experience, suicidal women want to look their best when they die—a kind of final curtain on their life. But again, women don't usually use guns and they don't usually kill themselves when their children are home or in a place where their children might find them, he said, displaying the knowledge gained through his twenty-plus years of criminal justice experience.

Whitehead didn't doubt Paul suffered emotional pain from the death and prosecution. "Even people who get angry and shoot somebody suffer trauma."

Still, Whitehead maintains Paul shot Monica.

APPENDIX 3

A STUDY IN TUNNEL VISION

Long before the Court of Appeals rendered their verdict, Fackler and Welch made forensic history after they pieced together some of the information in Monica's case. They published two articles in the 1996 *Wound Ballistics Review*, the journal of the International Wound Ballistics Association. Fackler is the president of the association and edits the journal. One of the articles stated, "We hope that a sober consideration of the facts outlined will give pause to some, and demonstrate to those charged with collecting and evaluating physical evidence the dangers of a too rapid jump to judgment."

The articles showed the omentum and grex at length as well as showed a picture of Welch's trajectory study with the dowels matched up from holes in the plasterboard and then the brick wall. Welch's wife was the model in the photo. The state police hadn't bothered gathering these items to look at trajectory.

In fact, firearms examiner Larry Warehime, then of the New Mexico Department of Public Safety Crime Laboratory, told grand jurors and trial jurors trajectory studies aren't viable when a body is struck because the pellets move around in the body instead of forming a straight pattern.

Fackler hit the ceiling when he heard about Warehime's testimony. "He doesn't know about organs in the body. He shouldn't go out of his field. He's right, they spread out, coming out in a cone shape. It's a regular spread, but you can still get some directionality out of it. That's what Nelson did in his very nice set-up."

Warehime was way out of his league at trial and knew it, Fackler surmised. "Larry was really embarrassed. He was just saying whatever came into his head."

Fackler used another finding in the case to solve other crimes where he had to determine whether a wound was close-range or a distance shot. The condition of the shotcup petals in Monica's body helped with this. The petals were deformed in the body, especially the tip of the petal Fackler surmised struck her body.

Fackler, Welch and two other firearms examiners did tests firing shotguns at a distance and found the petal tips weren't damaged. Fackler explained that happens because within a distance of one to three feet, all four petals of the shotcup have opened, meaning the tips will not strike the skin.

"What is surprising is that the obvious and striking difference in shot cup petal deformation has not heretofore been noticed as an indicator to separate contact wounds [from distance shot wounds]. We suggest that the application of this finding might be at least as useful as the appearance of the skin wound in distinguishing contact from one to three foot distant shotgun wounds," Fackler wrote in his *Wound Ballistics Review* article.

Never one to miss an opportunity, Fackler has used this finding in other cases. For instance, he helped solve a 1960s murder in Northern Pennsylvania. A lawyer and a doctor were trap shooting and the lawyer was killed.

The lawyer had been shot in the middle of the chest.

The doctor told police they were trap shooting when he heard a noise. It was the lawyer's gun firing. When the doctor ran over, he discovered his friend had accidentally shot himself.

Fackler's investigation showed no damage to the tips of the petals and they had opened fully. Fackler estimated the gun had to be about three or four feet from the lawyer's body when it went off.

"There was too much distance for him to have done it himself. After I presented my findings, [the doctor] confessed."

Fackler had spent an hour talking to Jiles before Paul's trial. Mitchell told him to explain exactly what evidence he would present to jurors.

"Convince him," Mitchell said.

Fackler didn't hold anything back. Welch had already shown Jiles and Carnell the display with the dowels. This didn't seem to make a difference. Fackler explained the wound ballistic evidence, the petals, the problems with the autopsy report, the omentum—the list was endless. Jiles listened as if he just wanted to know what to expect at trial.

Fackler believes the case should attract wide-ranging attention. The facts frighten him in a world where expert testimony is supposed to make a difference in cases. Instead, he believes well-respected medical examiner's testimony was based on tainted evidence. An "awful" flawed report gave jurors incorrect information. A prosecutor couldn't accept the overwhelming evidence. Or refused to for political reasons. The firearms examiner showed weakness and inability to admit he was wrong.

"It's easy to pull the wool over your own eyes. One finds it hard to differentiate between fools and frauds," Fackler observed.

APPENDIX 4

INTERVIEW WITH GRAND JURY FOREMAN

The grand jury foreman in Paul's case was upset that Monica Dunn's letter was never introduced as evidence to the grand jury.

"That's distressing to me. It seems there were things we didn't know about and, of course, that's not fair to Paul. Things disclosed to the grand jury should be the same things as proposed at trial. That's going to exonerate him."

Leonard Gallegos feels if they had been given that information, the jury would either have deadlocked or decided not to indict him.

Although the purpose of a grand jury is to determine if there is probable cause to take a case to trial, Gallegos thinks grand jurors should get all the facts. But usually grand juries just get to hear the prosecution's side of the case. The defense isn't even allowed to be present during a grand jury hearing.

Gallegos knew Monica and Paul. He knew Monica's family and he knew Paul during Paul's police career.

Gallegos says he always heard Paul had a ruthless side to his manner of dealing with people. He heard that Paul was hard-nosed and got into some fights. He saw Monica as a gentle, easy-going person. He never saw in her a woman with the disposition to kill herself.

A work release compliance officer for twelve years, Gallegos interviews and screens all candidates for work release at the jail in Aztec. Monica's brother was in Gallegos's work release program several times at San Juan County Detention Center. Gallegos once revoked him from the program, yet he viewed Monica's family as easy-going, religious, God-fearing people.

His interpretation based on the evidence the grand jury was presented was that Paul and Monica were fighting over the gun. Gallegos doesn't believe Monica could grab the gun and hold it, then press the trigger. He also wondered what in the world Paul was doing when Monica supposedly pulled the trigger. Gallegos felt if it were him, he could stop anyone from pulling a trigger.

There were many facts not presented to the grand jury. Gallegos explained he never heard that Monica might've been holding the gun to her abdomen as Paul walked in the door. Again, he said it would be different if they had been presented with that scenario as grand jurors.

Yet even considering the information withheld from the grand jury, some facts about the case still bother Gallegos. For example, he doesn't like the idea that Paul gave Monica the shotgun for home defense. Double ought buck shot is for killing people. Gallegos wonders why the gun would be loaded with such ammunition.

He also understood that Monica hated guns. He believes firearms don't belong in the hands of people who don't know how to use them properly, people who don't know the potential danger of the weapons.

It didn't make much sense to Gallegos that Monica was dressed up and that the kids were in the car ready to leave that day when Paul showed up at the house. "That doesn't say to me she meant to commit suicide. There's something sinister here."

The expert witnesses, especially one who photographed

the crime scene persuaded Gallegos that Paul had killed Monica.

"Paul was arrogant. I knew that just from knowing him. They did have a history of physical abuse—she had bruises on her body from a previous confrontation. And she had told people he was going to kill her."

Despite his opinions on the case, Gallegos, who always tries to be open-minded, did his best to keep his thoughts to himself while grand jurors were examining the case evidence and making their decision.

"I'm the kind of person who tries to look for the truth," Gallegos explained. To achieve this, in part, he tried not to remember Monica or think of how he knew her. He always would look for truth, he said, truth and nothing else. He wanted to be fair to the victim and the defendant.

"That's what justice is all about. You can't be prejudiced and be on a jury. If you're prejudiced, you don't belong on a jury."

Gallegos sees Paul on the streets of Farmington from time to time. Paul never acknowledges him. Gallegos doesn't believe it's up to us to judge each other. He believes people should not be burdened by feelings that can only drag you down.

He also sees Victor Titus quite often. Titus often refers to Gallegos as "Uncle Leonard." They've talked about a variety of things but never about the Dunn case. Titus has never asked him about it, and Gallegos has never brought it up. Gallegos thinks the world of Titus as a friend and an attorney.

APPENDIX 5

COLLECTION OF LETTERS ON THE PERFORMANCE OF POLICE OFFICER PAUL DUNN

January 10, 1990

Chief Calvin Shields
Farmington Police Department
Farmington, NM 87401

Dear Chief Shields:

My five-year-old son was in the hospital emergency room last Monday night being treated for an asthma attack when Officer Paul Dunn came over, gave him a toy police badge and talked to him for a few minutes.

Officer Dunn apparently was there on a vehicle accident investigation, but he took the time to make a little boy feel a lot better.

We have tried to teach our children that the police are their friends. But telling them is one thing. Officer Dunn's actions left a far greater impression on a five-year-old than his parents could ever accomplish.

In fact, whenever we encounter one of your officers, such as in a restaurant, they are always happy to talk with our kids and shake their hands.

Our police officers are rarely thanked for the excellent job they do in often trying circumstances. If Officer Dunn is an example of the rest of the police force, then the entire city certainly can be proud.

Sincerely,
George H. Johnston

Paul Dunn
Farmington, NM 87401

Officer Paul Dunn:

Thank you so very much for all you did in trying to save our father's life. We know you did your very best for him and that is a great comfort for us. May God bless you for being such a caring person. We are so very thankful that dad spent his last few moments in life with you and we'll always remember you in our prayers.

The Waters family

February 27, 1985

Mr. Calvin Shields
Farmington NM Chief of Police
Farmington, NM

Dear Chief Shields:

Please accept this belated letter of thanks for the excellent job done by three of your officers on April 6th last.

If you remember this date, this was the day I had a massive heart attack while astride a horse in the parade. I would personally thank and commend Officers Clifford L. Ollum, Paul C. Dunn and Lawrence Downs. These well-trained and dedicated officers were immediately on the spot and without hesitation started CPR and continued same until arrival of the local paramedics. Without their competent aid, I would not be alive today. Believe me, their Red Cross training was well worth the effort.

From me, my wife and son, thanks to each of you from the bottom of my nine times damaged heart.

Sincerely,
C. O. "Ken" Kendrick

Chief R. Melton
Farmington Police Dept.
Farmington, NM 87401

Dear Chief Melton:

This letter is to commend one of your officers. While they all deserve commendations, this particular officer, Mr. Paul Dunn, deserves special recognition.

Mr. Dunn was one of the investigating officers of our school bus accident on August 26, 1992. Mr. Dunn performed his duties in the most professional manner possible.

Since this was the first serious accident involving a school bus for our district, it had a very negative impact on many of our drivers. This being so due to the many rumors that were going around.

I requested Mr. Dunn to attend a short debriefing of all the drivers concerning this accident on the 26th.

Mr. Dunn made an excellent presentation at this meeting. He discussed the feet per second a vehicle covers at "X" miles per hour and the difficulty of judging the speed of an oncoming vehicle. He also emphasized the importance of being sure what another vehicle about to enter traffic is going to do.

After his presentation, many of the drivers stated how much they appreciated his input and they now have a better outlook.

Once again, our thanks to Officer Dunn, yourself and the entire department for all your help over the years concerning "School Bus Safety."

Sincerely
Robert L. Bevers
Transportation Supervisor
Farmington schools

May 22, 1986

Mr. Shields
Chief of Police
Farmington, NM 87401

Dear Mr. Shields:

Many policemen do not get a pat on the back often enough and sometimes a pat on the back goes a long way. That is why I thought I would write this letter and bring this incident to your attention.

On May 20, 1986, a young traffic officer stopped me, thinking I was speeding. After talking with the officer, he voided the citation and left. A few minutes later, he returned and apologized for pulling me over.

Mr. Shields, this young officer was very polite and courteous, which shows a great reflection on our Farmington Police Department, as well as a great reflection on you as our Chief of Police. The man's name is Paul Dunn.

Again, I express my thanks.

Elaine M. Henley
A-1 Automotive

Family Crisis Center, Inc.
Farmington, NM 87401

December 28, 1987

Chief Calvin Shields
Farmington, NM 87401

Dear Chief Shields:

On Saturday, December 19, at Wal-Mart, Officer Paul Dunn distinguished the Farmington Police Department by handling a volatile situation with one of our families with such professionalism. His voice and manner were so calming. His intervention prevented a child from being injured further and the 100 or so spectators from reacting inappropriately.

On behalf of the Family Crisis Center, we wish to commend Officer Dunn for his extremely helpful and timely intervention and commend your department for providing such caring and professional officers.

Many, many thanks.

Sincerely yours,
Marge Atkinson
Executive Director

February 3, 1984

Capt. Ben Sanchez
Farmington Police Department

Dear Ben:

On the 14th of January, my family buried our mother. Bertha Salisbury had just celebrated her 74th birthday.

As is often the case, Mom lived a number of years after she retired. The last eight years she lived without the husband who had been her constant companion. She was surrounded by grandchildren and great-grandchildren who loved to hear her talk about her days as a police officer.

I'm sure her heart would have swelled with pride for at sight of the two strapping, handsome young motorcycle officers who were her honor guard and the pride of her grandchildren and great-grandchildren. No longer was their grandmother just an old lady "out of contact with the world around her" but at the funeral, the memory of her as a police-lady lived in those of us who remembered her and was born in the younger children.

The shiny shooting trophies and newspaper clippings (now yellow with age) are shared among the children and grandchildren, but the memory of her police honor guard will surely be the most pleasant and long-lived memory of all.

To the young officers who were her honor guard, "We salute you," and I must say, "you did a much greater service than you may have imagined."

Thanks again, Ben, and thank you, Farmington Police Department.

Bruce L. Salisbury
(for the family of Bertha Salisbury)